CONTEMPORARY INEQUALITIES AND
SOCIAL JUSTICE IN CANADA

CONTEMPORARY INEQUALITIES AND SOCIAL JUSTICE IN CANADA

Edited by Janine Brodie

UNIVERSITY OF TORONTO PRESS

Toronto Buffalo London

Library and Archives Canada Cataloguing in Publication

Contemporary inequalities and social justice in Canada / editor: Janine Brodie, University of Alberta.

Includes bibliographical references and index.
Issued in print and electronic formats.
ISBN 978-1-4426-3408-4 (softcover).—ISBN 978-1-4426-3409-1 (hardcover).—
ISBN 978-1-4426-3410-7 (EPUB).—ISBN 978-1-4426-3411-4 (PDF)

1. Social justice—Canada. 2. Equality—Canada. 3. Canada—Social conditions.
I. Brodie, M. Janine, 1952–, editor

HN110.S6C66 2018   303.3'720971   C2017-905827-4
                                                    C2017-905828-2

We welcome comments and suggestions regarding any aspect of our publications—please feel free to contact us at news@utphighereducation.com or visit our Internet site at utorontopress.com.

North America
5201 Dufferin Street
North York, Ontario, Canada, M3H 5T8

2250 Military Road
Tonawanda, New York, USA, 14150

ORDERS PHONE: 1–800–565–9523
ORDERS FAX: 1–800–221–9985
ORDERS E-MAIL: utpbooks@utpress.utoronto.ca

UK, Ireland, and continental Europe
NBN International
Estover Road, Plymouth, PL6 7PY, UK

ORDERS PHONE: 44 (0) 1752 202301
ORDERS FAX: 44 (0) 1752 202333
ORDERS E-MAIL: enquiries@nbninternational.com

Every effort has been made to contact copyright holders; in the event of an error or omission, please notify the publisher.

This book is printed on paper containing 100% post-consumer fibre.

The University of Toronto Press acknowledges the financial support for its publishing activities of the Government of Canada through the Canada Book Fund.

Printed in the United States of America.

Funded by the   Financé par le
Government   gouvernement
of Canada   du Canada

Canada

CONTENTS

ACKNOWLEDGEMENTS

The idea for this edited volume began to take shape at the Royal Society of Canada's Annual Research Symposium, which I organized in Banff, Alberta, in late 2013. Attended by distinguished social science researchers and over 200 participants, the theme of the symposium was "Social Justice in the 21st Century: Toward a New Intergenerational Social Contract." Many of the chapters in this volume began as presentations to this forum. This book project could not have been completed without the generous support of the Pierre Elliott Trudeau Foundation, which awarded me a fellowship in 2010, and the Canada Research Chairs Program in which I hold a Tier 1 Chair in Political Economy and Social Governance. The contributors to this volume are grateful to the two anonymous reviewers that provided invaluable comments to improve their chapters, as well as to Michael Harrison and Mat Buntin at University of Toronto Press, who have expertly and patiently guided this project to its completion. At various stages, exceptional doctoral students in the Department of Political Science at the University of Alberta have assisted in the production of this volume. We owe a big thank you to Chad Cowie, Janet Phillips, Brent Epperson, and Justin Leifso.

PART I

Contemporary Perspectives on Social Justice

CHAPTER 1

INEQUALITIES AND SOCIAL JUSTICE IN CRISIS TIMES

Janine Brodie

Introduction

The contributions to this volume explore the diverse and intersecting social inequalities that are shaping a renewed social justice agenda in twenty-first century Canada. For more than a generation, our daily horizons have been deeply configured by crisis-ridden neoliberal governing strategies, which have compounded the persistent disparities generated by racism, sexism, and colonialism. Initially injected into national and international political conversations and policy agendas in the late twentieth century under such aliases as restructuring, globalization, and austerity, the neoliberal project has rested on the foundational claim that "there is no alternative" to its ever-evolving prescriptions for market-focused governance and crisis management. This radical experiment in market fundamentalism promised to end what it condemned as unjust redistributive social policies and the "unnatural" social engineering of the welfare state, to free entrepreneurs from the smothering constraints of regulation, taxation, and national boundaries, and unleash a new era of global entrepreneurialism, consumer choice, and prosperity for all.

The realities of neoliberal governance, however, tell quite different and unsettling stories. Across its short and troubled history, neoliberal governance has often strayed from its neoclassical economic foundations, discarding some rationales that no longer fit with turbulent economic realities, and subverting others with new and inventive strategies of crisis management (Brenner, Peck, and Theodore 2010, 184). Contrary to its core promises of self-regulating markets and trickle-down prosperity for all, the neoliberal governing formula has been implicated in a series of financial crises, which in turn have prompted severe recessions, uncompromising austerity programs, and even harsher realities for the most vulnerable and marginalized. Invariably, these crises have been interpreted as anomalies, the product of unanticipated market forces, or, more often, as the failure of national governments to curb spending and suppress public demands for social programs. The neoliberal model itself was rarely implicated in the regular (approximately every five years) and destructive path of these successive financial implosions. However, as Dani Rodrik argues, these booms and busts are "hardly a sideshow or a minor blemish on international capital flows; they are the main story" (quoted in Ostry, Loungani, and Furceri 2016, 39).

The neoliberal project stands indicted for a long list of governing challenges and outright policy failures, among them egregious inequalities in income, wealth, and life chances; precarious employment; underemployment and unemployment, especially among youth, women, and marginalized people; and political volatility, often fanned by racial, ethnic, and religious intolerance. Waves of right-wing populism, fuelled by xenophobia, nativism, misogyny, and outright racism, have spread across advanced democracies in recent years, but contemporary politics also is increasingly populated by broad-based social justice movements, seeking alternatives to the growing insecurities of daily life, environmental degradation, and the injuries of colonialism and racism. As this chapter explains, the neoliberal project has consistently aimed to decentre citizenship claims to redistribution, recognition, and representation, and to reshape popular understandings of the ideals of social equality and social justice (Fraser 2013). These ideas inspired social movements and progressive public policy for much of the twentieth century, and, as the contributions to this book describe, they have never been fully erased by decades of neoliberal assaults. In what follows, we explore why many social scientists use the term "crisis" to describe the contemporary moment, the origins of the idea of social justice, and the ways in which neoliberal theory and policy have positioned the market as the arbiter of what is just and fair. Finally, the chapter turns to the concept of diversity, which has emerged as a core theme in Canada's national narrative in recent years. As the contributions to this volume explain in greater detail, however, the recognition of Canada's growing diversity must be accompanied by tangible strategies that open avenues of inclusion and representation, begin to repair the damages of racism and colonization, and expand the idea of social justice beyond twentieth-century redistributive frameworks. The social and political upheavals of the contemporary moment signal that neoliberalism has lost its hold on the public imagination. "Something new is brewing" (Lascelles 2016, A12), but it is far from certain whether a renewed social justice politics will prevail among the competing discourses and the political uncertainties of this moment. Canada needs an informed and honest conversation about what social justice should look like in the twenty-first century.

The Anatomy of Crisis

Social scientists and international policy networks increasingly use the term "crisis" to describe the complex and interdependent currents of instability, inequality, and insecurity that define contemporary neoliberal times (Fraser 2014; Bauman and Bordoni 2014; W. Brown 2015; Oxfam 2016; WEF 2016). The lingering consequences of the 2008 Great Recession, the longest and deepest global economic crisis since the 1930s, betrayed the gospel of self-regulating markets as a self-interested and privileged myth. But, contrary to many predictions at the time, this profound global crisis did not immediately sound a death-knell for neoliberal fundamentalism, or provoke a pronounced shift in political allegiances or governing practices. Some five years after the financial meltdown, Kahler and Lake remarked that the striking feature about the Great Recession was that "the economic crisis [provided] few signs of fundamental political realignment, policy experimentation (apart from central banks), or mobilization by new political actors in any of the most seriously affected economies" (2013, 1–2).

At the beginning of the crisis, G8 governments quickly coordinated strategies to restore the system and return to business as normal. Massive public bailouts of private financial institutions, substantial public borrowing for "shovel-ready" stimulus packages, unconventional monetary policies such as historically low interest rates of indeterminate duration and quantitative easing (QE), and public austerity were unveiled in quick succession. These extraordinary measures, while preventing a full-blown financial collapse, set in motion a chain reaction from which the global economy has yet to recover. The crisis unravelled European financial markets and the political cohesion of the European Union; negative or tepid growth in combination with public austerity measures widened the gap between the rich and the rest, effectively denying a new generation a pathway to a good job and a secure future; emerging markets accumulated new debt as massive flows of capital scoured the globe for more promising investment sites and higher returns; and migrants pressed on borders to find some measure of economic and physical security.

In the view of many political economists, disequilibrium, economic stagnation, indebtedness (both public and private), and unsustainable income and wealth disparities constitute the "new normal" in the post–Great Recession economy (Streeck, 2016; Piketty 2014; The Economist 2014). The cover page of The Economist on 14 November 2015 underlined the point that neoliberalism's systemic crises were ongoing. The illustration showed three large books, entitled Volume I, The Great Subprime Crash (2007–2009); Volume 2, The Euro Crisis (2010–2012); and Volume 3, The Emerging Market Bust (2015–?). Volume 3 appeared poised to knock over an as yet untitled Volume 4. There was no bookend in this illustration, no suggestion of containment, which would signal that the worst was over. Instead, there was only the uncertainty that a question mark can convey.

The decade of uncertainty since 2008, however, has ultimately transformed the political landscape. Both defenders of the status quo and twenty-first century social justice movements confront a wave of right-wing populism, which, rather than providing an alternative to market governance, promotes a toxic brew of xenophobia, racism, and nativism as a response to the ongoing crisis. Such populism masterfully converts private economic insecurities and social anxieties into public animosities toward others, among them, faceless elites, women, immigrants, refugees, equity-seekers, and the marginalized. It cultivates and feeds on fear and division rather than offering tangible policy roadmaps to alternative futures (Bauman and Donskis 2016). As a result, contemporary politics in many parts of the liberal democratic world has become increasingly fractious and volatile, devoid of a middle ground, fatalistic, and, for many, hauntingly reminiscent of the politics of the 1930s.

In a telling account of the 2008 Great Recession, John Clarke (2012) poses a singular but critical question for citizens and policy-makers alike: "What crisis is this?" This is a difficult question to answer in the midst of ongoing economic instability and still unfolding political uncertainty. Increasingly, however, analysts suggest that this is not one of many recurrent crises *in* neoliberalism, but instead, a crisis *of* neoliberalism, which is deeply lodged in the cumulative and corrosive legacies of market-driven governance (Streeck 2016). Social movements and international policy networks emphasize that this crisis is multidimensional, as economic instability overlaps and interlocks with climate change, the growing precariousness of everyday life for so many, the legacies of colonialism and racism, the mounting frustrations of the marginalized, and growing strains of intolerance and extremism (Oxfam 2016; WEF 2016).

Wolfgang Streeck argues that the contemporary neoliberal regime of financialized capitalism has lost the capacity to "constitute a predictable order around which people could build stable identities and secure lives," or indeed to "reproduce itself as the core of a stable political order" (Streeck and Roos 2015, n.p.). Echoing Karl Polanyi (2001), Nancy Fraser (2014) similarly explains that unregulated markets have progressively undermined the economic, ecological, and normative foundations of contemporary society, challenging our collective capacity to sustain livelihoods and communities, social solidarity, and the ecosystem upon which all life depends. The stakes, Fraser suggests, have never been so high or so unforgiving. Neoliberalism's legacy, in short, is one of pervasive uncertainty and insecurity (Standing 2014; WEF 2016): we live in a "post-certainty" world (Bauman and Bordoni 2014, 139).

In periods of relative calm, instabilities are understood as policy challenges that are responsive to tried and tested manoeuvres in the usual policy repertoire. In crisis times, in contrast, an unanticipated triggering event exposes incommensurates: things that simply do not fit or could not and should not have happened according to the tenets of the prevailing governing logic (Gourevitch 1986). Often the result of gradual, almost imperceptible shifts in economic and social organization, and the cumulative impact of the prevailing governing model itself, these anomalies are initially misunderstood, misnamed, and misdiagnosed (Brenner, Peck, and Theodore 2010). Ultimately, they do not respond to the standard policy instruments. Policy-makers then scramble for inventive and experimental solutions that offer little certainty that the crisis will be resolved (Kahler and Lake 2013).

This feeling of uncertainty only intensifies as conventional and then experimental measures prove ineffective in the face of new realities. Antonio Gramsci, imprisoned by Italian fascists in the 1930s, referred to this time of groping for new solutions as an "interregnum." Gramsci argued that a crisis consisted "precisely in the fact that the old is dying and the new cannot be born." In an interregnum, he observed, "a great variety of morbid symptoms appear" (1971, 275–76). This in-between-ness is a time of "social nakedness . . . when we don't know where we are heading" (Bauman and Bordoni 2014, 83), when "several things might happen but only one actually does" (Gourevitch 1986, 9–10). In such times of pervasive uncertainty, citizens lose faith in the system, believing that it is rigged against them, in conventional political leadership, and in formal political institutions and processes. Alienated from the status quo and lacking clear alternatives, they become vulnerable to political scams, and the frenzied voices of demagogues with fantastic promises of greater tomorrows. This too is an integral part of the anatomy of a crisis.

Stable times are identified as such principally because the prevailing governing paradigm has successfully embedded itself in the popular political imaginary as "common sense"—as the way things are and should be—and because political aspirations and interests are "readily intelligible." They conform to a discernable grammar that specifies what a political claim looks like, who legitimately can make a claim, and how claims should be addressed (Fraser 1996, 393). These "readily intelligible" claims, of course, are mediated by power imbalances and political grammars that undermine, delegitimize, and render invisible many residual, competing, and emergent forms of claims-making (R. Williams 1977). Politics in normal times is always already a site of potential contestation, not the least, as described below, because of expansive dynamics of social justice claims-making.

In crisis times, in contrast, political expression and organizations proliferate outside of familiar political idioms, prevailing political organizations, and formal institutional channels. As Karl Polanyi (2001) explains in his enduring analysis of the ultimate breakdown of laissez-faire capitalism in the 1930s, the social and political fissures opened up by this earlier experiment in market governance generated the "spontaneous eruption" of all manner of counter-movements—revolutionary, progressive, regressive, and pathological. These countermovements shared a common point of departure—the system was broken and political leaders either would not or could not fix "the problem" as they defined it (Brodie 2012). But the solutions they offered were contradictory and contentious. It took almost two decades of grinding despair, fascist genocide, and a world war before a new political and institutional order and new grammars of claims-making consolidated around the ideas of equity, shared fate, and social security programs, such as universal health care, unemployment insurance, and social welfare (Polanyi 2001; Brodie 2012).

Polanyi's work reminds us that a governing paradigm in crisis unleashes myriad alternative political and social imaginaries, some built on the injuries of social inequalities, others focused on shoring up the crumbling edifices of common sense, and still others promoting transformative visons of more equitable and sustainable futures. The contemporary age of uncertainty similarly has witnessed the "spontaneous eruption" of an array of countermovements across advanced democracies. These countermovements are diverse, reflecting local and national contexts and leadership styles, and their analyses of the crisis embody deeply divergent orientations to political change, ranging from malignant framings of difference (e.g., xenophobia, Islamophobia, anti-Black racism, and homophobia), to transformative agendas focused on redistribution and environmental sustainability, to anti-racist and decolonized futures. Crisis times fuel social polarization and contentious politics.

It has become a familiar lament that neoliberalism's consistent enforcement of the dictum that "there is no alternative" to market governance (the so-called TINA principle) has left little conceptual or political space for imagining or articulating alternative futures. Fraser, for example, observes that we are "living through a crisis of great severity," but "we lack a conceptual framework with which to interpret it let alone to act in an emancipatory way" (2014, 541). Similarly, Leonidas Donskis explains that "we live in a world without alternatives. It's a world that proposes a single reality and a world that labels as lunatics—or, at least, eccentrics—all those who believe that everything has an alternative, including even the very best models of governance and the most profound ideas" (Bauman and Donskis 2016, 2).

We are living through uncertain times, on this we can all agree. As the chapters in this volume variously explore, however, our crisis times are generating alternatives, especially in the form of renewed social justice thinking and organizing that stretches beyond the redistributive focus of many twentieth-century social movements. The social justice lexicon is "infinitely more common now than it was even a couple of years ago" (Kamier 2015), and promises to intensify in response to growing currents of authoritarianism and populism. Contemporary grammars of social justice typically dissect pressing social issues such as income inequality and precariousness at the intersections of race, indigeneity, sexuality, gender, and ecology where they are often experienced most intensely (Kamier 2015). This emerging grammar of social justice is both inclusive and complex, opening possibilities for new coalitions, and demanding a broader societal, indeed, global debate about what social justice should look like in our times. As discussed later in this chapter, contemporary Canadian national narratives, unlike those, for example, in the United States and beyond, purport to recognize these complexities through the celebration of diversity. However, the idea of diversity, as the contributions to this volume underline, promises little to the marginalized unless it walks with substantive public policies that advance the goals of inclusion and social justice. The next section of this chapter explores the shifting parameters and potency of the idea of social justice.

The Idea of Social Justice

All societies, from the distant past to the present, rest on assumptions about fairness and just rules for living together, but these rules are also constantly challenged. The idea of justice, and its political descendent, social justice, constitute what Walter Bryce Gallie (1956) called "essentially contested concepts." These concepts have generated deeply invested political struggles over their meaning and have been differently institutionalized across time and cultures. Essentially contested concepts generate normative and political debates that cannot be settled with appeals to empirical evidence or deductive logics (Bauman and Bordoni 2014, 53). Rather, they reach deeply into our perceptions of who we are, how we should govern ourselves, and what our obligations are to each other. The latter question takes on critical importance for settler societies such as Canada, which, until very recently, has typically suppressed or ignored questions about its obligations to Indigenous peoples.

These formative questions about political collectivity are especially germane in crisis times. Indeed, the very idea of social justice, as we commonly understand it in Western political thought and practice, emerged out of the profound social upheavals and displacements that accompanied the protracted transition from feudalism to capitalism in Europe, and especially, the consolidation of the industrial revolution, which drew vast rural populations to urban factories and to the Americas in the early nineteenth century (Brodie 2007). During these years, new waves of modernist thinking celebrated the idea of progress and improving the human condition, and as Polanyi recounts, "people began to explore the meaning of life in a complex society" (2001, 88–89). The abject destitution that characterized early industrialization "fixed attention on the incomprehensible fact that poverty seemed to go with plenty." The growing realization that ordinary people need not and should not be preordained to a life of poverty and servitude, Polanyi argued, was "as powerful as the most spectacular events of history" (2001, 89).

As industrialization consolidated, so too did the idea that the unequal distribution of wealth, power, and well-being was a systemic problem—a social problem—that was rooted in unregulated capitalism, exploitation, and colonial dispossession. These early traces of a social way of thinking intensified across the nineteenth century, and became a familiar rallying call for both revolutionary movements determined to overthrow capitalism, and workers' collectives, trade unions, and social democratic parties that struggled to improve the lives and political representation of the burgeoning urban working class and the destitute. Whether revolutionary and reformist, these new political currents embodied a transformational shift in political literacy, which enabled people to evaluate foundational social institutions on the basis of their social justness and fairness, and to imagine alternatives (B. Jackson 2005, 360; Barry 2005). This significant shift in political thinking led Polanyi to conclude that "social not technical invention was the intellectual mainspring of the industrial revolution" (2001, 119).

Academics who have tracked the evolution of the idea of social justice emphasize that its transformative power grew out of two breaks with the governing logics of early capitalism. First, social institutions, including markets, were opened to critical assessment on the basis of their capacity to allocate resources more equitably across society. Second, glaring social problems, such as endemic poverty, were no longer seen primarily as a personal deficiency or moral failure, or as the exclusive responsibility of religious organizations or private charities. Instead, individuals and groups were empowered to seek redress for structural inequalities and unjust institutions on the basis of their social membership, which was increasingly expressed and implemented on the basis of national citizenship (B. Jackson 2005, 360). It also followed that those who were excluded from citizenship status—at various times, men without property, women, Indigenous peoples, the colonized, and the racialized—did not have claims-making status. Neither were their social justice claims to representation, redistribution, or recognition "readily intelligible" in dominant discourses. However, these exclusions and silences in early social justice thinking were immediately (and continue to be) challenged and destabilized by the critique embedded in the concept of social justice itself. As Wendy Brown explains, the idea of social justice has been inherently dynamic and expansive because it "harbours ideals in excess of itself" (2015, 206). Social justice is not a stable state to be achieved, but instead is a way of thinking and governing that prioritizes the elusive and shifting goals of fairness, equality, and inclusion. The social justice lexicon has consistently provided a common grammar for identity formation and claims-making stemming from exclusions and inequalities, and social and political practices were challenged on the basis of equity and fairness. Across the twentieth century, the grammars of social justice became more inclusive and complex as the promise of social justice made ever-widening claims, not only intelligible, but morally and politically inescapable. From the anti-slavery movement, to women's rights, to same-sex marriage, "social movements of every kind" have consistently emerged out of and used social critiques grounded in the logics of social justice (W. Brown 2015, 206).

Social Literacies

The trajectory of social justice politics during the past century was generative, expansive, and contentious, especially after the collapse of laissez-faire thinking in the 1930s. That decade witnessed an explosion of countermovements and experimentation with divergent alternatives, including "new deal" work-fare, fascism, communist central planning, and social democracy. After World War II, however, some variant of social liberalism took root in most advanced democracies. The architectures of some post-war social states were more elaborate and inclusive than others. The Canadian social state, for example, was late to develop, with its major pillars only set in place in the 1960s, and was less expansive and generous than some of its European counterparts. All post-war social states, however, projected an understanding of social justice that broke with prior logics of laissez-faire and market-friendly governance. As Bauman explains, the social state aspired to insure all citizens "against the vagaries of fate, individual fear of indignity in any of its many forms (as fear of poverty, exclusion and negative discrimination, ill health and unemployment, homelessness, ignorance) that haunted pre-war generations" (Bauman and Bordoni 2014, 8). As important, the social state cultivated new social literacies—ways of thinking and talking about social organization, which understood that markets were inherently unstable and inequitable, and that governments should cushion hardships, reduce poverty and insecurity, and create opportunities for the systemically disadvantaged (Brodie 2012, 129–30). Post-war social literacies also rested on the principles of shared fate—an understanding that anyone could fall on hard times through no fault of their own, and that no one should be resigned to a life of abject poverty or oppression.

There is always a yawning gap between the imaginable horizons of an ideal and what is tangibly achieved through public policies. Government, as

Peter Miller and Nikolas Rose remind us, "is a congenitally failing operation" (2008, 71), in which ideals consistently run up against entrenched power,
rival discourses, and emergent claims. Such was the case with the social state.
As feminist, critical race, and Indigenous scholars have long underscored,
the social state opened discursive and institutional spaces for some forms of
social justice claims-making and ignored or actively suppressed others. These
regimes were built on the unpaid reproductive work of women, the exploitation and marginalization of racialized minorities and immigrants, and in
settler societies such as Canada, the ongoing oppression of Indigenous peoples.
Indigenous claims-making, grounded in the injuries of dispossession, assimilation, and cultural genocide, were unintelligible to the post-war social justice
project, not the least because these claims challenged the very foundations of
the settler state (Coulthard 2014).

Yet, in many ways, these vital critiques of the post-war social state were
part of the broader dynamics of social justice politics, which invariably generate deeper and different understandings of social justice, more inclusive social
literacies, and often resistance and backlash. The politics of the 1960s and 1970s
reverberated with waves of social justice claims-making on the state and on
society more broadly for recognition, representation, redistribution, and self-
determination. Anti-racist, feminist, LGBTQ2S, environmental, and Indigenous
claims-makers mobilized to push against the biases and limits of the post-war
social state with more expansive visions of social justice. The explosion of
so-called identity politics during these years challenged both dominant framings of the social justice project, and political and economic interests that were
deeply invested in the maintenance of social hierarchies of inequality. Some in
the traditional left, for example, lamented that "identity politics" was a distrac-
tion from the redistributive ambitions of the post-war social justice project
(Fraser 2009). Making claims about gender discrimination or systemic racism,
they argued, were second-order questions that diverted attention and energy
away from the universal goal of redistributing wealth and providing social
security for all. This argument, however, was met with allegations of white,
heterosexual, and settler privilege. The social injustices endured by people
of colour, women, Indigenous peoples, sexual minorities, and marginalized
ethno-cultural groups, detractors rightly argued, could not be so easily catego-
rized as either a matter of redistribution or recognition (Malinda Smith 2003,
2008). Misrecognition through discriminatory legislation or corrosive cultural
stereotypes and discrimination, dispossession, and exclusion from centres of
social and political prestige and power, and invisibility in dominant discourses,
they argued, were inseparable from poverty, social marginality, and economic
insecurity. The intensification of social justice claims-making during these
years, however, also threatened entrenched political and economic interests.

Business-funded think tanks warned that liberal democracies were staggering under the weight of excessive claims-making, and were rapidly becoming ungovernable (Crozier, Huntington, and Watanuki 1975). Twentieth-century expressions of social justice would thus fall into the crosshairs of neoliberal social imaginaries as the century drew to a close.

Social Justice in Neoliberal Times

The story of the ascendency of neoliberal governing strategies in Western democracies, and, indeed, around the globe, has been often told. This governing formula was initially conceived in crisis, during World War II, by a small group of theoretical economists who raged against the dangers they saw in growing strains of collectivism that differently informed communism, socialism, and social democracy (Brodie 2010a). Key figures in this intellectual movement such as Ludwig von Mises, Friedrich von Hayek, and later Milton Friedman argued that government planning and redistribution threatened individual liberty and freedom, distorted the capacities of markets to promote innovation, competitiveness, and choice, punished entrepreneurs with unnecessary regulations and wrong-headed confiscation of private profit, and expanded the state and its many bureaucracies at the expense of free enterprise. These themes were progressively fine-tuned by small groups of like-minded academics, journalists, and businessmen, and broadcast by a blossoming network of business-funded think tanks. But, their "neo" liberal message did not gain much traction with governments or voters in the mid-twentieth century who saw the role of governments and markets quite differently (Monbiot 2016). By the late 1970s, however, amidst the compounding tremors of two global oil price shocks, stagnant economies and mounting inflation (stagflation), and growing talk of ungovernability, confidence in the post-war social state began to crumble. Typical of crisis periods, uncertainty and ignorance about how to respond soon prompted an urge to intervene in new ways and with different governing logics (Bauman and Bordoni 2014, 7). This pivotal moment was well understood by Friedman, who recounted the shift to neoliberal ways of thinking in the preface to the second edition of *Capitalism and Freedom*. Originally published in relative obscurity 20 years earlier, it is widely considered a canon of contemporary neoliberal thought. Friedman writes, "Only a crisis—actual or perceived—produces real change. When that crisis occurs, the actions that are taken depend on the ideas that are lying around. That, I believe, is our basic function: to develop alternatives to existing policies, to keep them alive and available until the politically impossible becomes the politically inevitable" (1982, ix).

Neoliberal prescriptions for a new era of market-friendly governance were multifaceted and ambitious. New governing strategies such as the privatization of state-owned enterprises and services, the relaxation of regulations on financial markets and industry, expanded international trade through constitution-like trade agreements (Gill 1995), so-called active social welfare programs (workfare), and massive tax reductions for corporations and the very rich were embraced by major global economies and core international financial institutions. These were imposed on developing countries through debt reduction (structural adjustment) programs or new and encompassing international trade agreements. Underpinning all of these changes, however, was a concerted campaign to dismantle and transform the social literacies of the post-war era.

The dismantling of post-war social literacies took many forms, beginning with the social state. Neoliberal theorists identified state intervention as a threat to individual freedom, a constraint on innovation and consumer choice, and as a distortion to otherwise self-governing markets. Popularizing these propositions, Margaret Thatcher would famously repeat, "There can be no liberty unless there is economic liberty," while Ronald Reagan oft-repeated in his down-home style, "Government is not the solution to our problem. Government IS the problem." As Bauman recounts, "In popular perception, aided and abetted by the chorus of a growing part of the learned and opinion-making public, the state was downgraded from the rank of the most powerful engine of universal well-being to that of a most obnoxious, perfidious and annoying obstacle to economic progress" (Bauman and Bordoni 2014, 9).

The battery of policies most commonly associated with neoliberalism eroded public rationales and capacities to provide social protection and advance social equity. State services were eliminated or "shifted sideways" (through outsourcing and partnerships) to the market (Bauman and Bordoni 2014, 9), while "large scale problems . . . were sent down the pipeline to small and weak units unable to cope with them technically, politically or financially" (W. Brown 2015, 132). In Canada, for example, federal social spending was progressively reduced to levels not seen since the 1940s, before Canada's post-war social architecture was set in place. At the same time, discursive and political spaces for social justice claims-making were systematically eroded, if not closed. Equality-seeking groups were discredited as "special interests," institutional hubs in government and civil society were defunded and dismantled, and equity-based political grammars and activists progressively disappeared from the political stage (Brodie 2010b). This disappearing act unfolded gradually and unevenly with respect to different equity-seeking groups and across jurisdictions. Over the course of a generation, however, "political discourse [was] 'cleansed,' so that the public interest, public ownership, common goods, equality, the redistribution of wealth, the stubborn facts about poverty and inequality, etc., all became 'unspeakable'" (Hall and Massey 2012, 59).

In part, social issues became unspeakable because equity-seeking groups were systematically excluded from policy-making processes, but, more important, neoliberals advanced their own definitions of social justice that turned post-war social literacies upside down. According to this contentious reframing of the concept, the role of the state was not to cushion citizens from the vagaries of the market, or to dismantle entrenched gendered, racialized, and colonial hierarchies. Instead, the state was charged with facilitating and creating markets so they could distribute rewards to those deemed most deserving. Von Hayek, for example, argued that market forces were impersonal—they operated according to the inexorable nature of supply and demand and thus could not be implicated in subjective decisions about fairness and social justice. He insisted that redistribution of income, security, and opportunity through political mechanisms such as social security programs was, in fact, decidedly unjust because it undermined the symbiotic relationship between reward and contribution that free markets purportedly achieved (UNCTAD 2012, 33). In this reframing, justice demanded that those who made greater contributions to society, which viewed through a market-affirming lens meant economic entrepreneurs and so-called job creators, should be rewarded with a bigger piece of the pie. Justice not only demanded that people get to keep what they produce (Nozick 1974) but also that "neutral" market mechanisms ensure that everyone get what they deserve (Monbiot 2016). The legacies of inherited wealth or the many vectors of structural inequality that preoccupied post-war social movements were ruled inadmissible in this reformulation of social justice. Equity-seekers, in the neoliberal formulation, were undeserving.

Economic inequality, which has reached previously unimaginable levels in recent decades, also was entirely consistent with neoliberal ideas about the generation of economic growth. Neoclassical economics dressed up inequality with the fineries of marginal productivity theory, which pronounced that higher incomes for some merely reflected their greater contributions to the success of an enterprise and, since economic growth was the new barometer of progress, to broader society (Stiglitz 2012, 29; W. Brown 2015). Among other things, this rationale justified an outrageous and rapid escalation in corporate executive compensation since the 1990s, which Thomas Piketty (2014, 2016) identifies as a significant factor underlying the sharp escalation in income inequalities in the neoliberal era.

Trickle-down theory was another innovation in the neoliberal toolkit that justified and celebrated income inequality. Market fundamentalists asserted that in a free society inequality fuelled entrepreneurialism. Markets rightly paid an entrepreneurial risk premium for those who dared to innovate, to invest in an idea, to find efficiencies, and to open new markets—all of which had broader social and economic benefits. Trickle-down theory painted a win–win scenario for governments, investors, workers, and consumers. If governments freed up entrepreneurs by cutting red tape, reducing taxation rates, and dismantling collective bargaining and employee benefits, they would create more jobs, enhance competitiveness, provide cheaper consumer goods, and grow the economy. Ultimately, accelerated economic growth would generate more revenue for governments to provide better public services and build more robust infrastructures. The tax cuts, as the trickle-down cheerleaders remain convinced, would pay for themselves many times over. Taxes, especially on the rich and the corporate sector, and regulation were thus recast as deterrents to economic growth, while the legitimacy of the state increasingly hinged on its capacity to "grow the economy" rather than protect citizens from either market failures or predictable life risks such as illness or aging (W. Brown 2015, 40).

This foundational reframing of the relationship between the state and markets gradually but surely transformed the social literacies and grammars of post-war social citizenship. As Carlo Bordoni describes, citizens and equity-seeking groups were subjected to incessant processes of "demassification," which is to say, left to fend for themselves. Social guarantees, once "the backbone of individual existence," were "phased-out, diminished, and emptied of meaning" (Bauman and Bordoni 2014, 16, 56), public goods and services were progressively commodified, available only to those with the money to purchase them, and individuals were "cajoled to become entrepreneurs of the self"—to take risks and self-invest in skills that markets valued and demanded (W. Brown 2015, 40). This neoliberal individualization dictated that individuals be self-sufficient market actors and assume full responsibility for themselves, their families, and their personal fortunes and failures—in effect, to find "biographic solutions" to the dictates of the market and other risks beyond their personal control (Beck and Beck-Gernsheim 2002, 22–26).

The problem with this formulation is not that individuals do not work hard to find personal solutions to the daily challenges of the contemporary (dis)order, not the least, paying for school, securing a job, arranging for child or elder care, investing in a home, saving for a rainy day or skills-upgrading, or planning for retirement. Rather, the problem with individualization is that the knowledge and resources we bring to these life choices are "not themselves a matter of choice" (Bauman 2002, 69). In a highly unequal society, many people simply do not have the money, resources, connections, or information to find personal solutions to the multifaceted problems generated by a highly volatile global environment. Neither do singular individuals have the power to change the rules of the game. Yet neoliberal discourses over the years have been highly successful in "bundling agency and blame" (W. Brown 2015, 134). The neoliberal moral tale configures the rich as self-made and deserving winners

(witness Donald Trump), the ones who made the right choices in a competitive global economy, and the vast majority of others as struggling to make
ends meet and personally responsible for their failure to thrive and get ahead.

The powerful narratives of trickle-down, entrepreneurialism, and individualization have progressively lost their sway, however, since the 2008 Great
Recession and the decade of uncertainty that it has left in its wake. Then,
global leaders had argued that there was no alternative to the unconditional
and massive public bailouts of financial and corporate entities: they were
simply too big to fail. The contradictions of this moment in the short history
of neoliberal governance were palpable, even to the most disinterested observer.
Corporate entities, both responsible for the crisis and fundamentally antagonistic to government intervention and the social state, were thrown a lifeline
by governments and largely unprotected taxpayers, many of whom saw their
jobs, savings, pensions, and home equity vanish into thin air. The resuscita-
tion of purportedly self-regulating markets, or as Chris Hedges (2013) puts it
more pointedly, this "insidious affirmative action for the rich," strained public
finances and ballooned public debt, which soon was reframed as the core
obstacle to global recovery. In 2010, G8 countries abruptly shifted course from
fiscal stimulus to "fiscal consolidation"—put simply, public austerity (Brodie
2014). Ordinary folks, still reeling from the aftershocks of the 2008 crisis, were
set up to pay for the corporate bailouts with their government services, social
programs, and opportunities for public sector employment (Blyth 2010). Again,
the public was told that there was no alternative to the wave of austerity that
swept across advanced democracies. And, not surprisingly, precarious economies
stagnated, others fell into recession, and unemployment and underemployment,
especially among youth, grew to levels reminiscent of the Great Depression.

In these post-crisis years, citizens are no longer cajoled to be entrepreneurs of the self—this idealized neoliberal subject who had been betrayed
by the miracles of the market. The market consistently benefited only top
income earners while the rest, regardless of their self-investments and other
biographic solutions, found themselves falling behind and implored to sacrifice their personal security and futures in order to help the market recover.
The "sacrificial" subject of neoliberalism in crisis endures cuts to wages, working hours and benefits, precarious employment, currency devaluations, and
the further erosion of social programs and state investment in public services
in order to help revive the global economy, replete with its uncertainties and
inequalities. The whole community, as Wendy Brown explains, is called upon
to sacrifice "in order to save particular elements within it" (2015, 213, 210–16).

In the intervening years, neoliberalism's familiar refrain that "there is no
alternative" to the latest market-affirming experiment has been increasingly
rebuked by international policy networks, volatile electorates, and a broad

spectrum of emergent countermovements that challenge the foundational assumptions of the neoliberal model. In an ongoing environment of economic fragility and political contestation, neoliberalism finds itself on the discursive ropes, with all but a handful of its long-time advocates expressing dissatisfaction with its legacy and future. In 2016, senior International Monetary Fund (IMF) economists analysed decades of economic data to answer the question of whether the promises of neoliberalism had been oversold to governments and broader publics. They concluded that the alleged benefits of neoliberal policies "in terms of increased growth seem fairly difficult to establish when looking at a broad range of countries," "the costs in terms of increased inequality are prominent," and "increased inequality in turns hurts the level and sustainability of growth" (Ostry, Loungani, and Furceri 2016, n.p.).

Inequality, whether measured in terms of income, wealth, well-being, or life opportunities, has been the defining legacy of neoliberal market-affirming discourses, policies, and practices. Reversing the moderate but sustained reduction in income inequalities realized by the social state, the past three decades have witnessed an unprecedented transfer of income and wealth from the vast majority of humanity to a small global plutocracy, a process that has intensified since the 2008 Great Recession. Statistical evidence that globalization was producing a few winners and many losers first emerged in the 1990s, but so-called inequality apologizers "brushed aside the yawning gap between the rich and the rest" as a brief and transitory phase in the relentless unfolding of global markets—an unfortunate consequence of the restructuring of supply chains, new production and information technologies, and the formation of high-income dual-earner families (Stiglitz 2013, 29). In the wake of the Great Recession, however, income inequality became the rallying call for a growing wave of social justice movements from the Indignados in Spain to the Occupy Wall Street movement (OWS), which, in 2012–13, spread from New York City to 900 cities around the world. Although OWS faded from the headlines within a few months, its powerful narrative of an unjust neoliberal global order, which is divided between an extremely privileged 1 per cent and everyone else, is a core theme informing both contemporary social justice claims-making and, increasingly, international policy missives. By 2016, leading international policy networks such as the Organisation for Economic Co-operation and Development (OECD), the IMF, and Oxfam conceded that we are "living through an inequality crisis" that has reached unsustainable extremes (Oxfam 2016, 1, 6). To better appreciate the depth of this crisis, Oxfam reported in 2017 that 62 of the world's richest people own as much as 3.6 billion of the world's poorest people: 8 men own more than the poorest one-half of the world.

The social justice implications of these unsustainable disparities are as obvious as they are immediate, especially for the millennial generation and the marginalized, who, unable to secure a good job, save for the future, or get ahead, will carry the scars of the contemporary crisis of inequality for decades to come. This crisis, however, is unique and demands more complex interventions than the redistributive strategies deployed by the post-war social state, although income redistribution and the renewal of social security policies is clearly part of the solution. The post-war social architecture was constructed on and sustained by the transfer of social income (i.e., welfare, family, and unemployment benefits, social programs, public services) from working and middle-class workers with stable (often lifetime) employment and employment benefits (i.e., collective bargaining, paid vacation, disability benefits, private pensions) to those temporarily or permanently marginalized in labour markets due to unemployment and underemployment, age, illness, ability, or caring responsibilities. Contemporary labour markets and the broader social terrain, however, have been profoundly altered by decades of neoliberal policy interventions, the globalization of production, and technological change. Well-paying manufacturing jobs have moved offshore, only to be replaced by low-paid or part-time positions in the retail or service sectors; employment has become more "flexible" and contractually limited with few, if any, employment benefits or opportunities for advancement; and the social safety net has been rolled back or put out of reach for those who need it the most. Most workers in Canada, for example, pay unemployment premiums, but less than half actually qualify for benefits when they lose their jobs.

Guy Standing argues that a new social hierarchy has emerged from decades of neoliberal governance and the globalization of production, which has been superimposed on the twentieth century industrial model of owners and directors, white-collar workers and professionals, and industrial workers. According to Standing, the contemporary social terrain consists of a global plutocracy (the 1 per cent), a diminishing salariat (white-collar workers with long-term contracts and employment benefits such as private pensions and extended health care), a small cadre of proficians (young, project-oriented self-entrepreneurs), and a mushrooming precariat (with low-paying and insecure jobs and few private or public benefits) (Standing 2011, 2014).

The precariat, Standing argues, is not meaningfully captured in the old political grammars of a squeezed or declining middle class, an underclass, or even a lower class. The precariat is a diverse social group, which includes the young and educated who are unable to find a place in their chosen profession, remnants of the old industrial working class whose jobs have disappeared through globalization or technological change, and those who have been consistently marginalized in labour markets—the low-skilled, women, migrants, racial minorities, Indigenous peoples, and the differently abled (Standing 2011). Many among the ranks of the precariat cannot get into or have been pushed out of the salariat and the security and social mobility that it has traditionally provided. Professions in the health, education, and public sectors that were once secure have been made flexible and contractual, and stripped of employment benefits. Some in the precariat cobble together several part-time jobs to survive, while others engage in serial employment, moving from one limited-term contract to another, from one indeterminate period of unemployment or underemployment to another, and from one pay cheque to another. Still others live in poverty at the margins of the labour force with little hope that life will change for the better.

What coheres this burgeoning group of so-called losers in the global economy is profound uncertainty, insecurity, and anger. They are confined to dead end, career-less, part-time, and unfulfilling jobs; they have insecure social incomes, often deemed ineligible to participate in or benefit from existing social welfare and social security programs; and they have no roadmap to a better future or hope of social mobility (Standing 2014, 386). They are the embodiment of successive neoliberal policy failures and the incessant individualization of systemic injustices. Regardless of how individuals in the precariat might build their personal portfolios of human capital, becoming "entrepreneurs of the self," they are expected to sacrifice their well-being and futures for a fragile, inequitable, and crisis-ridden governing formula, which by most measures is simply unsustainable (W. Brown 2015, 214; Fraser 2014).

The precariat is defined by diverse biographies of insecurity, frustration, and increasingly anger, among them the former unionized industrial worker resigned to part-time employment in the service sector, the newly minted college graduate unable to find a path into his or her chosen field, the immigrant trapped at the margins of the labour market, and the single mother unable to secure child care and a full-time job. These biographies of uncertainty also intersect with and weave through persistent exclusions grounded in the cumulative legacies of colonialism, racism, and ableism. These are distinctive bundles of frustration and insecurity; the precariat does not speak from a shared location, or with a single voice. This diversity, Standing (2014) argues, also makes the precariat a "dangerous" class that is vulnerable to extremist voices, offering simplistic solutions and blaming the "other" for their insecurity. Similar to the experience of the 1930s, these crisis times have witnessed the widespread repudiation of political elites and core political institutions, and the growth of populist movements, leaders, and political parties that point their accusatory finger at globalization, intellectualism, racial minorities, multiculturalism, feminism, and, especially, refugees and immigrants as being responsible for the very real insecurities of daily life in contemporary times. These increasingly racist

and illiberal discourses have moved from the margins to the centre of political debates in many Western democracies, all the while veiling the profound
inequalities that put the vast majority in the same precarious boat. As the
contemporary social order becomes evermore deeply divided by the politics
of "us versus them," fear and recrimination, and racism and violence, the spec-
tre of political failure haunts our collective future (Monbiot 2016). Our times
call out for alternative political imaginaries and necessary, if difficult, conversations about inequalities and social justice in Canada.

Diversity and Social Justice

Many Canadians can readily identify with the insecurities of the precariat, even if they do not use this term when they talk about themselves, their
families, or their fears for the future. Secure jobs have disappeared, nearly half
of Canadians live from pay cheque to pay cheque, and many others (40 per
cent) feel overwhelmed by debt (Chevreau 2016). Canadians also have been
subjected to the politics of ethnic and racial division, which, in more intense
forms, are unsettling politics in many European democracies, and especially in
the United States. For a decade, the Harper government quietly cultivated the
antagonistic politics of "us versus them," not the least by disavowing Canada's
history of colonialism, marginalizing Indigenous voices, increasing restrictions on immigrants and refugees, raising the bar for citizenship, referencing
so-called old stock (white) Canadians, banning the hijab during citizenship
ceremonies, and proposing hotlines to identify "the barbarians" in our midst.

Prime Minister Harper was defeated at the polls in 2015, in part because
his opponents provided voters with a clear alternative to the politics of division. Justin Trudeau, in particular, celebrated Canadian citizenship equality
and diversity. Diversity clearly is not a new theme in Canadian politics: in
fact, it is hard-wired into its settler-colonial foundations, depending as it does
on already existing diversity among Indigenous peoples, as well as successive
waves of new immigrants who are also increasingly visible minorities. For the
past half-century, however, this diversity typically has been viewed through the
lens of culture rather than through the lenses of race and colonialism. Canada
has imagined itself as a bicultural and bilingual community, and as a multicultural community, which not only tolerates, respects, and celebrates different
cultural traditions and practices but also identifies cultural difference as a defining feature of Canadian identity. In recent years, Canada also has represented
itself as having three founding cultures—Indigenous, French, and English.

Scholars and activists alike have been critical of these cultural (whether
bi-, tri-, or multi-) formulations of identity and difference, because they gloss

the heaviness of difference, whether experienced as racialization, racism, colonialism, xenophobia, marginalization, or exclusion. It is significant, then, that Canada's federal government has reframed the way it talks about differences among Canadians by emphasizing diversity rather than multiculturalism. The claim that "Diversity is Canada's strength" echoed throughout the 2015 federal election campaign, which elected more visible minorities, Indigenous peoples, and women than ever before, and resulted in a uniquely diverse federal cabinet with gender parity. Justin Trudeau proudly announced, "This is what Canada looks like," and has consistently elaborated on this diversity narrative since his election. As an example, Trudeau explains that "Canada has learned to be strong not in spite of our differences, but because of them" and that "Canadians understand that diversity is our strength. We know that Canada has succeeded—culturally, politically and economically—because of our diversity, not in spite of it" (Trudeau 2015). Canada has also been celebrated in the international press for its approach to diversity, especially after it opened its doors to Syrian refugees, while its southern neighbours took steps to close theirs. An Economist headline proclaimed, "Liberty Moves North" (29 October 2016).

Canada is an increasingly diverse country: this is an irrefutable axis in contemporary Canadian politics. The language of diversity, thus, is fundamental to a renewed social justice project, because it stretches our political imaginations and policy agendas beyond mosaic multiculturalism to take into account all kinds of perceived differences among Canadians, including those grounded in race, colonization, religion, sexual orientation, gender identity, and ability. However, the contributors to this volume ask: What work is the idea of diversity actually doing in contemporary Canadian politics?

Critical race and equity scholars who have studied diversity programs in various organizational settings find that the term's meaning shifts substantially depending on who is talking. Diversity, many argue, is simply a euphemism—a cliché that gestures at recognition, representation, and inclusion, but actually works to obscure and reproduce deep and historically entrenched inequalities. Sara Ahmed, for example, assigns the term "diversity" to a class of words that she calls "non-performative" (2007b). These are words that imply an action that does not follow—words that reproduce social hierarchies by appearing to transform them. Many ideas and words gain force and content only when they travel with other words that give them a mandate to advance social and political change. Consider, for example, the different meanings and actions that are implied when the word "social" walks with words like justice, solidarity, equality, responsibility, sustainability, and inclusion. Each of these pairings prescribe particular forms of claims-making and policy-making. Diversity, in and of itself, is only a descriptor, a way of describing a group, organization, or population. Left standing alone without a walking partner to give it substance and direction, the term can generate anti-diversity counter-narratives that attempt to reassert racial and social hierarchies by, for example, promising to test immigrants for "Canadian values," or to "Make America Great Again." Our task is to animate non-performative words like "diversity" by linking them to robust strategies of recognition, reparation, and redistribution.

In settler societies such as Canada, however, the challenge of diversity also necessarily demands stretching social justice imaginaries to long-neglected and uncharted territories. A social justice agenda, which I have just argued must be attached to diversity discourses, is always already imagined and enacted on the tenuous and fragile foundations of the pre-emptive sovereignty of settler societies. These forms of political imaginaries also are in crisis, not the least because of ever-stronger assertions of Indigenous self-determination, and growing conflicts about land, water, and the environment. These conflicts demand more from a diversity imaginary than can be provided by either conventional social justice politics or, even, a politics of reconciliation that focuses primarily on the restoration of mutuality and respectful relationships between settler and Indigenous peoples. Instead, these conflicts invite us to expand our understanding of diversity itself, beyond compositional markers of diverse groups, to include different forms of governance, different political geographies, and different obligations to the environment as foundational pillars in our collective project (A. Simpson 2014; Coulthard 2014).

This Volume

Crisis times, as noted earlier in this chapter, are spaces of in-between-ness when multiple and conflicting visions of the future compete to shape public discourses, political allegiances, and policy outcomes. The contributions to this book advance the case that these crisis times call for a renewed and expansive social justice agenda, which addresses the multiple challenges of the early twenty-first century in progressive and sustainable ways. As David Robichaud discusses in **Chapter 2**, a renewed social justice politics necessarily begins with a critical interrogation of common notions of fairness and justice that have dominated political thinking in recent decades. Using the analogy of Robinson Crusoe, he argues that neoliberal prescriptions for individual reward inaccurately depict the ways societies actually work and progress. Robichaud makes the case that redistribution is both necessary and just because every member of society contributes to "individual" success stories. All of these contributions should be recognized and valued. In **Chapter 3**, Malinda Smith examines the "great experiment" that has fundamentally transformed the Canadian social landscape in the past four decades. The Canadian population has become

increasingly racially and ethnically diverse, while statistical projections anticipate that within a generation, one-half of Canadians will be either immigrants
or children of immigrants. Considering this shift as well as existing diversity
among Indigenous peoples, Smith recounts the ways "diversity stories" have
been deployed in contemporary political discourses and policies. She provides
stark empirical evidence, which clearly demonstrates that Canada's core institutions are failing to embrace the advantages of diversity by continuing to
under-represent Indigenous peoples, visible minorities, and women in key
decision-making and authoritative roles. Diversity policies, she concludes,
only appear to "diversify whiteness."

The three chapters in **Part 2** of this volume provide case studies in precariousness by differently posing the question "social justice for whom?" In
Chapter 4, Judy Fudge explores shifting regulatory regimes that have been
applied to migrant workers in Canada in recent years. Migrant workers, she
explains, have been represented as threats who take jobs away from resident
workers, but, as Fudge explains, these discourses divert attention away from
the erosion of wages and employment conditions for everyone. In **Chapter 5,**
Grace-Edward Galabuzi focuses on the case of Canadian universities to
assess the impacts of equity, diversity, and inclusion initiatives. He argues that
so-called post-racial and colour-blind policies do not reflect the lived experiences of Indigenous or racialized students and faculty, but instead, often
reinforce "whiteness" and the inherently colonial foundations of these institutions. He concludes that a renewed social justice politics must reach beyond
dominant norms of Eurocentrism, and pursue transformative strategies to indigenize and decolonize the academy. In **Chapter 6,** Hayden King argues that
a renewed social justice politics in settler societies such as Canada necessarily
requires a new social covenant with Indigenous peoples. King explains that
settler colonial models of governance are in crisis, not the least because of the
profound precariousness and inequalities that define the daily lives of so many
Indigenous peoples, broken treaty relationships, and an unprecedented surge
in Indigenous activism that is focused on land claims, land use, and our relationship with the environment. King outlines several principles of Indigenous
political economy, including reciprocity, sustainability, and mutual autonomy,
which could form the foundations to begin to meaningfully decolonize social
relations in Canada.

The contributions to **Part 3** of this volume focus on the critical role of
activism in shaping new futures in Canadian politics. In **Chapter 7**, Meenal
Shrivastava demonstrates that, despite the election of new governments both
federally and in Alberta, Canada continues to manifest many of the key
markers of a "petroculture." These markers include inordinate reliance on
resource extraction (especially oil), income inequalities, democratic deficits,

and environmental degradation. Shrivastava points to the emergence of political alliances between Indigenous peoples and the environmental movement
as a potentially powerful point of resistance to the seemingly relentless expansion of resource extractive practices. Alexa Degagné, in **Chapter 8**, reflects
on the history of lesbian, gay, bisexual, queer, and trans politics in Canada as
examples of "anger activism." She argues that, confronted with social injustice, discrimination, and violence, anger activism can help forge new alliances,
build communities, empower previously silenced voices, and challenge hierarchies of social and political power. Her case study emphasizes that our personal
anger and the anger of others can be channelled to realize more just and inclusive social outcomes. Finally, in **Chapter 9**, Judy Rebick reflects on both her
long and distinguished history of social justice activism in Canada, and the
emergence of what she terms "21st-century social justice movements" in the
wake of the 2008 financial crisis. Rebick applauds the bottom-up and inclusive strategies of these new movements, and argues that these new forces are
progressively reshaping the perspectives and politics that are necessary to meet
the multiple challenges of these crisis times. All of the contributors to this
book invite us to think, act, and talk openly about what social justice should
look like in contemporary Canada.

Further Readings

Bauman, Zygmunt, and Carlo Bordoni. 2014. *State of Crisis*. Cambridge:
    Polity Press.
Brodie, Janine. 2014. "Elusive Equalities and the Great Recession: Restora-
    tion, Retrenchment and Redistribution." *International Journal of Law in
    Context* 10 (4): 427–41.
Brown, Wendy. 2015. *Undoing the Demos: Neoliberalism's Stealth Revolution*.
    New York: Zone Books.

CHAPTER 2

SOCIAL JUSTICE AND THE EXTINCTION OF *HOMO CRUSOECONOMICUS*

David Robichaud

Introduction

Never before have inequalities of wealth been so huge either within our societies or between rich and poor societies. A 2016 Oxfam briefing paper argues forcefully that the global inequality crisis, which it has documented in recent years, "is reaching new extremes." Data obtained from Credit Suisse indicate that the richest 1 per cent of the world's population have more wealth than the rest of the world combined. In 2015, the richest 62 individuals in the world, down from 388 individuals in 2010, had wealth equivalent to the bottom half of humanity (Oxfam 2016, 1–2). In Canada, the top 10 per cent own almost half of all wealth, while the top 1 per cent of income earners receive 12 per cent of all taxable income (A. Jackson 2013, 1). These statistics are not simply shocking to our sense of fairness and economic justice, but they flag important economic and social problems that might span generations. More and more economists are warning us of the problems we will face if we do not put an end to this accelerating enrichment of the wealthy (Stiglitz 2012; Piketty 2014). Less economic growth, more financial volatility, increasing indebtedness among the middle class, and chronic poverty are among the many contemporary challenges that have been attributed to the growing gap in income, wealth, and life chances. Epidemiologists also have bad news for us all: societies with higher levels of inequality appear less healthy on a broad range of indicators, including obesity and drug and alcohol abuse (Wilkinson and Pickett 2009). It is important to stress the most amazing element of their findings: it is not poorer societies that face more problems, but instead, societies with higher levels of economic inequalities.

This situation did not happen suddenly. For decades, neoliberal politicians fed on the discourse of right-wing economists and encouraged us to modify our fiscal structures and to decrease taxes on the wealthy, under the assumption that this windfall would be reinvested in the economy, create jobs, and fuel growth. According to this optimistic story, it does not matter who gets the resources at first, since consumption and investments trickle all the way down to the poorest people, raising living standards for everyone. Unfortunately, despite impressive economic growth in the 1990s and massive increases in the earnings of the wealthiest of our societies, the average North American has lost purchasing power since the 1980s.

In the past three decades, neoliberal politicians have relied heavily on libertarian philosophy and political objections to distributive justice and their intuitively attractive arguments to justify rising inequalities. The libertarians argue that individuals are entitled to everything they produce, that we need incentives to produce wealth, and that giving money to unemployed or unproductive individuals will decrease their motivation to work. These ideas weave through public discourses and informal conversations about social and redistributive policies. The poor are represented as lazy, negligent, and undeserving of social transfers from the state. Lazy teenagers playing videogames, undeclared workers, and immigrants abusing social programs are for many the new representations of those getting help from the state. More and more people feel that it is unjust to have to pay high taxes for social programs for people who, according to this view of undeserving poor, basically choose to become dependent on the state. Libertarian ideas also inform everyday conversations about taking money from hardworking and successful members of our society. We value hard work and productivity, so the argument goes, and people who work harder should receive more than others. They create goods and produce wealth, and thus should get all the benefits from what they produce. A worker is entitled to every cent he or she receives for his or her economic activity.

These popular arguments for rejecting redistributive policies are in large part grounded on a misunderstanding of how individuals create and acquire wealth. Our understanding of wealth production is based on the myth of *homo crusoeconomicus*. According to this myth, each individual is like a Robinson Crusoe on an isolated island. We each produce, in relative isolation from others and within the limits of our capacity, different goods with different values in different quantities. People choose freely to make the most of their unequal talents in different contexts, and what they make out of these talents should legitimately belong to them, without consideration for how others are faring. The most talented produce more than the less talented, and therefore should obtain higher compensations. According to this picture, it is *just* for hardworking and talented people to have more than untalented and lazy people; it is *unjust* for the state to arbitrarily take money legitimately earned by the wealthy to redistribute it to the least well-off. The assumption underlying this position is that justice relates to individual contribution: contributing a lot entitles one to a large share of the collective wealth; contributing nothing entitles one to ... nothing. From here, it is easy to criticize distributive justice and the redistribution of resources as taking too much from the deserving rich to give to the undeserving poor.

In this chapter I do not challenge the idea that we are entitled to the goods we produce in isolation from others, using only our talents. Rather, I challenge the idea that such an argument can justify the level of inequalities observed today. By looking at the libertarians' rejection of distributive justice, I will show that they are right when they consider that the distribution of wealth should reflect individual contributions, but that they are wrong in their understanding of what should count as "relevant contributions" to the production of wealth. By focusing solely on individuals producing wealth and by explaining success and failure by reference to hard work, talent, and virtues, we miss the background that makes these individual contributions possible. We also fail to appreciate that this background is made possible only by a thick web of subtle but complex contributions from every single member of society. I will try to highlight the thickness of these contributions to society and to collective wealth in order to show that they are much more equal among individuals than we may believe, and therefore that the distribution of wealth should legitimately, for reasons of justice as libertarians understand it, be made much more equal as well.

Libertarianism in Contemporary Debates on Justice

In normative philosophy, many theories have tried to demonstrate that economic inequalities are not justified and that we have a moral duty to redistribute wealth. The mid-twentieth century was dominated by a debate between utilitarians and liberal egalitarians over the proper justification for a just distribution of wealth. According to utilitarians, a more equal distribution of wealth is required due to the decreasing marginal utility of some goods, including money. The idea is quite simple. If I give you a coffee, you will get some benefits and obtain some well-being from it. If I give you a second, then a third, then a fourth, each additional coffee will produce less well-being than the previous one, to the point where it will produce no well-being at all or even create harm. Many goods are subject to this phenomenon and money is one of them. According to utilitarians, the reason why we should aim for a more equal distribution of wealth is that it is the best way to produce a maximum of well-being and happiness in a given society. It follows then that if one is in favour of well-being and happiness (and who is not), then one also should favour more equality since it is the best way of achieving these social goals.

The liberal tradition has been critical of the utilitarian approach. John Rawls, for example, identified what we will call "the separation of persons" as the main flaw in the utilitarian approach (1999, 19–24). Utilitarians approach problems at the collective level and are willing to sacrifice some people's well-being in order to maximize overall well-being. Every redistribution is justified, no matter who suffers or how badly, as long as it maximizes overall utility. This is unjust according to Rawls. He proposed instead a theory that protects an individual's freedom but, at the same time, allows for redistribution from the wealthy to the least well off. The argument is once again quite simple. Imagine we find a way to hide part of your identity from yourself. You know the society you live in, the ways people think and get motivated, and how rich people and poor people live, and so on. You know everything there is to know about your society, but are unaware of your personal situation in this complex and diverse society. You are then asked to identify the principles of justice according to which rights and wealth should be distributed in order to create a just society. You do not have to choose the just principles, simply the ones that you prefer.

According to Rawls, in such an "original position," people would be risk-averse and would try to make sure that no matter who they happen to be, they would have enough to enjoy decent lives and pursue meaningful life projects. Individuals would make sure that nobody is left behind, just in case it might be them. Rawls suggested that under these conditions, people would first require extensive rights protecting a sphere of liberty, and second they would require that only competence and talent, rather than cronyism, discrimination, or prejudice, opened access to opportunities and to coveted social positions. Third, they would require that the distribution of wealth be equal among all, unless some inequalities are necessary to create more wealth and improve the situation of the least well off. Inequalities can be permitted, if they seem necessary to motivate people to work harder, take risks, study, and work in stressful and demanding roles. However, we would only allow inequalities that improve lives of the poorest people in the society.

This is another convincing justification for the redistribution of wealth. If you are impartial and resist defending your personal interests, you will prefer a more equal distribution of wealth and a society where the poorest are as comfortable as possible and where the richest can only get richer if they improve the situation of the least well off. This argument convinced many people, but not Robert Nozick (1974), one of Rawls's colleagues working a couple of doors down the corridor in Harvard's philosophy department in the 1970s. Nozick came up with an objection that is extremely simple but also extremely convincing. He basically took the argument of the necessity of the separation of persons more seriously than Rawls.

Nozick (1974) argued that the money Rawls proposes to redistribute is not lying there in nature waiting to be distributed, but that it already belongs to people who obtained a right of property over these resources through acts of production and exchange. In other words, they made, sold, and traded things. If we cannot demonstrate that this production or exchange involved theft, threats, fraud, treachery, or any kind of behaviour that one judged to be illegitimate, then we are obliged, Nozick argued, to acknowledge the legitimate owners of these resources, no matter the level of inequalities that are created by these activities. They have complete ownership of these resources, and this complete ownership follows from the complete ownership people have of their own bodies. Through owning their bodies and their talents, they acquire unowned external resources with which they mix their labour. For example, an apple on a wild tree is unowned and can be appropriated by anyone, but once I cook it and make an apple pie, it is absolutely mine and I would be wronged if someone took it from me.

Nozick's (1974) theory of justice is an entitlement theory, not a distributive theory. What matters morally is the acquisition and transfer of property rights over external resources, not the final social distribution that we end up with. The only legitimate reason we might have to impose redistribution is if some individuals have been wronged in the past and have claims to restitution. Otherwise, the social distribution of resources is a by-product of individual choices and activities, which must be protected using absolute rights. If resources are acquired in a morally irreproachable way, and if they are freely exchanged, trying to reach a certain kind of distribution will necessarily amount to violating people's freedom and rights over and over again. This is a violation of the separation of persons: we allow some to take from others in the name of a collective project, namely social equality. For transfers to be legitimate, individuals must consent to it. Rawls would say that we would consent if placed in a hypothetical situation of partial ignorance. Nozick would say, along with Ronald Dworkin, that a "hypothetical contract is not simply a pale form of an actual contract; it is *no contract at all*" (Dworkin 1977, 151).

In a nutshell, a just society for libertarians is one in which individuals enjoy equal liberty understood as absence of interference from others. Justice requires that people be left alone with their possessions, by others and by the state, unless these possessions are acquired illegitimately. In what follows, I intend to show that following Nozick's logic, we can put forward strong arguments in favour of state intervention and redistribution of wealth through taxation.

The Libertarian Desert Island: Home of the *Homo Crusoeconomicus*

Libertarians commonly resort to the Robinson Crusoe tale to ground their claims to the legitimacy of individual property rights and appropriation. To imagine the moment of acquisition, the precise moment when an unowned object becomes someone's property, and the reason why it becomes his or hers to do with as he or she wishes, many scholars propose the image of a single person on an otherwise deserted island. Nozick (1974), Milton Friedman (1982), David Gauthier (1986), and other proponents of libertarian positions have used this thought experiment to ground a justification of absolute individual property rights and to question the legitimacy of state intervention or duties of redistribution.

The story usually unfolds as follows. Imagine you land on a desert island after a shipwreck with nothing but your knowledge, your talents, and your preferences. After a couple days of waiting for help, you realize that you might be there for a while and that it might be worth building a shelter and fashioning some tools. This will demand time and effort beyond simply looking for food, watching for boats, or enjoying the beach, but it will improve your situation and chances for survival in the long run. Limited only by resource availability and your knowledge, talents, and skills, you build a hut, tie some fishing nets, and make a reservoir to collect rain water. You also may capture some animals in order to get eggs and meat, or maybe work on a garden for accessible fruits and vegetables. You still hope to be rescued, but your life is far less miserable now.

Suppose that a couple years after your arrival on the island, another castaway washes up on your island. He is in bad shape and, of course, owns nothing, except his own body, and the talents and knowledge that come with it. He claims that since you possess so much more, you should redistribute some resources to him for reasons of justice. Libertarians question whether we should consider such a claim legitimate. Let us be clear: you have no right to ask the newcomer to leave the island. Appropriation is submitted to the Lockean proviso, requiring that one leave enough for others when appropriating a good. We may also think that you have a duty of charity to help him in order to avoid misery or death. But would it be intuitively acceptable to argue that, out of a duty of justice, you owe a share of what you possess to this person *because* he is poorer than you?

Most libertarians would argue that you have absolutely no duty of redistribution. Why? Because the distribution of wealth is not something you controlled; all you did and could do was decide what portion of your time and resources you were willing to invest in making your future better, and you should be responsible only for the results of these decisions. You stole nothing from anybody, made nobody's situation worse by your behaviour, exploited no one's talents or resources, and therefore you can legitimately call everything you possess your own. As Nozick argues, "no one else can make a claim of justice against this holding" (1974, 185).

I think that this argument is sound and that justice cannot justify a redistribution of wealth in such a situation. The first islander acquired resources legitimately, left enough to others for them to pursue any project they might deem desirable, and justice cannot justify taking some resources from the first islander. I think libertarians are wrong, however, when they describe our societies as aggregations of such islanders. Picturing our society as a multitude of free and isolated *homo crusoeconomicus*, pursuing their individual interests, each of whose success depends solely on their talents and good fortune, is a false depiction of social life.

There is something important missing from this portrait, which is obvious when we consider the wealth we would expect an individual to produce if left alone on a desert island. Even by picturing the brightest human left alone on an island rich with resources, it is hard to imagine that he or she would survive his or her first few years, let alone produce anything more than rudimentary infrastructures and tools. How then can we explain that our brightest minds are working on sending robots to Mars or solving complex global problems, when the very same brilliant minds would hardly be able to build a hut on a desert island? How can we explain the success of our civilization when we compare it with past civilizations, if individual talent is not the answer? We will now make explicit that individual talent is a necessary element to succeed in a competitive environment, but not a sufficient one. Talents can only be developed and produce desirable goods in a certain kind of context, and this context is made possible by the contributions of many, if not all. Contrary to libertarian assertions, *individual success is a collective accomplishment*.

Desert Island: A Nice Story Teaching Us Nothing

What makes the island story so intuitively appealing is that we think that since the islanders produced some goods without any help from anyone, without abusing or stealing from anyone, they are entitled to those goods. They simply "mixed their labour" with unowned resources, transforming free and common resources into privately owned goods. However, there is a big problem in thinking that today's wealth is due to free individuals producing and exchanging in isolation from one another.

In order to understand why libertarians are wrong in thinking that redistribution is morally indefensible in our societies, we must highlight how we managed to go from a period in our development where sharpening rocks was a great accomplishment to one where we routinely send satellites into orbit in order to communicate on Facebook with "friends" on smartphones connected to the web via public Wi-Fi. It has little to do with the improvement of our capacities as individuals. We rather have to look at three interrelated determinants of our collective success: (1) division of labour; (2) material and immaterial heritage; and (3) normative heritage. These determinants of success were inaccessible to *homo crusoeconomicus*. When he or she was no longer alone on his or her piece of land, he or she had to adapt to a more complex world, which presented new threats but also offered a multitude of diverse and complex opportunities. *Homo crusoeconomicus* and others similar to him or her collectively adapted to and helped create these new opportunities. The figure of *homo cooperativus*, rather than that of *homo crusoeconomicus*, better approximates the social world in which we live.

Divisions of Labour

For an individual to become excellent at any demanding task in our society, others have to perform other tasks necessary for survival. If we had to grow vegetables, attend to farm animals, sew clothes, build houses, and educate our own kids, we would probably be very bad at all those things. We certainly wouldn't have time to develop philosophical theories, or send satellites into orbit, or do any of the other things that we consider to be admirable achievements.

Some social positions (professions, political positions) are more closely tied to some of our preferences and our interests. Some are more demanding, involving more stress and responsibilities, or more investment in learning and practice. Specialization is costly but necessary to produce highly valuable goods. These specialized positions tend to come with better compensation, higher social status, and more recognition. The competition for these positions and for the social benefits they provide is fierce, and those who occupy them should be rewarded substantially. Their talent, superior knowledge or skills, character, and many other attributes made them more capable than others in accomplishing important and difficult tasks, and it is important to reward their investment and talents.

Although the particular virtues of these workers explain in part their success and their exceptional knowledge, we still have to consider how this knowledge was acquired and made relevant. Specialization in very technical skills or very detailed knowledge only makes sense in a complex division of labour. The banker, the writer, and the professional athlete, for example, can only spend the thousands of hours necessary to acquire their unique comparative advantage once others make sure that their basic (and not so basic) needs are filled. The division of labour makes possible and encourages the specialization of each worker, providing huge benefits to all members of society. If we are successful, it is in a very particular, very precise role that only makes sense when placed in the context of a complex social division of labour.

If division of labour was the whole story, libertarians could still argue that we are free to try to occupy the most favourable places in this complex structure, that some contribute more than others to this cooperative venture, that only talent and work can explain why some contribute more than others, and therefore, that they are entitled to more of the collective product than others. We explained that the production of a highly demanded good depends on the provision by others of a whole lot of other goods. Now, let's try to explain why our situation in the whole system is not a question of individual merit alone. For now, we can say that to be successful, one has to specialize, and this is only possible if others do the "dirty work."

Material and Immaterial Heritage: Standing on the Shoulders of Giants

I invented nothing new. I simply assembled the discoveries of other men behind whom were centuries of work. Had I worked fifty or ten or even five years before, I would have failed. So it is with every new thing. Progress happens when all the factors that make for it are ready and then it is inevitable. To teach that a comparatively few men are responsible for the greatest forward steps of mankind is the worst sort of nonsense.

—Henry Ford

This famous quote from Henry Ford captures the importance of the division of labour and heritage, which is another necessary aspect of any success story. People do not take their first breath alone in a cavern. They are born into a society, and this society necessarily has a heritage to offer newcomers. This heritage is mainly of two types. The first and most obvious is the material heritage of a society. It comprises houses, roads, infrastructure, and all other objects useful in our everyday lives. The second, more abstract type of heritage is immaterial. It includes culture, languages, and all the knowledge acquired and "stored" by members of the society. Not every individual has to go through the Bronze Age and then the Iron Age to arrive at the Internet revolution. Having gone through these previous eras, our society is able to benefit from and build upon the knowledge and skills it has made possible. We do not have to start from scratch: we can start from where previous genera-tions left off and keep pushing forward.

This heritage was created by previous generations, but it is also kept alive and made available by present generations. If we are successful, we owe a large part of our success to previous generations who worked hard in order to create and maintain this heritage. This "cumulative cultural heritage" is theoretically accessible to every human being from the moment he or she can communi-cate with others (Tomassello 2001). However, access to this heritage is neither identical nor equitable. First, we will have access to different domains of this material and immaterial heritage, depending on who transmits the knowl-edge and where we live. All other things being equal (and they rarely are), it is easier for a Canadian to become a professional hockey player and for a Hawaiian to become a surfer. But more importantly, access to immaterial heri-tage is unequal. Individuals are not born equal in relation to the heritage that we share collectively. The content of this heritage and the access that individ-uals have to it varies considerably across social locations, thus making success much more difficult to achieve for some than others. Living far away from infrastructures will likely make life more difficult and more costly for some, not having access to knowledge will keep some options unknown until it is too late to invest time and energy in developing skills in some domains, and so on. Having people who can mentor or inspire us will affect the likelihood that we follow one course of action and not another.

The lengthy debate between Nozick and Rawls on the absolute property of our talents is relevant here. According to Rawls (1999), redistribution of wealth should reflect individual choices but not individual chances. We should aim at levelling the impact of chance on people's lives, and this covers the impact of talents. It is legitimate, from a moral point of view, to redistribute from the talented to the not-talented since nobody choses his or her talents or is responsible for them, and therefore no one should benefit or suffer from them. For Nozick (1974) and libertarians, in general, this is nonsense. Even if they are not responsible for their talents, people own their bodies and their talents.

Nozick's (1974) position seems more intuitively appealing, even if the conclu-sion is not necessarily the one we prefer. However, as soon as we distinguish between raw talent and developed talent, the position of each philosopher gets much closer. We could easily consider that talents are unequal and unmerited, but that individuals have nonetheless full property rights over them. However, we might also consider that the development of these talents will depend on access to the material and immaterial heritage provided by society, and therefore that highly developed talent will necessarily mean privileged access to this heritage and a favourable position in the division of labour that allows time to develop these talents. In order to be successful, one needs talent, but more importantly, one needs privileged access to the material and immaterial heritage created and transmitted collectively by generations and made available by contemporaries.

Normative Heritage: From Wolf-Free Desert Islands to Tamed-Wolf Communities

> Look, if you've been successful, you didn't get there on your own. You didn't get there on your own. I'm always struck by people who think, well, it must be because I was just so smart. There are a lot of smart people out there. It must be because I worked harder than everybody else. Let me tell you something—there are a whole bunch of hardworking people out there.
>
> If you were successful, somebody along the line gave you some help. There was a great teacher somewhere in your life. Somebody helped to create this unbelievable American system that we have that allowed you to thrive. Somebody invested in roads and bridges. If you've got a business—you didn't build that. Somebody else made that happen.
>
> —Barack Obama, 13 July 2012

In the above quote, American President Barack Obama gestures to the material and immaterial heritage discussed above, as well as to a third type of heritage that we will call "normative heritage." It is composed of sets of norms and rules that we follow as members of a specific society. Some of them might be subject to discussion, even criticism, but we all inherit a set of more or less coherent norms and rules from past generations. These norms range from shaking hands to not killing others, from monogamy to driving on the right, from dressing in black at funerals to holding doors for people walking behind us. Norms also regulate the preferred way of behaving in particular roles such as a parent, a clerk, a teacher, or a doctor. Some of these norms are made explicit by law while others remain implicit. When we think of the "unbelievable American system" that Obama describes in the above quote, we think of material and immaterial heritage as well as particular norms, regulations, and laws that make our interactions smoother and more efficient, including individual rights, specific roles in the family, duties of patriotism, and many other norms that constitute the normative landscape.

Although these norms are challenged and modified across time, they do impose limits on our behaviour. Enforced by different mechanisms, ranging from angry looks to imprisonment, they make our world more predictable and safer and create new opportunities for cooperation. The libertarian's imaginary of a world as composed of Robinson Crusoes living side by side dismisses two factors that are central to social life—social norms and the benefits of cooperation.

Everything Robinson Crusoe does on his island is intended to increase individual well-being. Since Robinson Crusoe is alone, he does not have to invest resources and time in defence and protection. It is a world devoid of predators and predatory behaviour, and thus there are no costs in producing a peaceful environment suitable for the production and accumulation of goods and knowledge. As soon as we interact with other people, however, we must cope with a new type of self-interested and individually rational behaviour: predation. The peaceful environment offered freely to Robinson Crusoe is not free when, as the Latin proverb contends, "man is a wolf to man." Peace is suddenly a collective good, which is costly to produce but offers collective benefits. I now want to illustrate the distribution of costs and benefits produced by this good.

Peace and freedom are not threatened as much by the nastiness of others as by so-called rational self-interest. If stealing your vegetables is less costly for me than growing them for myself on a desert island, it is rational for me to steal them from you. Individually, if the benefits outweigh the costs, it is a rational act. The problem is collective: if everyone thinks this way, nobody will grow vegetables, preferring to steal them (Hobbes 1996; Gauthier 1986). Of course, when nobody is growing vegetables they cannot be stolen and everyone starves. We must come to an agreement in order to make everyone's life better; that is, we must create a context where society is possible. To do that, we are going to need norms and lots of them. The nature of the norms constraining individual freedom and general compliance with these norms will determine what each one of us can expect to produce, accumulate, exchange, and consume.

We can think of two types of norms. First, there are norms of coordination. When we choose on which side of the road to drive or what our working hours will be, we agree to adopt the same way of doing things in order to create collective benefits and to make our collective living more efficient and predictable. People do not have strong incentives to violate these norms for obvious reasons: imagine what would happen to a store with unpredictable working hours or to a driver driving on the wrong side of the road. Second, there are norms of cooperation. These norms are more difficult to enforce since people have incentives to violate them. A thief, for example, benefits when he is the only one stealing, even though norms of cooperation dictate that not stealing is in everyone's interest. The same thing goes for norms prohibiting murder, driving through red street lights, excessive noise, littering, and so on. We all enjoy safety, calm, and clean environments, but we know that violating these norms once in a while will provide us with some extra benefits and will not prohibit us from enjoying these collective goods in the future.

There are two things that we must make explicit about norms. First, everyone's contribution is necessary for these norms to be effective. Generally, even when we have opportunities to steal with very low probabilities of getting caught, we do not even consider the option. This tendency to "normative conformism" is a precondition for individual liberty, private property, and of course, any form of social and collective production or exchange. All must refrain from pursuing their narrow self-interest in each and every opportunity offered to them and agree to adopt normatively adequate behaviour in order for these norms to be effective. Collective goods, including stable and predictable markets, rely on both formal regulations and normative conformism. Contrary to the libertarians' viewpoint, then, we understand the free market not as a natural institution existing prior to any convention, but as the result of many conventions and norms that are enforced by some form of coercive institution. A second thing we must mention is that norms do not benefit everyone equally. Some norms are overtly discriminatory by nature. Their utility is to create groups, restrict access to some goods, and organize our communities into manageable groups in order to provide services and distribute goods more efficiently. This discrimination can be legitimate or illegitimate, intended and recognized, or unintended and unrecognized.

Norms that create illegitimate and intended discrimination are usually displaced by others over the course of time. The exclusion of women and people of colour from universities, on grounds of gender and race, were intended to deny specific groups access to opportunity and mobility and were challenged as being discriminatory and illegitimate. A more implicit set of discriminatory norms are those that divide the load of domestic and productive work between men and women. Norms that structure the so-called normal division of labour in the family underlie gendered inequalities in earnings and opportunities, and as a result the status of women suffer in the workplace and beyond. Ranging from what we consider "normal" work for men or women, to what constitutes a good worker or a good mother, these norms will bias our decisions and judgments in often imperceptible ways to the benefit of some, here mostly men. But in some cases, discrimination is legitimate and intended, as when we restrict access to universities to those meeting some requirements in terms of academic achievements or linguistic capacity. Discrimination is deemed necessary in order to provide some goods efficiently, but it still creates unequal advantages for different individuals.

I want to propose two examples of norms creating intended discrimination but, at the same time, having unintended consequences. The first example applies to the creation and implementation of age cohorts. More than half of the hockey players in the NHL were drafted from the CHL, the major junior league in Canada. Now, professional sport is a pure meritocracy, and nothing but talent matters in determining who will or will not be drafted, right? Not necessarily. You may be surprised to learn that 40 per cent of the players in the CHL have something in common that has nothing to do with talent. They were born between January and March, while those born between October and December only represent 10 per cent of the players in the league. How can that be?

There is a norm applied in order to create cohorts of players. All those born during the same year will play together. This seems like an easy and transparent rule. But it is not. If you are born on the first of January, you are the oldest of your cohort. A couple of months does not mean much between adults, but when you are 11 years old and play at a peewee level, a couple of months can physically transform a boy into a young man. In turn, elite teams and trainers favour bigger and more physically mature players. Those bigger boys will be surrounded by better training staff, will play more minutes of hockey against better players, and will improve faster than others. Thus, what was at first a simple difference of a few inches will develop into real differences in talent a few months later. This cumulative effect explains why so many elite players were born in January and February (Barnsley and Thompson 1988; Nolan and Howell 2010). Relative age—how old an individual is relative to others in a cohort—will have a significant impact on relative success. The same applies to soccer players: research shows that almost one half of the players were born in the three months following the cut-off date (Helsen, van Winckel, and Williams 2005).

Perhaps you do not care about sports. What if I told you that school cohorts are created using arbitrary dates, such as the first of October in Quebec? An experiment comparing the grades obtained by fourth graders showed that the older students did better than the younger students—on average 12 per cent better—within the same cohort (Bedard and Dhuey 2006). A 12 per cent difference on a score sheet in the fourth grade may seem irrelevant to future success and failure in life, but remember that applications for secondary schools use marks from fourth and fifth grades. A couple extra points could make the difference between being admitted to elite secondary school programs and not. These programs also offer a cumulative benefit, transforming success due to maturity into differential access and opportunity in future endeavours, in part simply because of the month of the year in which one is born.

Other types of norms are biased in favour of some but are not discriminatory by nature. In many aspects of our collective life, we need norms to regulate and facilitate our interactions and to avoid producing inefficient collective results. In most cases, imposing the same norm on different individuals does not create any disadvantage. Driving on the right, wearing black clothes at funerals, and forbidding murder seem to be morally neutral and in everyone's interest. But some norms have different impacts on different people. We have laws protecting physical integrity and private property. No matter how strong or wealthy you are, you are better off if you happen to live in a society where these norms thrive. However, it is also clear that some get more benefits from these norms than others. For example, the norms regulating private property now disproportionately benefit the wealthy. The less you have, the less you need norms to protect your property. More than any other time, wealth today comes from capital rather than from work, from what you own or inherit rather than what you do (Piketty 2014). The norms in place do not care what the distribution of wealth is; they just contribute to ensuring that those who legitimately own things have exclusive right to choose what to do with them.

Conclusion: Promoting Justice, One Success Story at a Time

The liberal egalitarian justification for some form of economic equality that I have presented in this chapter recognizes the contribution of every member of society to the success of a few, as well as the fact that the market does not distribute wealth according to contribution, due in part to biased norms. The market is not a natural institution, but one made possible by norms generally observed. Individuals have unequal chances of thriving but each contribution is necessary to make collective success possible. It is therefore morally legitimate to use redistribution to correct for illegitimate and collectively undesirable inequalities. Libertarian assumptions about entitlements to the product of our work constitutes only a partial theory of justice. These assumptions rule out the relative contributions of others to individual wealth and success. Borrowing words from the Obama quote above, it takes many people, inside and outside the country, to maintain "this unbelievable [Canadian] system that we have that allowed [some] to thrive."

This justification for significant redistribution seems more plausible and more likely to get support from a large portion of the population. But in order to rescue what is left of the welfare state and social policies promoting socio-economic equality, we need more than new moral justifications. What we need is a new story of success. Instead of explaining success by referring exclusively to individual talents and virtues, showing how great individuals start from scratch and become rich and famous, we must emphasize the context in which these individuals evolved and made their fortunes. This will not be easy, since this tendency to look at individuals and to forget about context is ubiquitous. We tend to explain people's moral behaviour by referring to their character and not to their circumstances. Unfortunately, we are wrong to do so. Social psychologists refer to this tendency as "fundamental attribution error." Studies show that different agents will act in likely manners when put in similar situations. However, even when people are presented with this data and are aware of their bias, they keep explaining the difference between two different behaviours in terms of the presence or the absence of positive character traits of the people involved. We must try to counter this unconscious tendency by consciously analyzing the contexts that create success stories.

Of course, part of any success story will involve individual talent and virtues. Being intelligent, agile, and athletic will dramatically improve your chances of getting access to jobs in domains where these talents are relevant. But without a proper peaceful context in which to express our talents, without access to shared heritage allowing us to develop these talents, without time and resources made available by a division of labour, and without help from (sometimes biased) norms, our talents would provide very little advantage. Just remember what the most talented individual could produce on a desert island and compare it with an untalented one. We can expect only slight differences.

Wealth is not created by a handful of hyper-talented people, but rather by efficient social institutions coordinating contributions from many and creating amazing opportunities for some. The societies in which we live create contexts for the creation of some goods and services and offer resources to create what is desired and needed. It is fundamentally important to find ways to motivate our most talented individuals to develop their talents and improve their skills in order to get the most out of this heritage that we share. We therefore need to accept that some inequalities will be created. But we must also realize that the wealth that these very talented individuals create is made possible by the labour and the heritage they inherit from others. From this perspective, it is entirely legitimate to tax the rich more heavily, since they benefited more from the social organization to which everyone contributes. It is also legitimate to redistribute some of that collective wealth in order to recognize every contribution, not only market contributions, from each and every member of society.

Why am I convinced that our way of explaining inequalities is problematic and that changing our storytelling about success will influence our support for distributive policies? A study conducted at Princeton University asked students about their social policies preferences. Before they were presented with selected social policies to evaluate, students were asked to write a short explanation of their academic success. The question mentioned that both good fortune and hard work were necessary for academic success. However, the first group was asked to emphasize the role of good fortune in explaining their success; the second was asked to emphasize the role of hard work in their success. Students of the first group expressed more liberal preferences for social policies, as opposed to those of the second group who expressed more conservative preferences (Bryan et al. 2009). There is no doubt that an ambient explanation of success in terms of individual virtues and hard work contributes to broader societal preferences for conservative social policies. This chapter has argued that we need to restore a balance between the importance of hard work and the importance of luck and good fortune in our understanding of individual success, in order for people to be in the right mindset when the time comes to vote on social policies that advance social equality.

Further Readings

Gladwell, Malcolm. 2008. *Outliers: The Story of Success.* New York: Little, Brown and Company.

Inequality for All. 2014. Film directed by Robert Reich. New York: Radius Studios. www.inequalityforall.com.

Rawls, John. 2001. *Justice as Fairness: A Restatement.* Cambridge, MA: Harvard University Press.

CHAPTER 3

DIVERSITY IN THEORY AND PRACTICE: DIVIDENDS, DOWNSIDES, AND DEAD-ENDS

Malinda Smith

Introduction

Canada is in the midst of a demographic revolution, one that is ushering in a great social transformation in the constitution of Canadian society. In this chapter I will show how this growing demographic, social, and cultural complexity paradoxically informs research both on the "upsides of diversity," including ingenuity, creativity, and innovation (Page 2015), and the "downsides of diversity," including undermining social trust and civic engagement (Putnam 2007). This great social transformation is shaped by diversity among Indigenous peoples, generations of established patterns of racial and ethnic diversity, and the intensification and complication of the latter through new waves of trans-border migration. These major demographic shifts are transforming Canadian society in indelible ways, and suggest a need to shift from often banal diversity thinking to an engagement with what has been termed "super-diversity" (Vertovec 2007) or "hyper-diversity" (Noble 2011), which increasingly characterize Canada's major cities and urban neighbourhoods. Despite this great social transformation, and the shifting diversity discourses, what remains remarkably resistant to change, particularly among Canada's ruling class and within its major governing institutions, is an "ethnic pecking order" (Woodsworth 1909) that preserves white normativity.

Many political scholars and policy-makers tend to focus on diversity primarily, if not exclusively, within the frame of immigration and how, over time, it has produced a racially and ethnically diverse citizenry. Few analyses engage societal diversity outside a migration frame and, consequently, ignore diversity that is indigenous to this territory we call Canada (Voyageur and Calliou 2000/2001). "Although there are many commonalties and beliefs held by Indigenous people, there are also many differences," Voyaguer and Callious write, and this diversity is "not only geographical (some living in the high Arctic while others reside on the plains) and linguistic but also legal, cultural, and social" (2000/2001, 111; see also Statistics Canada 2010). Indigenous peoples, constituted by First Nations, Métis, Inuit, and Non-Status Indians, and an expanding urban Indigenous population, are among Canada's fastest-growing and youngest populations. They are igniting renewed social movements for intergenerational justice, land, sovereignty, and the protection of water and the environment. What diversity may mean for socially heterogeneous Indigenous peoples, relative to established and emerging racial/ethnically diverse communities, or newcomers, may be radically different. This "Indigenous biculturalism," as former Inuit Tapirit Kanatami leader Mary Simon (2011) put it, means that Indigenous peoples and nations are always navigating with non-Indigenous peoples in complex social spaces as they struggle to reinvigorate Indigenous knowledge, histories, cultures, and languages.

This Indigenous resurgence is taking place in the context of another great, indeed unprecedented, social transformation shaped by intensifying migration. Since the 1970s we have been witnessing one of the largest social experiments in modern history. In less than two generations Canadian society has undergone a fundamental transformation from being a predominantly white majority society to one increasingly constituted by a majority-minority dynamic (Jedwab 2016). While migration is how we tend to begin conversations on social diversity in Canada, linking diversity primarily to immigration re-enacts Indigenous dispossession and discursive marginality. This erasure, in turn, reinforces the conventional political and sociological conceptual lenses that underwrite the settler colonial narrative of a tripartite society constituted by "founding races"—as the English and French were called in the first book on Canadian politics, *Le Canada, les deux races: problèmes politiques contemporains* (Siegfried, 1906)—Indigenous nations, and "the other ethnic groups" (Haque 2012; Malinda Smith 2014). This tripartite social construct and conceptual framing reinforces racialized social hierarchies and the "ethnic pecking order" (Woodsworth 1909) that has dominated Canadian political life since its inception. It was further entrenched in the Bilingualism and Biculturalism Commission (1963–69) and subsequent legislation promoting multiculturalism and bilingualism. "Canada is a country characterized by a 'diversity of diversities.' It recognizes the contribution of its two founding cultures, while seeking to design a new place for Aboriginal people living within Canada ... and recognizes a wide range of social and other axes of diversity" (Jenson and Papillon 2000, 1). This now common-sense formulation reproduces the social hierarchies of the white settler society and the political vocabulary of the English and French as "founding people" who want to craft a "new place for Aboriginal people" and for the "other axes of diversity." The idea of racial and ethnic diversity here coexists with, and indeed maintains, the resilience of the white settler colonial ethnic pecking order.

From diversity to a "diversity of diversities," we have recently shifted to a new political vocabulary of super-diversity and hyper-diversity. Over the decade since the concept "super-diversity" was first coined (Vertovec 2005, 2007), research has explored these new social demographic dynamics at the level of the city and the neighbourhood, which are increasingly shaped by majority-minority contexts that include a substantial increase in both the number and size of ethnic groups (Crul 2006). While most research on super-diversity focuses on the intensification of racial and ethnic diversity— Canadians have reported over 200 different ethnicities in various censuses (Momani and Stirk 2017)—and the emergence of new racial and ethnic formations, the concept is meant to connote more, including "a world-wide diversification of migration channels, differentiations of legal statuses, diverging patterns of gender and age, and variance in migrants' human capital" (Meissner and Vertovec 2015, 542). Super-diversity is also meant to include different lifestyles, attitudes, and activities (van Kempen 2013, 2–3). The idea of hyper-diversity aims to move beyond the standard examination of differences *between* groups to account for differences *within* groups, and to evaluate the spaces they inhabit with respect to life chances and oppor-tunities "to develop relationships, businesses, lifestyles, [and] new activities" (van Kempen 2013, 3). Beyond recognizing identity differences and hybrid-ity, this emergent diversity thinking seeks to engage "a dynamism that alters processes of interethnic identification and connection" (Noble 2011, 830) in personal relations, neighbourhoods, workplaces, spaces, and flows, and in the process, engenders something novel.

In Canada, this super-diversity increasingly is constituted by diverse non-white—"visible" or "racialized"—minorities and Indigenous peoples living in Canada's major cities. While scholars have begun to reckon with super-diversity, few have attempted to grapple with the implications of this emergent racialized-Indigenous social dynamic for how we think about diversity and social justice in the twenty-first century. One in five Canadians is a racialized minority, and projections show that by 2031, immigrants or children of immi-grants will constitute 50 per cent of the population—up from 38.2 per cent in 2011 (Grant 2017). Racialized minorities will constitute one-third of the Canadian population, with the majority living in Toronto, Vancouver, and Montreal (Statistics Canada 2017). Prairie urban centres such as Calgary, Edmonton, and Winnipeg are similarly undergoing social transformations in terms of ethno-cultural, religious, and linguistic diversity. While on a smaller scale, these same cities are experiencing an Indigenous resurgence. The rapid transformation from a primarily white and European majority to a primarily non-white and non-European majority-minority compositional diversity is unprecedented in Canadian history, and it demands more innovative ways of thinking about social diversity. Calling it Canada's "diversity dividend," Bessma Momani and Jillian Stirk (2017) argue that, although diversity represents a significant global advantage, Canadians have not yet fully recognized or leveraged it. What we make of this growing social diversity and complexity will have profound implications for good relations with Indigenous peoples and for the future of Canada.

In the remainder of this chapter I explore three stories of why and how diversity matters in contemporary Canada. For lack of better terms, I call these stories "the good," "the bad," and "the ugly." The first story on "the good" or upside of diversity draws on business and management research that stresses how diversity can yield "diversity dividends" by making us smarter, better problem solvers, and more creative and innovative. The second "bad" or downside of diversity story draws on research from political science and sociology that suggest that diversity can erode social trust, political participation, and voluntarism in society. The third or "ugly" story reports on diversity data and exposes the social diversity dead ends that arise from the durability of a racial-ethnic pecking order and white normativity, despite the growing empirical reality of super-diversity. In fact, this final story may speak to how not to promote diversity in a rapidly changing demographic environment. This chapter concludes with a reflection on the challenges of shifting concepts of diversity for social justice at the intersections.

Story 1: "The Good" or Upside of Diversity Matters

What are the implications of diversity in the classrooms, courtrooms, boardrooms, and cabinets worldwide? In this story of how and why diversity matters, I explore "the good" or upside of diversity. The research on diversity in economics, business, management, and innovation studies map the productive and transformative potential of diversity in groups, firms, and organizations across sectors (Page 2015). Too often under neoliberalism, this potential is framed instrumentally in terms of the profit motive. As such, this approach may be juxtaposed with a human rights or social justice perspective that understands commitments to diversity in terms of anti-discrimination or normatively in terms of "doing the right thing." Katherine Phillips (2014) argues that decades of multidisciplinary social science research demonstrates that there is a "diversity dividend," which flows from being engaged with people who are unalike or different from us rather that those who are cultural clones or facsimiles of us. I outline three claims about diversity: first, diversity makes us smarter;

second, diversity makes us better problem solvers and decision-makers; and third, diversity fuels creativity and innovation.

Research conducted in multiple settings has shown that racial diversity can improve critical thinking, the quality of decision-making, and performance in groups. Diversity can make us smarter, "more creative, more diligent, and harder working," and, moreover, "socially diverse groups (comprised of assorted races, ethnicities, genders, and sexual orientations) are more innovative than homogeneous groups" (Phillips 2014, n.p.). Let me provide a few illustrative examples. In 2014, Sheen Levine and colleagues conducted a cluster of comparative experiments on diversity in the United States and in Southeast Asia. Drawing on price bubbles, Levine wanted to assess whether diversity could mitigate ethnic homogeneity in the market. In a *Quartz* interview Levine explained, "Past research seemed to have involved situations that call for ethnic considerations. We wanted to take a setting that is completely unrelated to race—something that requires analytical thinking, where there is one correct answer, and see what role ethnicity could possibly play there" (quoted in Wang 2015, n.p.). In both the United States and Asia, the researchers constructed groups that were racially homogeneous and racially diverse. They found that racially and ethnically diverse groups demonstrated deeper and more critical thinking and overall outperformed homogeneous groups by 58 per cent (Wang 2015). Sheen Levine and David Stark (2015) further elaborated that diversity "brought cognitive friction that enhanced deliberation," while the more homogeneous groups demonstrated cultural cloning and copy-cat tendencies that ultimately generated less successful outcomes.

A comparative psychology study of racially homogeneous and racially diverse decision-making juries offers another illustrative example. Samuel R. Sommers's (2006) study found a significant difference in the decision-making of all-white juries in contrast to racially diverse jury compositions. Racially diverse juries that include, for example, white and Black members, tend to have more in-depth discussions than homogeneous juries with all-white jurors. As well, "diverse juries are often better decision makers than homogeneous ones," according to Sommers (2006, 599). In more diverse jury settings, the participants were less likely to voice racial prejudices that, for example, assumed the guilt of Black defendants or the innocence of white defendants. They were more likely to discuss whether race mattered and was, in fact, a factor in a particular outcome. The Sommers study suggests there is an exponential benefit or multiplier effect to decision-making in more racially diverse groups. Greater diversity in jury composition leads to a closer examination of the evidence, consideration of a wider range of explanatory factors, longer deliberations, and greater competency than more homogeneous jury compositions (Bailey 2006, 18; Marinakis 2015). Another study of 700 non-capital felony cases also found that when there was an all-white jury it was likely to convict Black defendants 16 per cent more frequently when compared to juries with at least one Black member in which the racial conviction gap closed (Anwar, Bayer, and Hjalmarsson 2012).

Lu Hong and Scott E. Page (2004) examined the impact of diverse perspectives on collective problem solving and understanding, and on solving human organizational and computational challenges. They found that diverse groups not only performed better than homogeneous groups at complex problem solving but also that "diverse problem solvers can outperform groups of high-ability problem solvers" (2004, 16385–89). The authors draw a distinction between identity diversity and functional diversity. Identity diversity, they explain, typically refers to differences in demographic characteristics, cultural identities and ethnicity, and training and expertise. Advocates of diversity in problem-solving groups claim a linkage among identity diversity and what Hong and Page term "functional diversity"—the differences in how people represent problems and how they go about solving them (2004, 16385).[1] In this study, Hong and Page shift the focus from identity diversity to functional diversity and a "perspective-heuristic approach," which focuses on "how people encode problems and attempt to solve them" (2004, 16385). The authors found that a randomly selected team of diverse, intelligent people can outperform the best-performing people (2004, 16389). Put differently, diversity can trump ability in some contexts because the interaction of individuals with different identities, perspectives, and functions "forces group members to prepare better, to anticipate alternative viewpoints, and to expect that reaching consensus will take an effort" (Phillips 2014, n.p.).

Diversity, particularly super-diversity, has been called "the mother of creativity" (Baumgartner 2010) and is widely recognized as a driver of innovation (Hewlett, Marshall, and Sherbin 2013). This relationship between diversity and creativity occurs in part because in diverse teams, individuals tend to ask more questions, thereby reducing groupthink, considering different possibilities and paths, and engaging in a wider range of critical thinking processes. Scott E. Page, author of *The Difference*, also argues that in contrast to affinity groups, "an outsider can be very helpful, not because they are necessarily smarter than you, but because they are different than you. And this difference is in how they naturally or innately think about what is important when they see a problem or situation." Page goes on to argue that divergent perspectives can "give you the equivalent of more brain power because they give you more search power. They give you more places you can look for ideas and solutions" (quoted in S. Kelly 2012, n.p.).

While some studies focus on friction in relation to interpersonal conflict, it is also a spark that can fuel creativity and the possibility of unexpected outcomes

(Higgs, Plewnia, and Ploch 2005). Organizations, firms, groups, and leadership teams that foster a diverse and inclusive culture are incubators for innovation because they encourage mavericks to swim against the tide, break down silos, promote cross-pollination of ideas, foster ingenuity, and strengthen intercultural intelligence and competency (Fan 2011). In *Leapfrogging*, Soren Kaplan (2012) explores the role of surprise and discomfort in creativity and argues that it is the unexpected that fuels creativity and discomfort and drives innovation. "The single most important factor in fostering true game changers," Kaplan argues, is "the way leaders and organizations handle the discomfort, the disorientation, and the thrill (and pain) of living with uncertainty, finding clarity from ambiguity, and being surprised" (2012, 10). Overall, these arguments suggest that being "comfortable with discomfort" and individual courage and risk-taking, rather than always playing it safe, are requisites for being competitive and innovative in a fast-changing world (Warrell 2009, 2013). Creativity and innovation thrive in uncomfortable environments that disrupt the familiar, unsettle old habits, and trouble the traditional status quo.

The aim of achieving diversity in the workplace, according to Yoram Solomon (2016), is to ensure equal opportunity for all, whatever their race or ethnicity, gender, sexuality, age, and the like. Diverse companies also better reflect their consumers, clientele, and the broader population. But how do we connect diversity to efforts to achieve better services, products, and more creativity and innovation? Solomon identifies nine diversity factors that increase team creativity and engender "diversity dividends": demographic, multidisciplinary and cross-functional, knowledge and education, experience, generalists and specialists (breadth versus depth), extra-curricular interests, cognitive preferences, risk-taking, and vision. While recognizing that diversity can be hard, can inhibit interpersonal communications and the development of social trust, and can delay team bonding—factors needed by teams in order to speak and act freely—it also significantly increases a team's ability to see problems and solutions from unconventional perspectives (Solomon 2016).

Diversity, particularly direct exposure to multicultural experiences, can also spark and enhance creativity in the learning environment. In one of the first studies to empirically test the hypothesis that exposure to diversity and multiple cultures enhances creativity, Leung and colleagues (2008) found that simple exposure to multiple cultures alone enhances creativity. We can assume that this assumption partly informs internationalization initiatives, studies abroad, and faculty and student exchange programs promoted by many universities and schools. Exposure to cultural diversity can be related to creativity in two instances: first, "extensiveness of multicultural experiences was positively related to both creative performance (insight learning, remote association, and idea generation)," and, second, "creativity-supporting cognitive processes (retrieval of unconventional knowledge, recruitment of ideas from unfamiliar cultures for creative idea expansion)" (Leung et al. 2008, 169).

A correlation between diversity, productivity, and profitability is consistently confirmed across a range of studies. While correlation does not equal causation, another study of 366 public companies shows a "diversity dividend" and greater profitability for companies with a diverse workforce and corporate board (Hunt, Layton, and Prince 2015). In an examination of various metrics, including the companies' senior management, boards, and financial performance, Vivian Hunt and her colleagues (2015) found that more diverse companies outperform those that are socially homogeneous: "More diverse companies, we believe, are better able to win top talent and improve their customer orientation, employee satisfaction, and decisionmaking, and all that leads to a virtuous cycle of increasing returns" (Hunt, Layton, and Prince 2015, 1). In the United States, greater racial and ethnic diversity on senior executive teams yield better financial performance, whereas in the United Kingdom gender diversity appears to yield the best financial results. Hunt and her colleagues conclude that the unequal performance of companies in the same industry and the same country suggests diversity is a competitive differentiator that shifts market share toward more diverse companies. At the same time, however, they observe that while certain industries perform better on gender diversity and others on ethnic and racial diversity, no industry or company is in the top quartile on both dimensions (Hunt, Layton, and Prince 2015, 2–3). Similarly, the Catalyst Information Centre (a collective of educators committed to social justice education) found that companies with women in senior executive positions and as board directors financially outperform non-gender diverse boards in three areas: return on investment, sales, and equity (2013, 2). Gender-diverse boards also correlate with better corporate governance, lower corporate fraud, increased corporate social responsibility, and better corporate reputation (2013, 8–9).

Both gender and racial diversity matter to performance, yet many companies seem to focus either on gender or racial diversity rather than both. Despite the decades-old myth that because of diversity initiatives "men are endangered," as John Allan, the chair of Tesco, stated in Rawlinson (2017), there is no evidence from the past decades to support this claim (as the data below will show). There is even less evidence to support the corresponding myth that intersectional identities are privileged, as Allan also argued: "If you are female and from an ethnic background and preferably both, then you are in an extremely propitious period" (quoted in Rawlinson 2017, n.p.). Yet few, if any, companies report on diversity at the intersections; that is, whether the women and men on boards are racially diverse and what the research suggests about the implications of such difference for board governance, performance, productivity, and innovation. What we do know generally, however, is that diversity ignites greater deliberative thought that leads to better decisions, and that multicultural friction can be a driver of creativity and innovation (Agrawal 2016). Overall, diversity is a social reality that can be good, whether in the workplace, groups or teams, classrooms, or boardrooms.

Story 2: "The Bad" or Downside of Diversity Matters

The political, economic, and sociological research on diversity is contested from a variety of perspectives, but these divergent positions generally tend to be ordered along a liberal–conservative continuum: Is diversity a strength and a source of excellence as liberals claim, or is diversity a source of division, mediocrity, and misery as conservatives tend to claim? How do we reconcile these competing stories of diversity? The stories told in this chapter suggest, instead, that the very same dynamics of diversity can produce either or both outcomes. Diversity is, in large part, what we make of it (or not). It is precisely because diversity is used in so many and often contradictory ways that we need to be attentive to its uses, and understand what is at stake when we use particular narratives about diversity.

It has become somewhat common sense to claim that "diversity is a strength." This relatively recent conception of diversity, however, is also a deeply contested and resisted claim, especially when tied to immigration in advanced democratic societies in the European Union and North America. For example, while appealing for religious and cultural tolerance in her 2004 Christmas address, Queen Elizabeth II told her subjects, "Discrimination still exists. Some people feel that their own beliefs are being threatened. Some are unhappy about unfamiliar cultures. They all need to be reassured that there is so much to be gained by reaching out to others; that diversity is indeed a strength and not a threat" (BBC News 2004, n.p.). "Everyone is our neighbour," she continued, "no matter what race, creed and colour."

Over a decade later, Anglo–American democracies like Canada continue to make this claim. "Diversity is Canada's strength" has become integral to Prime Minister Justin Trudeau's vision of the country. In a November 2015 speech at Canada House in London, England, Trudeau stated that diversity was a fact of life and foundation of Canada, and was so much like "the air we breathe" that we may well take it for granted. Gesturing to Canada's international reputation for politeness, Trudeau insisted the contemporary "commitment to diversity and inclusion isn't about Canadians being nice and polite." Challenging critics of diversity, he argued that "diversity isn't a challenge to overcome or a difficulty to be tolerated. Rather, it's a tremendous source of strength." He acknowledged that the diversity of peoples, cultures, languages, and complex histories have been shaped by what he called "dark moments," among them, Indigenous dispossession and its continuing legacies, Canada's own unacknowledged history of slavery, the Chinese head tax, the wartime internments of Japanese, Italians, and Ukrainians, the rejection of boats loaded with Punjabi and Jewish refugees, and policies and institutions of redress. Quoting African American civil rights legend Martin Luther King Jr., Trudeau explained that "the arc of the moral universe is long, but it bends towards justice," though not always in a straightforward manner. Trudeau maintained that "Canada has learned how to be strong not in spite of our differences, but because of them." In Trudeau's vision, diversity is "a powerful and ambitious approach to making Canada, and the world, a better, and safer, place" (2015, n.p.).

In the economic realm, research by Bessma Momani and Jillian Stirk found "it is not enough to simply reap the dividends that come from attracting highly skilled immigrants to Canada" (2017, n.p.). It is necessary to go beyond the instrumental to offer the aspirational arguments for diversity, including that there is a societal dividend because we can "demonstrate how opening ourselves to the world benefits everyone" (2017, n.p.). Yet there is a yawning gap between the good that diversity does, or at least can do, and what diversity is able to do in practice. Despite all the recognized dividends of diversity, Momani and Stirk's research found that for many businesses there are fundamental "barriers to inclusion and what kind of policies and practices are needed so that diversity can be harnessed to drive innovation, productivity and global connectivity" (2017, n.p.). Examining 15,000 to 20,000 employees in 6,000 firms across 14 sectors, they found barriers, biases, and obstacles to a diverse workforce, including overqualified immigrants who were underemployed because of the failure to recognize their credentials or international experience, and because of businesses' "reliance on traditional networks, and unconscious bias in hiring. Underemployed highly skilled immigrants are in effect a stranded resource, something we cannot afford, in either economic or social terms" (Momani and Stirk 2017, n.p.).

This conception of diversity as a source of strength remains in large part aspirational, yet it has come under renewed scrutiny and contestation. When Prime Minister Justin Trudeau kept his commitment following the 2015 federal election to have gender parity in his 30-member cabinet, there was a notable pushback from conservative journalists and politicians who pre-judged that women and racial minorities necessarily meant less merit or competence and, by implication, reinforced the implicit bias that privileged white male normativity and preference for sameness. The response of many conservative critics was to argue that diversity would somehow impact merit or competence. Andrew Coyne (2015) wrote in the *National Post* that cabinet choices should be based on merit and not gender, reinforcing the myth that women are not equally meritorious and competent compared to white men, but also that white men are imagined as universal and outside identity diversity discussions. Paradoxically, Coyne begins the commentary by arguing that strict merit has never shaped cabinet choices, and historically factors such as party affiliation, region, and language have been taken into account in the appointment process. Moreover, cabinet insiders and outsiders were always shaped by social networks, friendships, even grudges and flattery, and have resulted in "numbers of the incompetent, the venal, and the merely mediocre among Her Majesty's ministers, most of them white men" (Coyne 2015, n.p.).

In the months following the 2015 federal election, conservatives continued to disparage the practice of diversity and inclusion; that is, moving beyond rhetorically supporting the idea without following through with the commitment to it. Conservative leadership candidate Kevin O'Leary, a businessman and reality television star on the Canadian Broadcasting Corporation's *Dragons' Den*, claimed Trudeau "ended up with a mediocre cabinet because he was more concerned about diversity than competence" (Canadian Press 2017, n.p.). The unsubstantiated equation of diversity with unqualified and incompetent women and racial minorities serves a function: it reinforces white male normativity. This kind of commentary tends to arise when there are efforts to break from white male normativity, which often goes unnoticed and unremarked. In challenging arguments put forth by Coyne (2015), and equally applicable to O'Leary's remarks equating diversity with mediocrity, Michael Laxer noted that historically, "white men were afforded positions of power and privilege not due to 'merit,' but due solely to being white men" (2015, n.p.). Raising questions about merit and competence precisely at the moment when efforts are made to disrupt this tendency is, according to Laxer, "a call for little more than business as usual and a call, not for 'merit,' but for continuing the white male hegemony that defines 'merit' solely in terms of the privileged qualities that its male commentators see in the mirror" (2015, n.p.). It is a call for the social reproduction of sameness.

Despite the diversity rhetoric, empirical evidence reveals that the ethnic pecking order persists among Canada's elites, and durable barriers to diversity endure in all major governing institutions. In 2017, Canadian university leadership, and to a large extent the professoriate, has remained overwhelmingly white and male despite the diversity of the student body and broader population (Malinda Smith 2016; Henry et al. 2017a, 2017b). The Canadian judiciary has been characterized as a "judiciary of whiteness", with 96 per cent of judges white and primarily male (Griffith 2016). A similar social segmentation shaped by white normativity is evident among elected offices (Tolley 2015; Black 2013), the police (Marcoux et al. 2016), the major media (Mochama 2016), and corporate boards (McFarland, 2014, 2015).

The sociological research on "whitopia" (Benjamin 2009) and so-called ethnic enclaves (Jiménez 2007) also raises questions about how we think about diversity. Such spaces can be sources of social capital, entrepreneurship, and cultural vitality, as the vibrant Chinatown or Little Italy exemplify in many cities around the world. Yet, whatever the rationale for these socially homogeneous spaces, they reinforce the gap between diversity rhetoric and, perhaps, diversity aspiration and everyday lived realities. Despite claims of living "in a multicultural society" and self-congratulatory "claims of tolerance and diversity," pollster Allan Gregg noted, "the evidence suggests that fewer and fewer of us are living in multicultural neighbourhoods," residing, instead, in "self-segregated communities, isolated along ethnic lines" (quoted in Jiménez 2007).

The "inconvenient truth" of diversity's downside was alluded to in Robert Putnam's work on social capital and particularly in his 2007 publication "E. Pluribus Unum." Based on interviews of 30,000 people in 41 communities across the United States, Putnam (2007) concludes that, in the short run, diversity can present a serious challenge to democracy, although he suggests these challenges can be overcome with time. Putnam pointed to the following dynamic in contemporary super-diverse neighbourhoods: declining distrust among neighbours, less voluntarism and contributions to charity, cynicism about leaders, lower voter registration and participation in electoral politics, and the fact that although they agitate for social change and reforms they seemed to "have less faith that they can actually make a difference" (Putnam 2007, 150).

Putnam's research appears to contradict the liberal story of diversity as strength and the related multicultural story of the benefits of diversity, as well as the "contact hypotheses" in sociology, which holds that increased interaction among racially and ethnically diverse peoples engenders greater social understanding. In contrast, Putnam argued that "the more ethnically diverse the people we live around, the less we trust them" (2007, 142). Diversity may reduce social trust, social solidarity, and social cohesion. While this is all quite troubling for civic life, it is important to historicize these tendencies. Putnam suggests every generation experiences a level of social distrust and discomfort. This was certainly true among earlier European immigrants and it remains true today, although the sources of immigration have changed.

Arguably, the upside and downside of diversity are, in fact, two sides of the same coin. On the one hand, conservative critics of diversity drew on Putnam's arguments to suggest, for example, that "greater diversity equals more misery" (Mercer 2007), and that "racial polarisation increases with social contact" as flowing from human nature (Dreher 2016, n.p.). Conservatives also draw on Putnam's finding to suggest racism and xenophobia are rational responses to living with social diversity. Rather than imagining that "provincialism and xenophobia are a product of ignorance, and that when people come into contact with one another they inevitably become more tolerant," Rod Dreher suggests this liberal view is "not at all representative of broader human nature" (2016, n.p.). On the other hand, and while insisting we cannot shy away from the challenges posed by diversity for democracy, Putnam insists diversity is good for society in the long run. Page also does not evade the challenges of diversity, insisting "when you interact with people who are different, it's difficult and trust goes down" (quoted in Greenblatt 2007, n.p.), but this is not an immutable condition. It can be overcome with time. Moreover, this very same difficulty and discomfort may have an upside in diverse workplaces and groups, because "there's strong empirical evidence that productivity goes up" (Page quoted in Greenblatt, 2007, n.p.). Diversity, indeed super-diversity, in the neighbourhood, the city, and workplace, is no more and no less than what we make of it.

Story 3: The "Ugly" or Diversity Data and Dead Ends

My third story examines institutional diversity initiatives which, paradoxically, function to reinforce white normativity. I draw on three illustrative examples from the public and private sector, which have long had diversity policies, programs, and even chief diversity officers. The evidence from the corporate sector, the judiciary, and police services reveal that diversity discourses and policies in private and public sector workplaces do not seem to produce results that reflect the everyday lived realities of super-diversity in cities and neighbourhoods. Rather—and despite four decades of equity policies—corporate boards, the judiciary, and the police continue to be shaped by racial and ethnic segregation, and remain overwhelmingly white and to a lesser extent male, thus maintaining the historic colour-coded ethnic pecking order even across gender and sexual difference. I have termed this social process "diversifying whiteness."

The data also suggest the need to examine social justice at the intersections, and to tease out how homosociality, cultural cloning, and imagined homogeneities can engender the "social injustice of sameness" (Essed and Goldberg 2002). The concept "intersectionality" was first coined by American critical legal theorist Kimberlé Crenshaw in 1989, and since then it has been used as a metaphor, a sensibility, a frame, a method, and a social policy lens. "Intersectionality is an analytic sensibility, a way of thinking about identity and its relationship to power. Originally articulated on behalf of Black women, the term brought to light the invisibility of many constituents within groups that claim them as members, but often fail to represent them" (Crenshaw 2016, n.p.). Without the relevant frame or lens to address inequities among diverse groups and within them, "the efforts to mobilize resources to address a social problem will be partial and exclusionary" and, moreover, "when there's no name for a problem, you can't see a problem. When you can't see a problem, you can't solve it" (Crenshaw 2016, n.p.). In this case, I am drawing on an intersectional sensibility and method to draw attention to how, for example, the category "women" can, and often does, obscure diversity among women, and how this may in turn obscure the fact that the only women represented are able-bodied white women.

Discussions of social cloning have been enabled by the normative assumption of social and cultural sameness that underpins modern thinking around politics, law, education, management, and processes of social reproduction and economic production (Essed and Goldberg 2002). Social and cultural cloning, like biotechnological cloning, leads to the repetitive reproduction of desired social characteristics (Essed and Schwab 2012), in this case the institutional tendency to selectively reproduce white male normativity. Consequently, we need to problematize the reproduction of racial and gender sameness in institutions not simply in terms of discrimination *against* women and racial minorities but, rather, "in terms of preference *for*, that is, practices sustaining imagined male homogeneity" (Essed 2004, 113). While Essed's 2004 work is centred on the university, it resonates across public and private institutions, particularly the author's account of how cultural cloning explains the durable persistence of the normative image of leaders as white and male. Despite decades of policies to achieve more equitable outcomes, cultural cloning and the privileging of white males continue to maintain senior management and leadership as socially and culturally homogeneous (Essed 2004). What this third story examines, then, is ongoing institutional cloning.

Diversity on Corporate Boards

Despite numerous studies that suggest boardroom diversity enhances productivity and profitability, and fuels creativity and innovation, corporate boardrooms remain socially homogenous. Studies by the Canadian Board Diversity Council (CBDC, n.d.) consistently show an under-representation of women, visible minorities, Indigenous peoples, and persons with disabilities as corporate board directors. The term "visible minority" is a legal term used by the Canadian government to identify people who are not Indigenous and "non-Caucasian in race or non-white in colour." While I use the term "visible minorities"[2] in this chapter, it is primarily because of its use for national data collection. It is used interchangeably with "racialized minorities," a concept that denotes the process by which groups are socially produced, and come to understand themselves, as distinct races despite the absence of correspondence with now disavowed preconceptions of biological races. For this reason, I also use "white" instead of the erroneous and pseudo-scientific concept of "Caucasian" (Hui 2013; Khan 2011).

Overall, corporate board diversity, particularly racial diversity, is not increasing. Few corporate directors are visible minorities and even fewer are Indigenous, and if there is any trend, it is one of declining representational diversity and the reassertion of white male normativity. While the percentage of women on corporate boards has increased marginally, there is a corresponding decline of visible minorities and Indigenous peoples, especially visible minority and Indigenous women. The data on corporate boards reveal a picture of homogeneity and cultural cloning, in which boards remain astonishingly white and male despite the discourses of super-diversity, and the empirical reality of social diversity of the broader population. Recent statistics underline this stark reality. Consider the following:

- In 2010 visible minorities constituted 5.3 per cent of board directors of Canada's 500 largest companies, but this number declined to 2.0 percent in 2014 (McFarland 2013, 2014; Dhir 2015).
- The percentage of Indigenous directors stalled at 0.8 per cent of board seats between 2010 and 2014 (McFarland 2014).
- The percentage of women directors gradually increased from 13.7 per cent in 2009 to 19.5 per cent in 2015 (McFarland 2013, 2014, 2015).
- The percentage of board directors with disabilities has steadily declined from 2.9 per cent in 2010 to 1.4 per cent in 2014 (McFarland, 2014).

The decline in visible minorities and persons with disabilities, juxtaposed against an increase in gender equity, suggests a trade-off in which "diversity initiatives" have largely become "gender diversity initiatives" rather than any notion of super-diversity on corporate boards.

"So why do old white guys continue to dominate boardrooms?" asks Joanna Pachner (2016, n.p.). "Why aren't Canadian corporate boards getting any less male, or white?" Rebecca Walberg (2014, n.p.) similarly asks. The research on how the old-boys network is maintained, on affinity bias, and on cultural cloning all provide partial answers to these questions. For example, Pachner's research found that "because nine in 10 directors rely on their personal networks of other senior male executives to fill board vacancies," recruitment to corporate boards is often based on friendships and informal social networks, which tend to reinforce cultural cloning and white male homogeneity (2016, n.p.). While a number of companies have made gestures to diversify their boards, there is a sense that some of these efforts are nothing more than token gestures to avoid public shaming. This "tokenistic mindset—let's get a woman, a minority and throw in some foreigners for good measure—misses the point" (Pachner 2016, n.d.). The vast majority of Canadian corporate boards not only lack significant diversity by gender, race, and ability—they also lack age diversity. In 2016, a full 93 per cent of board directors of the 500 biggest companies were over 50 years of age, while the average age for the S&P 500 companies was 63 years (Pachner 2016).

There is another dynamic at play here, one that requires us to pay closer attention to the uses and abuses of the language of diversity. Sara Ahmed argues that diversity-talk often only "supports existing organizational ideals or even organizational pride. What makes diversity useful also makes it limited: it can become detached from histories of struggle for equality" (2007b, 235). Institutions in the public and private sector have a vast discretion with respect to how they define or avoid defining what they mean by "diversity." It is thus no surprise, then, that despite the relatively small percentage of women, visible minorities, and Indigenous peoples on corporate boards, a CBDC survey found that 82 per cent of board directors thought their boards were diverse (McFarland 2015). As a result, as Christopher Chen of the Hay Group suggests, some companies define diversity in terms of perspectives or background, while most Canadian conversations on diversity focus almost exclusively on gender "with some attention paid secondarily to ethnicity" (quoted in Walberg 2014, n.p.).

The tokenistic diversity mindset, detached from the struggles for equality and social justice, has four significant implications: first, affinity bias and cultural cloning mean that boards maintain existing preference for sameness, thereby replicating and maintaining the status quo; second, the meanings of diversity and how and why diversity matters are highly contested but, also, not fully understood; third, the proliferating and inconsistent ways in which diversity is used across institutions means it often coexists with inequity; and fourth, growing evidence indicates that diversity recruitment strategies, where they exist, have yielded little change. This suggests the need for greater attention to rethinking the "value of diversity training that pins its hopes on educating people to rise above their prejudices" (Clegg 2017, n.p.). One suggestion by Harvard behavioural economist Iris Bohnet (2016) is the need to focus greater attention on designing processes that limit individual and group bias and cultural cloning tendencies.

Diversity in the Canadian Police Forces
What can we learn about diversity in Canada's major institutions when we examine it within the Canadian legal system? Here, again, we see the durability of white normativity across Canada's major institutions and power structures. Research on the Canadian justice system—the courts (Griffith 2016), the

legal profession (Canadian Centre for Diversity and Inclusion [CCDI] 2016a), and the police (Marcoux et al. 2016)—all reinforce similar white normativity dynamics we explored in the previous discussion of corporate board diversity. First, there has been slow progress on gender equity but also a persistence of white normativity across gender. Despite the rhetoric of diversity, the justice system is marked by representational homogeneity rather than social diversity. Second, we see that institutions are slow to change and lag significantly behind broader societal demographic diversity: the police force, the legal profession, and the courts do not reflect the demographic diversity of the populations they serve.

An investigative report by CBC News of 21 of Canada's largest municipal police forces found that with the exception of Halifax, "police diversity fails to keep pace with Canadian populations" (Marcoux et al. 2016, n.p.). Moreover, in some of the most socially diverse cities, police forces remain "overwhelmingly white" (Leavitt 2016a, 2016b). These findings are startling, especially when one considers that there is growing controversy about the relationship between minority communities and policing. Social movements like Idle No More and Black Lives Matter, both co-founded and led by women,[3] have drawn attention to the violence and abuse that Indigenous and racialized communities experience from law enforcement. Stop-and-frisk, carding, racial profiling, "starlight tours," missing and murdered Indigenous women and girls, and the disproportionate shootings and incarceration of Black and Indigenous peoples are obvious examples (Cole 2015; Palmater 2016). With the exception of Halifax, all "other major law enforcement agencies across the country fail to reflect their communities' diversity among their ranks, leaving large swaths of visible minorities and Indigenous populations without representation" (Marcoux et al. 2016, n.p.). Again, the statistics tell a disturbing story (Marcoux et al. 2016, n.p.):

- York region: 44 per cent of the population is non-white, but only 17 per cent of the police force is non-white.
- Edmonton: 35 per cent of the population is constituted by visible minorities or Indigenous peoples, but they make up less than 10 per cent of the police force.
- Vancouver: 54 per cent of the city's population are from social minority groups, but these groups make up only 22 per cent of the police force.
- Nunavut: 90 per cent of the territory is Indigenous, but only 12 per cent of the police force is Indigenous.
- Quebec City: just over 1 per cent of officers are racial minorities or Indigenous, whereas Quebec City is five times more racially diverse.

When we look at overwhelmingly white police forces that do not reflect the communities in which they serve then difficult questions need to be asked. A CBC investigative report found that over a nine-year period between 2007 and 2015, only five or 0.7 per cent of the 735 police officers hired by the Sûreté du Québec were visible minorities or Indigenous (Leavitt 2016b). The Quebec provincial police force is over 99 per cent white. This homogeneity leads to a credibility problem, argues Maria Peulso: "In any public office or public institution, it's important they reflect the diversity of the population that they serve" (quoted in Leavitt 2016b, n.p.).

Demographic diversity is necessary but insufficient for transforming socially homogeneous institutions like Canada's police forces. We already know from experience that approaches that attempt to change the face of police officers without a corresponding change to organizational culture have had limited benefits. As Sandy Hudson, a cofounder of Black Lives Matter Toronto, put it, "There has to be a real commitment to changing policy, to changing structure, and to changing the institution as a whole" (quoted in Marcoux et al. 2016, n.p.). The need to change the culture of policing in Canada, however, is easier said than done. While changing police culture is widely recognized as important for building social trust and transforming strained police–community relations (Leavitt 2016b), this message does not appear to be fully appreciated by police leadership and police unions. The Canadian Association of Chiefs of Police, for example, seemed unconcerned by the numbers showing that police forces do not reflect the communities they serve. For example, in the CBC investigative report, Clive Weighill, Chief of the Saskatoon Police Service, instead chose to highlight the comparably better representation of visible minorities and Indigenous peoples in the police compared to other sectors: "I think we've made a lot of progress. If you would compare policing to private corporations or other civic or municipal corporations, I think you'd see our numbers are drastically ahead of most people" (quoted in Marcoux et al. 2016, n.p.).

Diversity in the Legal Profession

The legal profession in Canada is also changing at a glacial pace with respect to the representation of women, Indigenous peoples, and racialized minorities. Since the 1980s, law societies across Canada have embarked on employment equity initiatives to increase diversity within the legal profession. For more than three decades, law societies have produced a series of reports on the status of women and on equity and diversity, which have focused on a range of issues, such as obstacles to hiring, workplace environment, work–life balance, and barriers to retention and advancement. Examples of these include the Law Society of Upper Canada's 1989 "Women and the Legal Profession" and 1996 "Barriers and Opportunities within Law" reports; the 2004 "Final Report on Equity and Diversity in Alberta's Legal Profession" by the Law Society of Alberta; the 2014 "Pour une profession inclusive—La diversité ethnoculturelle dans la profession juridique" by the Law Society of Quebec; and the 2016 Saskatchewan Justice Project's report on policies and practices to engender retention and advancement in the legal profession (CCDI 2016b, 18). However, while final reports were heralded for their significance upon their release, there has been a disjuncture between recommendations and outcomes. Too often, the reports and their expressed commitments are themselves taken as signs of success, reinforcing what Ahmed (2007c) refers to as "doing the document rather than doing the doing." Put differently, diversity advocacy requires us to pay attention to the politics of documentation and "how documents are taken up as signs of good performance, as expressions of commitment." Yet, beyond the document, little is done to effect change and this becomes clear when we "follow the documents around" to see how they are taken up by institutions or whether they are shelved. Yet Ahmed is right to argue that the production of the documents can be used strategically by diversity advocates, including to "expose the gaps between words and deeds" (Ahmed 2007c, 590) or "*how not to do things with words*" (Ahmed 2012, 1, emphasis in original).

Despite the efforts to generate reports and recommendations to improve the status of women in law and to socially diversify the profession, a study on demographic diversity by the Canadian Centre for Diversity and Inclusion (CCDI), in partnership with the Canadian Bar Association, found mostly stalled efforts to close the demographic diversity gaps. The objective of the report was to provide data that could better inform efforts to improve diversity and inclusion in the legal profession. As the CCDI noted, "The data does not tell us why a particular trend is happening or not happening," but drawing on experience and expertise, the report offers some potential reasons for particular trends. For example, between 2014 and 2016, the percentage of men among senior leaders in the legal profession increased, as did the percentage of senior leaders who are white (CCDI 2016a, 10):

- Male normativity: An increase from 2014 to 2016 in the percentage of senior leaders in the legal profession who were men: from 73.99 per cent in 2014, to 76.86 per cent in 2015, and 75.34 per cent in 2016.
- White normativity: An increase from 2014 to 2016 in the percentage of senior leaders in the legal profession who were white: from 89.78 per cent in 2014, to 88.91 per cent in 2015, and 90.78 per cent in 2016.

The CCDI's survey showed Indigenous peoples are under-represented, with barriers primarily being entry to the profession, and less so as obstacles to advancements once in the profession. In contrast, racialized minorities are entering the legal profession at increasing rates but remain absent at the top tiers of the profession. The CCDI report shows that women and racialized minorities are significantly under-represented among equity partners, income partners, and in senior leadership roles. Nevertheless, the report also found that regardless of gender, white lawyers were more likely to become an equity partner than a racialized person. When we look at equity at the intersections, white men had "the greatest odds of being an equity partner" and were "seven times more likely than racialized women" to secure such a status (CCDI 2016a, 10). This tendency reinforces structures of white normativity and suggests a racialized gendered social contract (Pateman and Mills 2007) that maintains power, privilege, and prestige among white men and secondarily white women. Regardless, there is a distinct social hierarchy and ethnic pecking order that is replicated across Canadian institutions and this will be clearer, still, from an examination of diversity in the Canadian judiciary.

Diversity in the Judiciary

Mi'kmaq lawyer Naiomi W. Metallic characterized the Canadian judicial system as a "judiciary of whiteness" (quoted in Tutton 2016, n.p.). This characterization is supported by the data from a study of diversity in the judiciary published in *Policy Options* in 2016, which showed that of the 2,160 judges in the provincial superior and lower courts, only 1 per cent were Indigenous and only 3 per cent were racial minorities (Tutton 2016). Conducted by Andrew Griffith, a former director of the Ministry of Citizenship and Multiculturalism, the study examined the backgrounds of federally and provincially appointed judges. Griffith found that provincially appointed judges were slightly more diverse than federally appointed judges but overall the results are dismal. There are no Indigenous or visible minorities on the Supreme Court or the Federal Court of Appeal. Indigenous judges make up 2.4 per cent of the Federal Court, and only 7.4 per cent of the Tax Court is composed of visible minorities. Women fare better in federal courts, comprising 44 per cent of the Supreme Court, 27 per cent of the Federal Court of Appeal, 31 per cent of the Federal Court, and 26 per cent of the Tax Court (Griffith 2016, Figure 1). These trends are reproduced in federal appointments to provincial courts. While women constitute approximately one-third of provincial Supreme Courts, Courts of Appeal, and Superior Courts, visible minorities constitute less than 5 per cent of provincial Supreme Courts and less than 1 per cent of the other two provincial courts. Indigenous justices are

virtually absent from this critical layer in the Canadian justice system, consti-
tuting less than 1 per cent of all three federally appointed provincial courts
(Griffith 2016, Figure 2).

Diversity is more apparent among provincially appointed justices but the
picture is mixed across the provinces, and, as Griffith notes, "overall the provinces resemble each other in their under-representation of these groups" (2016,
n.p.). For example, with the exception of Nova Scotia, there are no visible
minority or Indigenous judges in Atlantic Canada. Quebec has a few visible
minority judges but no Indigenous judges. Saskatchewan and Manitoba have
few Indigenous judges, and in the North, despite a large Indigenous population,
there are no Indigenous judges. With a few notable exceptions, the provinces
differ but generally do better with respect to the appointment of women, with
representation ranging from a low of 25 per cent in Alberta and New Brunswick
to a high of 44 per cent in Manitoba and Quebec (Griffith 2016, Figure 3).

There are at least two takeaways from this data. First, despite the growing
diversity of the population and the legal profession, the judiciary does not
reflect the people it serves. Second, the data comport with my argument on
cultural cloning, the durability of white normativity, and what I term as the
diversification of whiteness. The diversification of the judiciary has meant
inviting to the bench white women, but rarely visible minority or Indigenous
lawyers. White normativity in the judiciary is maintained despite diversity
policies because diversity has been reduced to gender, or perhaps even sexual
diversity, which benefit primarily white women or white LGBT people within
the profession. There is a notable absence of good data on representation and
experiences of persons with disabilities.

Does it matter if the police, the legal profession, and judges do not reflect
the diversity of the broader communities or the clientele who are most likely
to come before them? Metallic insists, and I agree, that all "powerful institutions
ought to reflect the societies they serve" (Metallic quoted in Tutton 2016, n.p.).
Those who often come before the courts and need legal representation—for
example, Indigenous people, Black people, and other visible minorities—are
least well represented in authority positions within the justice system and thus
risk being viewed as illegitimate to those communities. The current debate
over murdered and missing Indigenous women and police carding practices
exemplify this risk (Griffith 2016; Cole 2015).

Conclusion

Debates over the meaning and significance of diversity have been animated
within public and private institutions and public policy-making in Canada for

over a generation. Most stories of diversity are framed in terms of immigration but, in doing so, they tend to obscure existing Indigenous diversity and to reinscribe white settler colonial social imaginaries. This chapter has examined shifting conceptions of diversity, including a "diversity of diversities," super-diversity and hyper-diversity, and the implications of these terms for how we think about Canadian society and polity at the level of the city and the neighbourhood. This chapter has argued that these shifting conceptions of diversity reflect a lived reality in which Canadian society is undergoing a great and unprecedented social transformation. Canada is rapidly transforming from a predominantly white European social formation with a few major ethno-cultural groups to a predominantly non-white and Indigenous majority-minority society.

This chapter has examined the multiple and contested meanings and uses of diversity, super-diversity, and hyper-diversity in theory, policy, and practices across various sectors and institutions through three stories of diversity. It framed these three stories as "the good" or upside of diversity, "the bad" or downside of diversity, and "the ugly" or dead end of diversity evident in data on diversity practice. In the first story, I looked at the "diversity dividends" in economics, business, and management, and the studies that show how diversity leads to better decision-making and fuels creativity, innovation, and productivity. The research in this area also shows that the same dynamics that fuel the upside of diversity—for example, social friction, surprise, uncertainty, discomfort—also can inform the downside of diversity. In the second story of diversity I delved into the political and sociological research that associates diversity with mediocrity, misery, and declining social cohesion and civic engagement. The paradoxes of diversity are also evident in this story, including how the same dynamics fuelling super-diversity, entrepreneurship, and cultural innovations can also engender lower social trust, civic engagement, and political participation. The extent to which these diversity dynamics are new, or reflect age-old migration patterns, is open to contestation. What is new, however, is the great social transformation that has given rise to majority-minority social dynamics in Canadian cities and neighbours, and to an emergent Indigenous, non-white sociality in cities like Toronto, Montreal, Vancouver, Winnipeg, and Edmonton. The ways in which Canada navigates this novel dynamic will shape its future in the years to come.

The third and final story this chapter examined the ugly or dead ends of diversity, focusing on the disjuncture between words and deeds, rhetoric and policies, as evident in the lack of diversity among Canadian elites and within all of its governing institutions. In this third story I looked at diversity data with three illustrative examples—the corporate sector, the legal profession and the judiciary, and the police—pointing to the fact that these institutions do not reflect the identity diversity of Canada, and the communities and clienteles that they serve. This third story also revealed a durable tendency across time and space: Despite diversity talk and the emergent super-diversity majority-minority dynamic, white normativity and varied processes of socio-cultural cloning endure, and thus reproduce a durable racial-ethnic pecking order among elites and within major governing institutions. I also argued that dividing practices—the tendency to include either women *or* racial and ethnic minorities *and* Indigenous peoples—and inattention to intersectionality have given rise to the phenomenon in which diversity practices that often only benefit white women and thus only diversify whiteness. Individually, and together, these three stories reflect the productive possibilities of diversity. At the same time, they reflect the profound limits of the concept of diversity and the multiple and contradictory work it is drawn upon to do. It may well be the case that the productive possibilities of diversity have exceeded the performative capacity of the concept.

Further Readings

Ahmed, Sara. 2012. *On Being Included: Racism and Diversity in Institutional Life*. Durham, NC: Duke University Press.

Bendl, Regine, Inge Bleijenbergh, Elina Henttonen, and Albert J. Mills, eds. 2015. *The Oxford Handbook of Diversity in Organizations*. Oxford: Oxford University Press.

Henry, Frances, Enakshi Dua, Carl E. James, Audrey Kobayashi, Peter Li, Howard Ramos, and Malinda S. Smith. 2017. *The Equity Myth: Racialization and Indigeneity at Canadian Universities*. Vancouver: UBC Press.

Notes

1 Hong and Page also note that "identity diversity has been shown to correlate with functional diversity" but "we need to be acutely aware that identity-diverse groups often have more conflict, more problems with communication, and less mutual respect and trust among members" (2004, 16385–86). This is the thread that connects the "benefits of diversity" to the "downside of diversity" research of Robert Putnam (2007), but also the comfort thesis on why boards remain relatively homogeneous. Katherine W. Phillips (2014, n.p.) also notes that "social diversity in a group can cause discomfort, rougher interactions, a lack of trust, greater perceived interpersonal conflict, lower communications, less cohesion, more concern about disrespect, and other problems," making it appropriate to ask, "So what is the upside?"

2 Visible minority populations according to the Employment Equity Act and Statistics Canada include the following 10 groups: Chinese, South Asian, Black, Arab, West Asian, Filipino, Southeast Asian, Latin American, Japanese, and Korean (Statistics Canada 2010).

3 Black Lives Matter (BLM) in the United States was cofounded by Alicia Garza, Patrisse Cullors, and Opal Tomati in 2013 following the killing of Trayvon Martin and the acquittal of George Zimmerman who shot him. Since then the movement has expanded to a decentralized network of over 30 chapters. BLM has become an international social justice movement known on social media by the hashtag #BlackLivesMatter. BLM Canada has various chapters, including in Toronto, Vancouver, and Edmonton. The BLM Toronto chapter was cofounded by Janaya Khan and Yusra Ali in October 2015 following the police killing of Jermaine Carby during a traffic stop.

PART II

Living Precariously:
Social Justice for Whom?

CHAPTER 4

JUSTICE FOR WHOM? MIGRANT WORKERS IN CANADA

Judy Fudge

Introduction

In April 2014, a young Canadian working at a McDonald's in Victoria, British Columbia, complained to a Canadian Broadcasting Corporation (CBC) investigative reporting program that migrant workers from the Philippines were getting higher pay and better hours than Canadian citizens for the same work. He also accused his employer of reducing the hours of Canadian workers and turning away Canadians who were applying for jobs (Tomlinson 2014a). This story created a domino effect as reports began to emerge from across the country of other restaurant employers abusing the Temporary Foreign Worker Program (TFWP) (Tomlinson 2014b). The tipping point came when the story of Sandy Nelson, a waitress in Weyburn, Saskatchewan, who was terminated from her job after 28 years and replaced by a temporary migrant worker, reached the air. She was widely reported as saying, "How can that be right? They are not Canadian. I am Canadian" (Leo 2014, n.p.).

The federal government's response was quick; it imposed a moratorium on the use of temporary migrant workers in the food services sector (Employment and Social Development Canada [ESDC] 2014). Two months later, the government lifted the moratorium at the same time as Employment and Social Development Canada (ESDC), the federal department responsible for labour market policy, released "Overhauling the Temporary Foreign Worker Program: Putting Canadians First," a report that introduced significant changes to the TFWP (Government of Canada 2014). ESDC Minister Jason Kenney, who as minister of Citizenship and Immigration Canada between 2008 and 2013 had been responsible for the massive increase in the number of temporary migrant workers employed in Canada, complained that certain employers had started to rely on access to low-wage temporary foreign workers as an employment model (Curry 2014). Not only did he announce that the government was contemplating phasing out access to low-wage temporary foreign workers (Curry 2014), he also characterized the migrant workers as "quasi-indentured" (Wright 2014).

This controversy over the use of temporary migrant workers in the Canadian food services sector reveals a great deal about the relationship between labour markets and immigration in contemporary global capitalism as well as the charged relationship between "foreigners" and "citizens" in today's neoliberal governance regimes. Most research on temporary migrant worker programs in Canada focuses on the exclusions and inequalities experienced by migrant workers and does not consider how these programs influence local or national labour markets and their impact on Canadian residents' wages and working conditions (Lenard and Straehl 2012; Goldring and Landolt 2013). However, this story provides a point of entry into understanding how labour migration regimes are not only mechanisms for regulating national labour markets (Bauder 2006), but also are used to shape the legal and social entitlements of citizenship in this neoliberal era. After the global financial crisis that shocked advanced capitalist countries in 2008, governments in Canada and Europe began to scapegoat migrants as the "cause" of unemployment, rather than reforming financial institutions or confronting finance capital, in an attempt to mollify their citizens, many of whom experienced deteriorating standards of living.

This chapter explores the relationship between the social organization of migrant workers' unfreedom through the conditionality of legal status and how the creation and deployment of precarious migrant labour regulates national labour markets. It begins by drawing the connections between neoliberal labour regimes, immigration controls, and the exploitation of migrant workers. It shows how precarious migrant status is linked to precarious employment, and how the categories of "foreigner" and "citizen" are used to justify the unfreedom and hyper-exploitation of migrant workers. Focusing on "low-skilled" occupations within the food services sector in which precarious (low-paid and insecure) jobs predominate, this chapter then describes the "low-skilled" (since October 2014 called "low-wage") stream of the Temporary Foreign Worker Program, its growth, the "public" reaction to foreigners taking Canadian jobs, and the government's response to this controversy. This chapter charts how the federal government, which initially gave employers virtually unrestricted access to temporary migrant workers in order to dampen wage increases in certain parts of the country, changed its approach and began to attack migrants as undercutting Canadian wages, and the employers who sponsored them as using indentured labour. This chapter also probes the relationship between temporary labour migration and social entitlements to citizenship in Canada.

It concludes by raising the normative question of who the subject of justice is in a globalized labour market.

Globalism and Neoliberalism

Temporary migrant workers are foreign workers without a guarantee of permanent settlement (Surak 2013, 87). The drivers of temporary migration programs are often the contradictory needs of governments to protect both the economy and the nation. For the host state, the goal of temporary migration programs is to maximize "economic utility while minimizing social cost" (Surak 2013, 88). In the context of contemporary globalism, the flip side of capital's movement offshore to seek cheaper, harder-working, and more disciplined labour is the use of temporary migrant labour in the labour-intensive sectors in the global North (Lewis et al. 2014; Walsh 2014). The relationship between globalization and neoliberal policies, which promote "free" markets for employers at the expense of regulation to protect workers from risk, is destructive to the creation and recreation of cohesive and durable communities and societies. Thus, it creates both the necessity and desire for people to migrate across international boundaries in search of work. In turn, this surplus labour from beyond the national state can be hired, fired, and deported to meet demand without regard to social reproduction. In this way, the "on-going interplay of increasingly deregulated labour markets, characterized by employers' demands for low-cost 'flexible' labour and highly restrictive immigration and asylum policies that variously structure, compromise and/or remove basic rights to residence, work and welfare for all but the most prosperous migrants" create a supply of precarious migrants to work in precarious jobs (Lewis et al. 2014, 15). Thus, temporary migration schemes are "political-legal arrangements for producing labour markets that advance the neo-liberal agenda" (Walsh 2014, 4). They feed upon the profound inequality among workers and between national states in the global political economy.

In the global South, economic trends such as growing inequalities between high- and low-income countries and insecurity, instability, and vulnerability due to economic and political crises have increased the numbers of men and women who migrate in order to obtain paid work. Remittances are crucial for the survival of household, community, and country in large swathes of the developing world, and exporting workers is one means by which governments cope with unemployment and foreign debt. In the global North, falling fertility rates, increasing life expectancy, the shift from manufacturing to services, and changes in the expectations and living standards of citizen workers have led to growing demand for workers who are officially classified as "low-skilled" to perform jobs that are dirty, dangerous, and degrading. Despite this demand, citing concerns that include preserving the integrity of welfare and fiscal regimes, the wages and working conditions of national workers, as well as national identity and social cohesion, richer and more developed countries such as Canada refuse to grant low-skilled workers either (immediate) permanent residence or citizenship status.

drop in spaces

Precarious Migrants, Non-Citizens, and Flexible Labour

Although national immigration policies have always been shaped by each country's unique history of immigration, there is a convergence internationally toward temporary migrant programs (previously known as "guest-worker programs" but now called "managed or circular migration") for low-skilled workers (Surak 2013; Walsh 2014). Since the 1990s, there has been an intensification of migrant exploitation in low-wage sectors of core capitalist countries in the global North (Lewis et al. 2014). A distinctive feature of these temporary, circular, or managed migration programs for low-skilled workers is that these workers are often not entitled to the same rights as workers who are nationals of the host state. Typically, migrant workers are subject to a range of mobility, employment, and residence restrictions in the country in which they are working that do not pertain to workers who enjoy either permanent resident or citizenship status in the host state. While all residents who do not have either permanent residency status or citizenship are, to some extent, precarious (Goldring, Berinstein, and Bernhard 2009), some migrant statuses are much more precarious than others (Morris 2001). For example, entry to Canada as a high-skilled migrant worker provides a range of rights, such as family accompaniment and a clear path to permanent residence, which is simply not available to a migrant who is admitted under the low-skilled labour migration streams (Fudge and MacPhail 2009). The different migrant statuses are important in channelling migrant workers into different labour market locations. Through immigration law the state creates a differentiated supply of labour that produces precarious workers and precarious employment norms in the hospitality, construction, agricultural, and private household sectors (Fudge 2012). There is a hierarchy of desirability for certain occupations and sectors that depends upon the migrant worker's race, ethnicity, gender, and country of origin (Lewis et al. 2014, 4).

Nandita Sharma has pointed out how, in the latest period of capitalist globalization, it is the *foreignness* of both certain forms of capital and certain workers that becomes framed as the key problem of neoliberalism. "Within this framework, not only is the relationship between national states and

capitalists obfuscated, but the fortification of national state boundaries comes
to be seen as necessary for the protection of 'society' . . . [with] profound
effects in relation to the organization of national labour markets" (2006, 5).
National labour markets are socially constructed in and through the relations between capital, labour, and the state, which crystallize into durable
institutional structures (Peck 1996). In capitalist societies these institutions
are also sites in which the capacity to rule is organized and technologies of
governance—including legal technologies—are legitimized. Sharma highlights the ways in which particular national economies are constituted in
and through the simultaneous inclusion of foreign migrant workers in labour
markets, and their exclusion from the nation as citizens (2006, 54–55). As
Kristen Surak remarks, "what typically makes immigrants economically desirable to employers—their submissive malleability as rightless outsiders who
perform the undignified task that natives shun—are precisely the qualities
that make them undesirable as members of a society" (2013, 86). Placing
people in the category of "temporary foreign workers" allows for their differential inclusion as lawfully subordinated people in the host nation and host
labour market (Sharma 2012, 33). While it is unacceptable (and most often
illegal) to discriminate against people on the basis of their race or gender,
it is considered to be just to differentiate against workers on the basis of
their migrant status; that is, on whether they are "citizens" or "foreigners"
(Sharma, 2012, 28). As Jason Foster and Bob Barnetson explain, "by cast-
ing international migrants as 'others,' state-imposed limits on their rights
can be seen as an effort to 'protect' the jobs of Canadian workers from
the threat posed by international migrant workers" (2015, 111). Temporary
migrant workers, thus, are an extreme form of flexible labour (Fudge and
MacPhail 2009) who can be expelled when no longer needed. In this way,
the national state can simultaneously respond to the demands of the demos
and capital (Surak 2013, 86).

Unfree Migrant Labour

Sociologists have developed the concept of "unfree labour" to describe migrant
workers who do not have the right to circulate freely in the host country's
labour market since most are bound to a particular employer and can only
change employers with the host state's permission (Walsh 2014). Unfree labour
situates "unfreedom" in opposition to "free" labour, which is characterized by
agreement or "free" contractual relations (Lewis et al. 2014, 8). Sharma (2006)
considers the unfree migrant workers who cross national boundaries in order
to work to be the exemplary post-Fordist workforce. Her work contributes

to the scholarship of the last several decades that has sought to highlight the centrality of unfree labour to contemporary capitalism and conceptualize freedom/unfreedom as a spectrum rather than a binary (Shrivankova 2010; LeBaron 2015; Strauss 2013; Davidson 2010). In other words, unfree labour ranges from restrictions on migrant workers' mobility via the imposition of immigration controls to forms of chattel slavery. The unfreedom of migrant workers reveals the extent to which contemporary capitalism incorporates a range of regimes of labour control that do not fit the paradigmatic notion of "free" employment.

Unfree labour is related to but broader than "forced labour," which revolves around the notions of menace of penalty and coercion. For example, migrants who are tied to a specific employer as a condition of their residence in a host country are not free to circulate in the labour market, but neither are they coerced to remain with their employer. More recent definitions of forced labour also recognize that unfreedom can occur when a worker initially enters freely into an employment situation, but is deceived about the nature and conditions of work and/or is forced to remain in that relationship through coercion (Andrees and Belser 2009). In many situations of debt bondage, for instance, a migrant worker "freely" chooses to take a job, but later is unable to quit because of a huge debt owed to a recruiter, who may, in turn, threaten the migrant worker's family unless the debt is repaid in full. Neither situation precludes the payment of a wage; many forms of unfree labour and forced labour are in fact done in exchange for some form of payment. Slavery in all its forms, bonded labour, and other forms of forced labour are thus subsets of unfree labour that involve coercion of various kinds upon, during, or prior to the initiation of the work relation. They occur on a spectrum of unfreedom that not only encompasses a range of forms and relations of commodification and exploitation, but a variety of individual work relations that are not static across time or in place.

While temporary migration programs are touted as promoting a triple-win solution (Angenendt 2014)—for host states, employers, and the migrant workers—tensions between the temporal logics of national states, capital, and migrant workers inevitably surface (Surak 2013, 89–90). Employers prefer the rhythm of the business cycle, and temporary workers, who can only exit their employment relationship on pain of losing their migrant status, allow employers to avoid the cost of labour turnover. By contrast, national states do not want migrant workers to develop ties or entitlements that accrue with the passage of time so that foreigners are assimilated into citizens. Migrants want to earn money and expand their life chances, and the temporality of their life choices differ from those of capital and the host state. Moreover, they sometimes seek to evade the requirement that they return to their country of origin, and courts, as well as public opinion, can mitigate the harshness of government immigration policies.

The Shift from Immigration for Settlement to Temporary Migration for Work

Beginning in the 1990s, Canada shifted from recruiting immigrants for permanent settlement through the points system to using temporary migration programs for skilled workers as a transition to permanent residence (Alboim 2009). Although low-skilled temporary labour migration programs date to the 1960s, they were small in size and targeted specific sectors (agricultural) and specific occupations (domestic work in private households) as well as specific source countries (initially Caribbean counties) (Fudge and MacPhail 2009). The first official temporary migrant worker program, which was established in 1973, was used primarily for filling shortages in high-skilled occupations. The Immigration and Refugee Protection Act, which came into effect in 2002, established the Temporary Foreign Worker Program (TFWP), which simply incorporated most of the key features of the earlier temporary labour migration program (Sharma 2006; Fudge and MacPhail 2009).

The different streams of the TFWP can be broken into two broad categories: those requiring a labour market assessment before an employer can hire a temporary migrant worker, and those that dispense with this requirement. The latter stream, which since October 2014 has been called International Mobility Partnerships, tends to be linked to multi- and bilateral agreements or pertain to international students. Of the 221,273 foreign nationals entering Canada in 2013, 62 per cent (137,533) entered under International Mobility Partnerships, while the other 38 per cent (83,640) came in under the TFWP (Government of Canada 2014, 2). What was new, however, was the introduction of the Low-Skilled Pilot Project in 2002. This initiative did not replace either the Foreign Domestic Movement Program (renamed the Live-In Caregiver Program in 1992) or the Seasonal Agricultural Worker Program, but operated alongside them. It was a response to the demand for a much broader range of low-skilled workers to fill jobs across a range of sectors.

The TFWP, which since 2014 only refers to those streams that require an employer to obtain an employment authorization (known as a Labour Market Impact Assessment), is demand-driven, although prospective employers are required to satisfy a labour market test administered by the federal department that is responsible for the functioning of the Canadian labour market. The precise terms of the employment authorization have changed dramatically over the past decade, but in general employers must demonstrate that they have advertised for workers from within Canada, will pay the advertised job the prevailing wage rate, and, if they have previously employed migrant workers, have complied with the conditions of the work authorization and provincial employment standards legislation. In theory, the employment authorization safeguards that migrant workers do not take jobs seen as belonging to Canadians or undercut Canadian terms and conditions of employment, while ensuring that employers who have exploited migrant workers in the past do not continue to do so.

Under the TFWP, migrant workers are issued closed work permits that tie them to a specific employer at a specific location, and they are not allowed to work for any other employer or at any other location without first obtaining a new work permit, which requires a new labour market assessment. Migrant workers admitted through the TFWP are ineligible for welfare (social security benefits) and for contributory-based employment insurance benefits, even though employment insurance contributions are deducted from their pay cheques (Fudge 2012; Marsden 2011). They are entitled to contributory pension benefits, which are typically regulated under bilateral agreements with the sending country. They are also entitled to the same labour laws and standards, as well as access to enforcement regimes, as permanent residents and citizens.

These requirements, restrictions, and rights apply to all of the TFWP streams regardless of skill or wage level. In addition, employers of migrant workers admitted under the low-skilled scheme are required to pay the workers' transportation costs and medical insurance until the worker is eligible for public health insurance (Fudge 2012; Faraday 2012). However, unlike high-skilled migrants who are entitled to be accompanied by family members, who are eligible for open work permits, low-wage workers must demonstrate that they can support accompanying family members, who are not eligible for open work permits (Fudge and MacPhail 2009). Moreover, unlike the high-skilled program, workers admitted under the low-skilled program can only obtain permanent resident status through the Provincial/Territorial Nominee Program, which requires employers to nominate foreign workers for permanent residence status. Other eligibility requirements under this program, such as years of schooling, official language capability, and occupational classification, vary from province to province, and only a few admit limited numbers of low-skilled migrant workers (Nakache and D'Aoust 2012, 176).

Opening and Closing Access to the Hospitality Sector

When it was introduced in 2002, rigorous requirements for employers to obtain an employment authorization combined with the one-year duration of the work permit kept this labour migration stream small (Fudge and MacPhail 2009). However, in 2006, the newly elected Conservative government changed the program from one that had very restrictive demand-side requirements to one that was effectively employer-driven. Construction and hospitality businesses in Western Canada were particularly vocal in their demand for quick and easy access to low-skilled migrant workers, claiming that it was important to capitalize on the economic boom while it was underway, and that training Canadians to do the jobs would simply take too long. The government responded by easing the advertising requirements on employers to obtain an employment authorization, expediting the authorization process, and extending the duration of the work permit from one to two years, with no limit on the number of times a visa could be renewed. There was a dramatic increase in the number of low-skilled workers who were admitted through that program, jumping from 15,309 in 2007 to 25,660 in 2008, and they were employed in many sectors, including fish processing plants, meat processing plants, full-service restaurants, retail stores, fast food establishments, coffee shops, ski resorts, and hotels (Fudge and MacPhail 2009; Government Canada 2014, 3).

The recession that hit Canada in 2008 after the global financial crisis undermined popular support for the TFWP. At the same time as unemployment began to edge up, stories recounting the abuse of temporary foreign workers by recruitment agencies and employers appeared in the national and international media. Labour unions were vocal in their criticism of the program, as was the Parliamentary Standing Committee on Citizenship and Immigration and the Auditor General. The government was urged to implement greater protection for migrant workers and greater oversight.

Although the number of migrants entering under the low-skilled program dropped to 19,011 in 2009, and even more dramatically to 14,122 in 2010, the stock increased, as the duration of work permits had been extended (Government of Canada 2014, 3). In 2013, there were 84,630 low-skilled migrant workers in Canada with a valid work permit. What is surprising is how quickly the numbers rallied after the immediate effects of the financial crisis diminished. The demand was fuelled by the emergence of a cluster of new industries and sectors, including retail trade, accommodation and food services, and transportation and warehousing, which were using migrant workers more regularly to address labour market needs (Foster 2012, 36). Migrant workers were employed as cooks, fast food servers, clerks, cleaners, truck drivers, and warehouse labourers. These workers tended to be recruited from the Philippines, India, China, and Mexico (Foster 2012, 29).

In a delayed response to the earlier criticisms, in 2011 the government began to impose greater restrictions on the use of low-skilled migrant workers and the residency rights of migrant workers (Fudge 2012; Faraday 2012). In 2012, however, the government allowed employers to pay low-skilled migrant workers 5 per cent below the prevailing wage so long as the wage was the same as that being paid to their Canadian employees in the same job and in the same location (Foster 2012). This shift in the wage policy for migrant workers has to be understood in light of the first austerity budget introduced by the Harper Conservative government once it won its first electoral majority. As Ann Porter (2013) recounts, the 2012 budget contributed to the privatization of risks and responsibilities associated with unemployment and a more coercive role for the state vis-à-vis working people and the unemployed.

In 2012, the Harper government introduced regulations to Employment Insurance (EI) that forced workers to adapt to a low-wage labour market (Porter 2013). Frequent users were required to accept employment involving a 20 per cent pay cut or lose benefits. After seven weeks, workers would have their benefits terminated if they refused a job that paid 30 per cent below their previous wage. The impact of this change was most notable in areas with high seasonal unemployment.

In introducing the change to eligibility for EI, the federal government explicitly linked it to the TFWP (Porter 2013). Diane Finley, the minister of Human Resources and Skill Development at the time, stated that in January 2012 Albertan employers received approval for 1,261 TFWP positions for food counter attendants, while at the same time, "nearly 350 people made a claim for EI who had cited significant experience in the same occupation and province" (Porter 2013, 16, quoting Canada News Centre 2012). Finley noted that "what we want to do is make sure that the McDonald's of the world aren't having to bring in temporary foreign workers to do jobs that Canadians who are on EI have the skills to do" (Porter 2013, 16, quoting Harper 2012). This linkage between the two programs can be seen as a threat to unemployed Canadian workers to accept lower paid work, or to be replaced by a "foreign" worker. It is a clear example of how the federal government used migration policies to justify changes to well-established social policies that have long been regarded as a social entitlement of citizenship.

"Foreign" Workers Replacing Canadians

In 2013, stories about a Chinese-owned mining company bringing Chinese workers on temporary visas to work in the mines of British Columbia (Nuttall 2013) and the Royal Bank of Canada's use of migrant workers employed by a US outsourcing company touched a nerve (Tomlinson 2013). The United Steelworkers, which represents mineworkers in Canada, complained that foreign workers were doing the jobs that their unemployed members could easily perform. The bank was criticized for moving good Canadian information technology jobs to India. What distinguishes the migrant workers in these stories from most of the others in the media, which tended to emphasize how poorly migrant workers are treated in Canada, is that they were not doing the jobs, such as farm and domestic work, that Canadians often refuse to do. Instead, migrant workers were represented as taking jobs away from Canadians. The federal government's response to the public outcry was quick; it imposed more requirements on employers to establish a labour market shortage in order to gain access to the program, transferred some of the costs of processing applications from the public purse to employers, blacklisted employers who had violated the program, and prohibited employers from offering wages to migrant workers below the prevailing wage rate, an innovation that the Conservative government had recently brought in. Employers who lie on their employment authorization applications about their efforts to hire Canadians face serious criminal sanctions, including additional fines and jail time.

The TFWP was also changed to stipulate that English and French are the only languages that can be identified as a job requirement, a measure that was introduced to ensure that language requirements cannot be used by an employer to exclude qualified Canadians from being able to apply because they would prefer to hire temporary foreign workers. Moreover, employers seeking employment authorizations were required to attest that they were not using the TFWP to facilitate the outsourcing of Canadian jobs (Government of Canada 2014, 17–18). These initiatives were allegedly designed to protect resident workers' access to jobs in the Canadian labour markets as well as prevailing wage and employment norms in Canada. However, in light of the fact that the federal government no longer had reliable labour force statistics, and thus was unable to ascertain that the TFWP had become a new business model, it appears that scapegoating migrants as the cause of unemployment and low wages was the government's underlying reason.

These stories helped shift the narrative about temporary migrant workers from the economic needs of Canadian employers and the exploitation of vulnerable migrant workers to how Canadian workers were being displaced by "foreign workers" (Foster 2014). But it was the scandal concerning the McDonald's in Victoria in particular and the hospitality sector more generally that led to wholesale changes to the TFWP. The day after the McDonald's story broke in April 2014, ESDC launched an investigation into the three Victoria McDonald's franchises that were involved, which resulted in the restaurants being blacklisted from the TFWP (Tomlinson 2014a). By the end of the same month, ESDC placed an immediate moratorium on all government approvals to hire temporary foreign workers for food services employers in order to conduct a full review of the TFWP.

The response to the scandal and moratorium was divided. Employer associations supported the continuance of the TFWP. For instance, Restaurants Canada (which represents about 30,000 employers in the food services industry) took the position that there were not enough Canadian workers available to fill vacant positions and that restaurants needed low-skilled temporary foreign workers in order to keep their businesses open. The industry association even began an online petition against the federal government's April 2014 moratorium on access to the TFWP for food services employers (Restaurants Canada 2014). The Canadian Federation of Independent Business (2014) has proposed a special stream, based on bilateral agreements, such as the Seasonal Agricultural Workers Program, for hospitality and retail workers that would provide a pathway to permanent status, enable migrant workers to switch employers within the sector, a bill of rights for temporary foreign workers, stricter enforcement rules, lower fees, and wages based on those paid to Canadian residents who work in the same establishment. What the restaurant sector wanted was to reduce labour turnover, and migrant workers fit the bill as they were prohibited from changing employers as a condition of their visas.

Labour unions were divided on whether the TFWP should continue. The BC Federation of Labour and the United Steelworkers Union supported a moratorium on the entire TFWP (both high-skilled and low-skilled streams) so that the program could be re-evaluated. The BC Federation of Labour argued that the TFWP takes away jobs from Canadian workers, and that temporary foreign workers have fewer rights on the job than Canadian workers due to their precarious immigration status (BC Federation of Labour 2013). Unions in British Columbia have a long history of opposing migrant, especially Chinese, workers (Goutor 2007). In contrast, United Food and Commercial Workers Canada (UFCW), which had long attempted to organize all—including migrant—agricultural workers, supported the continuance of the TFWP, and argued the program should be changed to allow low-skilled temporary foreign workers to remain in Canada and become Canadian citizens. The UFCW also complained that low-skilled TFWs are denied workplace rights due to their precarious immigration status, such as the right to form a union (UFCW 2014).

Migrant advocacy groups like Justicia for Migrant Workers and the Migrant Workers Alliance for Change supported the continuance of the TFWP. However, these groups called on the federal and provincial governments to work together to ensure migrant workers admitted under the TFWP have the same rights in practice as all Canadian workers. They wanted the Canadian government to issue open work permits so migrant workers are not tied to one employer, and extend pathways to citizenship to all temporary foreign workers (Ramsaroop and Smith 2014). Finally, the C.D. Howe Institute, a conservative think tank, came out with a report arguing that the TFWP increased unemployment in BC and Alberta between 2007 and 2010. During this time period, employers in BC and Alberta were given easier access to temporary foreign workers in certain occupations including food and hotel services due to alleged labour shortages. The report's author, Dominique Gross (2014), argued there was, in fact, no labour shortage during this period.

The range of responses to the reforms to the TFWP largely reflect the short-term interests of particular groups of employers and longer-term concerns about economic growth, and few took into account the interests of migrant workers. At the heart of the scandal were conflicting views on what role government should play in regulating how employment relationships and immigration policies intersect, and questions about where migrant workers and new immigrants should fit in the Canadian labour market. The scandal also underscores the significance of Bridget Anderson's observation that "labour markets are a key site for the construction of us and them, and foreigners taking jobs has been a trope of concerns about aliens and immigrants for generations" (2013, 10).

The suspicion that employing TFWs had become a business model was confirmed by the statistics provided in "Overhauling the Temporary Foreign Worker: Putting Canadians First." Of the 12,162 employers who used the TFWP in 2013, 21 per cent (2,578) had a workforce comprised of 30 per cent or more temporary foreign workers. For almost 10 per cent of employers (1,123), temporary foreign workers accounted for fully half or more of their workforce (Government of Canada 2014, 9–10). Seeking to end this practice, the government introduced a quota on the proportion of low-wage temporary foreign workers that a business can employ. This cap is designed "to significantly restrict access to the TFWP, while ensuring that Canadians are always considered first for available jobs, reducing employer reliance on the program and increasing wages offered to Canadians" (Government of Canada 2014, 10).

Employers with 10 or more employees applying for a new employment authorization are subject to a cap of 10 per cent on the proportion of their workforce that can consist of low-wage temporary foreign workers. The cap is applied per worksite of an employer and is based on total hours worked at that worksite in order to ensure that large employers with multiple locations cannot exceed the limit for low-wage temporary foreign workers at any one of their locations. The government estimates that by the time this quota is fully implemented, the size of the intake under the low-wage migration program will be reduced by one-half from 31,099 in 2013 to an estimated 16,278 in 2017 (Government of Canada 2014, 10). Notably, the cap does not apply to high-wage migrant workers. In addition to the cap, the government imposed a moratorium on the hiring of temporary foreign workers for positions that require little or no education or training in the accommodation, food services, and retail trade sectors in economic regions with an unemployment rate at or above 6 per cent. This initiative, which became effective in June 2014, is designed to reduce youth unemployment, and the government estimated that it would reduce the number of temporary foreign workers by approximately 1,000 each year (Government of Canada 2014, 11).

The labour market test that allows employers to bring temporary foreign workers to Canada was renamed the Labour Market Impact Assessment (LMIA) and the process is more comprehensive and rigorous. Employers must now also attest they are aware of the rule that Canadians cannot be laid off or have their hours reduced at a worksite that employs temporary foreign workers. The duration of the LMIA was reduced from two years to one, and the length that a temporary foreign worker can stay in Canada was reduced from four to two years. Moreover, the fee for processing LMIAs was increased from $250 to $1,000 per migrant worker.

A centrepiece of the federal government's overhaul of the temporary workers program is its commitment to enforce the terms of the employment authorization. It announced that it was massively increasing the number of inspections, which will be targeted by the use of tips, random audits, and risk assessments, and it dramatically expanded the authority and powers of inspectors. In addition, the enforcement toolkit was enlarged to include administrative monetary penalties and bans. The federal government has also announced that more criminal investigations will be conducted in order to prosecute employers who lie on employment authorizations, and it has increased the severity of the criminal sanctions associated with violations of employment authorizations.

These initiatives are designed to protect Canadian nationals whose jobs may be displaced by migrant workers hired by unscrupulous employers rather than to protect migrant workers, although banning unscrupulous employers from the program may somewhat curtail the future exploitation of migrant workers. Since labour standards are a matter of provincial and territorial competence, the federal government lacks jurisdiction to enforce migrant workers' rights. However, it has encouraged its provincial and territorial counterparts to develop more effective enforcement strategies. Notably, the federal government has not promised to do what it can to improve migrant workers' rights, such as ending the closed work permit that ties a migrant worker to a particular employer or providing a pathway to permanent residence and citizenship that does not depend upon the employer's support. In Canada, precarious migrant status tends to exacerbate the underlying problem, which is ineffective or non-existent labour market regulation in jobs located at the bottom of the labour market.

The major problem is that labour law enforcement is complainant-based. Migrant workers are very dependent upon their employers; their work permits

are tied to their employer, many are required to live on their employer's premises, and many depend upon their employer's nomination in order to obtain
permanent residence. Very few migrant workers are unionized. Thus, despite
the existence of anti-retaliation provisions in employment-related statutes,
most migrant workers simply do not lodge complaints if their labour rights
are violated (Fudge and MacPhail 2009; Nakache 2013).

Jobs in the food services sector illustrate how institutional and regulatory frameworks shape both labour demand and supply. Such jobs are
often seasonal and temporary, and how unemployment insurance regimes
treat seasonal workers will effect whether or not there is a demand for migrant
workers to fill these jobs. Similarly, since the wages for these jobs are low and
conditions of employment are poor and labour standards are difficult to enforce
(Matulewicz 2015), permanent residents and citizens do not consider these
jobs to be attractive. In Canada, employers have been unwilling to improve
the terms and conditions of work in the food services sector and have sought
to recruit unfree migrant labour. But instead of seeing the "problem" as poor
terms and conditions in the sector, conditions that are created by a combination of employer practices, government policies, and social expectations,
migrant workers are identified as the threat.

Conclusion

Canada's labour migration system is complex, opaque, and subject to short-
term political pressures. With the shift to demand- and employer-driven
schemes, the Canadian government has delegated important administrative
functions—determinations of skill and labour shortages and worker recruitment and selection—to market actors. Under such privatized models, policies
are less concerned with aggregate economic consequences or distributive issues,
and more with localized short-term benefits at the firm and industry level.

Different immigration controls and migrants' rights contribute to the
creation of a highly segmented labour market for migrant workers (Fudge
2012). The government's response to scandals that migrant workers are displacing Canadians has been to impose restrictions, including quotas, on employers
who use the program, rather than to grant rights to migrant workers in order
to protect Canadian workers' jobs and standards of employment. This decision is more likely a political response to negative public opinion rather than
a real attempt to address the complex problem of designing an efficient and
fair labour migration regime that targets the bottom half of the labour market.

In introducing the raft of restrictions in 2014, the federal government
blamed employers, rather than its own policies, for the profound increase in the

use of low-skilled migrant workers, despite the fact that its previous policies facilitated employers' reliance on low-skilled migrant workers. During the oil-fuelled economic boom, wage increases for occupations in British Columbia and Alberta that were designated as experiencing profound labour shortages were no higher than other occupations (Fudge and MacPhail 2009, 26). This finding runs contrary to conventional labour market thinking, which predicts that occupations experiencing labour shortages would experience higher than average wage increases. While employers clearly have a short-term interest in suppressing wages, the fact that in 2012 the federal government permitted temporary foreign workers to be paid less than the prevailing rate suggests that it was not adverse to wage suppression. Access to migrant workers creates incentives for employers to delay the introduction of productivity-enhancing investments that would enable them to offer higher compensation in order to attract workers with permanent residence or citizenship status (Lemieux and Nadeau 2015, 21). In the long run, this practice is detrimental to the economy. There is also evidence that the increase in low-skilled TFWs in Alberta and British Columbia accelerated the rise of unemployment rates (Gross 2014).

Canada's immigration policy has been quietly shifting away from permanent settlement toward the use of foreign workers with limited citizenship rights. The low-wage stream of the TFWP serves to differentiate migrant from resident workers. The migrant workers admitted under it form a different category within the Canadian labour supply because they are more precarious than resident workers, either because they are assigned fewer rights or because the rights they are entitled to are not effectively enforced. Their precarious migrant status is used to assign them to jobs that are precarious and this limits their ability to improve their terms and conditions of employment. Precarious migrant worker programs permit employers to establish conditions of employment in the sector that residents would not tolerate. Domestic workers are overwhelmingly female, and the vast majority are from the Philippines. Workers admitted under the Seasonal Agricultural Workers Program are from either the Caribbean or Mexico, and almost all of them are men. Workers admitted under what was formerly known as the "low-skilled program" tend to be recruited from the Philippines, India, China, and Mexico, and they work as cooks, fast food servers, cleaners, and warehouse labourers (Fudge 2012). In this way, Canada's low-wage stream institutionalizes precarious employment norms, and contributes to the creation of segmented labour markets that are racialized and gendered.

What impact does low-skilled temporary migration have on national identity and social cohesion, concepts which are hard to define "and even harder to measure in practice" (Ruhs 2013, 28)? In Canada, the media reports of Canadian workers being displaced by foreigners fuelled a protectionist response, but, in general, Canadians support immigration (Reitz 2011). Using Canada as a case study, Keith Banting addresses the critical question of how to "reconcile growing levels of multicultural diversity and the sense of a common identity which sustains the norms of mutual support, the capacity to pursue collective projects and social solidarity" (2010, 793). He argues that the welfare state in combination with immigration and integration policies "set a frame that helps shape public attitudes and expands or narrows the opportunities for political elites to mobilize public attitudes and inject them into political debates" (2010, 802–803). This analysis is important because it suggests that xenophobic and nativist responses to migration are not the "authentic" attitudes of national populations, but instead, are themselves shaped by a combination of immigration, integration, and welfare policies, as well as by labour market institutions. Thus, it is important to consider how institutions shape public opinion. By linking deterioration in the benefits provided under Employment Insurance to temporary foreign workers the federal government explicitly scapegoated migrant workers. An institutional approach to understanding public attitudes also suggests that a troubling consequence of Canada's segmented labour migrant program is that by imposing different rules concerning access to both the labour market and to citizenship it may undermine Canadian's commitment to "democratic arrangements and citizenship's reciprocal and solidaristic ethos" (Walsh 2014, 17).

Historically, in Canada, a white-settler economy, it was critical to forge bonds of social solidarity across national origin and ethnic identity. Social justice was both a reason for, and consequence of, a Canadian identity in which settlement and citizenship were available to newcomers who were willing to work. Under neoliberalism, the ability and willingness to work is a necessary condition for admission into national boundaries, but it is not enough to be entitled to citizenship. Low-skilled or low-waged temporary migrant workers are the ultimate just-in-time and disposable workforce. Admitted at the behest of employers, they are not entitled to become permanent residents or citizens. Simultaneously, they are vilified in public discourse and blamed for unemployment and stagnant wages. Constructed as "foreigners," migrant workers are easy distractions from government policies that deregulate and liberalize labour markets, and employer practices that take advantage of unregulated competition in the labour market. Over the past 10 years, the federal government's policies toward temporary foreign workers are a classic example of pitting "them" against "us."

Closing the border to low-wage migrant workers and detecting and deporting the thousands of migrant workers whose visas expired (and are not eligible for renewal) on 1 April 2015 will not solve the deeper problem of the growth in precarious work in the Canadian labour market. In fact, focusing on the "threat of foreign workers" distracts attention from the broader institutional factors (such as the decline in private sector unions and the lack of enforcement of labour standards) that have contributed to the deterioration in jobs over the past several decades (Lynk 2009; Workers Action Centre 2015). Social justice cannot stop at the borders of the nation state but, instead, depends upon stretching and thus strengthening the bonds of social solidarity. The challenge is to transform our image of migrant workers from dangerous foreigners into citizen workers.

Further Readings

Choudry, Aziz, and Adrian A. Smith, eds. 2016. *Unfree Labour? Struggles of Migrant and Immigrant Workers in Canada*. Oakland, CA: PM Press.

Justicia for Migrant Workers (J4MW). http://justicia4migrantworkers.org/justicia_new.htm.

Migrant Dreams. 2017. Documentary by Min Sook Lee. Ontario: TVO. http://tvo.org/video/documentaries/migrant-dreams-feature-version.

CHAPTER 5

POST-RACIALISM AND THE "EQUITY, DIVERSITY, AND INCLUSION" PROJECT

Grace-Edward Galabuzi

Introduction

The first decade of the twenty-first century saw a proliferation of equity, diversity, and inclusion (EDI) initiatives in many Canadian universities. These initiatives were a response both to the realities of increasingly diverse student populations and society, and to long-standing critiques of the academy as Eurocentric, colonial, and racially defined. These critiques, levelled by communities of difference, among them Indigenous and racialized academics, women, LGBTQ, and academics with disabilities, sought to culturally diversify the academy. In response, Canadian post-secondary institutions have voiced their appreciation of diversity and pursued policies aimed at advancing equity and inclusion. It appeared that a major shift was set in motion, from the reflexive hostility that routinely greeted findings or charges of racism and demands for decolonizing the curriculum in previous decades, toward active engagement with equity, diversity, and inclusion concerns.[1]

Inspired in part by the ascendency of neoliberal governing values, the turn to diversity is often justified using the business case, especially in light of increasing competition for student enrolments. It has been argued that it just made good business sense to brand a university as open to all manner of diversity as a way of growing enrolments and attracting international and culturally diverse Canadian students. "Managing diversity" seemed to signal a modernization of the academy as an increasingly global and cosmopolitan institution, not unlike the transnational corporation whose ideological shadow was increasingly cast over corporatized Canadian universities. Supporting organizations such as the Canadian Association of University Teachers (CAUT), the Canadian Federation for Humanities and Social Sciences (CANFED), and the Ontario Conference of University Faculty Associations (OCUFA) also committed to addressing demands for racial justice in the academy (CAUT 2007), albeit with differing levels of intensity. York University sociologist Enakshi Dua (2009) has documented many of the "diversity"-related policy moves at major Canadian universities. The idea of diversity and inclusion even became a "stock story" in many Canadian universities (Aguirre 2010). There seemed to be a real opening for those interested in advancing equitable practices and outcomes in this new era of diversity. And yet many equity advocates remain dissatisfied and frustrated with the pace and direction of change.

In this chapter, I explore the juxtaposition between this proliferation of diversity programming, and their attendant celebrations of inclusion and race-lessness, and the persistent concerns of racialized and Indigenous academics about ongoing racial injustice within Canadian universities. I suggest that these contradictory impulses can be explained by the normalization of the idea of post-racialism in the Canadian academy. This idea is rooted in long-standing notions of colour-blindness and whiteness, on the one hand, and the ascendance of neoliberal managerialism and its demands for commodifying diversity, on the other. The seeming co-optation of the concepts of equity, diversity, and inclusion (EDI) as well as various attempts to institute diversity management regimes, however, stand in stark contrast to the experiences of Indigenous and racialized members of the academy and their ongoing demands for racial justice. This dissonance between institutional celebrations of EDI initiatives and the lived experience of their supposed beneficiaries has potentially adverse implications for the mission and operation of the academy.

One key implication of this transformation in management practices has been a major shift away from the politics of coalition associated with racial justice and, in the process, struggles against persistent racial disparity and inequality. As I argue in this chapter, this shift is rooted in a particular theorization of race, the hegemonic prominence of colour-blind ideologies, and the emergence of post-racial politics in this neoliberal moment. Together these factors serve to secure white privilege and diminish the claims of racialized people for remedial action. It is the convergence of these three developments that I argue is responsible for the fraying of anti-racism coalitions, and the reassertion of whiteness as a social order that unevenly distributes opportunities, often at the expense of racialized groups.

The twenty-first century academy's neoliberal operating logic is also consistent with post-racialism thinking, especially its embrace of individualism and individual remedies to experiences of racial discrimination. This in turn militates against an understanding of racial oppression as rooted in collective harm (structural racism) and the need for collective action for racial justice. Indeed, Susan Iverson has argued that, in the American context, the diversity project in the academy as conceived "is complicit in perpetuating the racial order as historically constructed" (2007, 587). I will argue that the Canadian academy cannot undergo fundamental transformation with respect to racial justice, while its historical, racial, and colonial foundations and the dominant social relations that arise from these foundations and ongoing practices remain largely unacknowledged. In the final analysis, the key observation here is that the project of racial justice and decolonization, whether as EDI or otherwise branded, cannot simply be grafted onto the racial institutional edifice through a process of diversity management. Such an edifice must be unsettled to make way for a new inclusive order.

Using critical race theory as an analytical framework, I explore the extent to which policies that appear to be well-intentioned attempts to create more diverse and inclusive institutions have instead reinforced a sense of marginality and exclusion for racialized and Indigenous peoples in the academy. Specifically, I argue that the ascendance of post-racialism is possible in large measure because of a growing gap between white allies and racialized and Indigenous people in the academy in their very conceptualization and practice of anti-racism. This includes a turn away from critical anti-racism as a dominant way of understanding the politics of racial justice toward what has been referred to as post-racial anti-racism (Paul 2014). The celebration of post-racialism effectively erases the significance of racial considerations in the daily lives of racialized academics and de-emphasizes threads of structural racialization in the academy, thereby undermining the legitimacy of racial justice projects.

I also employ a Gramscian analysis that provides critical assistance in exploring the hegemonic position of whiteness in Canadian universities and how dominant orders respond to critical pressure by constructing new modes of institutional organization and a common-sense logic that normalizes them through consent and coercion (Gramsci 1971). From a Gramscian perspective, the concept of passive revolution (a revolution without a revolution) helps us get at the essential contradictions that are the source of what I suggest is a failed racial justice project—stalemated in the tension between the aspirations of equity for racialized and Indigenous citizens of the university and commodified forms of diversity and inclusion. Stuart Hall's (1986) work has demonstrated how Gramsci is useful in addressing the structural-cultural tension when it comes to the question of race, racialization, and colonization. I follow his application of a historical and discursive approach and apply it to the question of racialization and academic institutions.

The Limits of the Equity, Diversity, and Inclusion (EDI) Project

In many universities across Canada, the debate about diversity and inclusion has gone mainstream, largely in response to critiques emanating from communities of difference, and in particular, Indigenous and racialized communities and academics who are defined by these identities. Indeed, my own institution has undertaken initiatives that seek to mainstream equity, diversity, and inclusion, as have many others, with varying degrees of commitment (Antone et al. 2010). In part, these EDI initiatives are a response to growing diversity in Canadian universities and in broader society, whether ethno-cultural or other dimensions of difference such as gender, sexual orientation, ability, race, and indigeneity. This inescapable fact of multiplying diversities, however, has yet to be reconciled with the history of Canadian universities as central agents of a Canadian project, which was historically understood as a white Canada project. As Dorothy Smith reminds us, "universities in Canada were founded in and were integrated with the ruling apparatus of imperial powers that were implicated in the genocidal treatment of the peoples native to the territory we call Canada, institutions of slavery, [and] the subjugation of other civilizations" (2002, 151).

Francis Henry and Carol Tator (2009) also have observed that, in the past, white-dominant culture was a given in higher learning, and the absence of people identified as the "other" was taken for granted. The curriculum was defined by Eurocentric perspectives, which are rooted in whiteness, and invariably treated cultural difference as a deficit and as somehow not measuring up to the European standard. In the contemporary period, however, "the needs, values and practices of Canadian society have become more diverse and pluralistic," opening up Eurocentric assumptions to challenges from new voices and perspectives on ways of knowing, learning, and being (Henry and Tator 2009, 5). This sets up a tension that necessitates a shift in the mission of the Canadian academy to address these new realities (Malinda Smith 2010).

Universities play an ongoing and critical role in all national projects by defining what constitutes knowledge and by producing and reproducing dominant social and political structures and leadership cadres. George Dei and Agnes Calliste (2000) further explain that "schools, colleges, and universities continue to be powerful discursive sites through which race knowledge is produced, organized and regulated. Marginalized bodies are continually silenced and rendered invisible not simply through the failure to take issues of race and social oppression seriously but through the constant negation of multiple lived experiences and alternative knowledges" (quoted in Henry and Tator, 2009, 3).

Educational institutions exist within societal contexts and invariably embody and reproduce dominant forms of social hierarchies, marginalization, discrimination, and social exclusion that persist in broader society. These structures are reproduced in the education system to the advantage of some and the detriment of others. This helps explain why unequal relations and outcomes persist in the face of often repeated pronouncements by elites, political leaders, and core institutions such as universities against systemic racism, classism, patriarchy, homophobia, and ableism. I want to suggest that we began Canadian time with the experience of colonization, both as national and global phenomena, which have generated social relations, institutional arrangements, and subjectivities that are still relevant today. It is not surprising that in the contemporary era, diversity projects have become a preoccupation in the Canadian academy. Diversity projects potentially represent a strategic compromise between historically dominant interests and the emerging interests of Indigenous and racialized populations. It is my contention, however, that the advent of official diversity and inclusion regimes, in their current form, actually undermine efforts to further racial justice rather than strengthen them.

The Old and New Academy

It has long been argued that racialized and Indigenous groups exist in spaces of marginalization on an academic terrain that is rooted in whiteness. The hegemonic position of whiteness generates tensions, especially when minoritized interests seek to assert counter cultural positions within the academy (Bannerji et al. 1991). Confronted with growing critiques from various so-called communities of difference (Indigenous and racialized academics, women, LGBTQ, and academics with disabilities), the Canadian academy has been put on the defensive. At the structural level, critics seek to transform the post-secondary institution into a more inclusive space and place where different people and interests can coexist in a culturally diversified academy. At the micro level, critics address the everyday lived experiences of racialized and Indigenous scholars and students, who often are confronted with hostile and unsafe working and learning environments, or denied equitable access to opportunities in the everyday practices, values, and norms of hegemonic whiteness (Henry and Tator 2009).

In the early twenty-first century, Canadian post-secondary institutions have responded to these pressures by embracing the ideas of diversity and inclusion, operationalizing them through a litany of institutions engaged in the mechanics of diversity (Ahmed 2004a, 2007b). These typically include diversity and equity reviews, diversity plans, diversity and equity advisory committees, the appointment of diversity and equity administrators, the declaration of diversity, equity, and inclusion statements, harassment and discrimination policies, and programs to bridge Indigenous and racialized students into the academy.[2]

Diversity initiatives typically acknowledge minoritized groups as outsiders in the academy, subject to whiteness as a standard, exclusionary policies and practices, chilly climates, and student and faculty attrition. These initiatives typically provide a discursive frame from which to propose strategies for inclusion and to compensate for the "social deficits" that are assumed to be associated with marginality (Iverson 2007). Generally, the initiatives apply to the way the university is organized and run, especially with respect to the representativeness of its faculty, administration, and students. But some also seek to address the pedagogical mission of the university. In fact, Shiboa Guo and Zenobia Jamal (2007) have identified three models that are common in doing diversity in Canadian universities: the intercultural model (based on individual intercultural education and positive attitudes toward difference to create change); the multicultural model (affirms the importance of culture in the learning and teaching processes and advances curriculum reform toward inclusive multicultural knowledge and perspectives, and multicultural competences); and the anti-racist education model (addresses the structural basis for the inequalities in education and confronts racism in the lived experience of students and faculty). This latter approach sees education as a racially, culturally, and politically mediated experience and calls for the integration of multiple centres of knowledge, recognition, and respect of difference as well as teaching for community empowerment (Guo and Jamal 2007). A corresponding approach, often referred to as the "decolonization of the academy" or "indigenization," attempts to address the colonial nature of the academy and knowledge production.[3] These approaches seek to change the institutional culture of the academy so that Indigenous faculty, staff, and students can thrive based on Indigenous values as opposed to opting out of post-secondary education as so many do today (Anderson and Hanrahan 2013). Decolonization, as Taiaiake Alfred (2004) argues, requires intentional and strategic confrontations with the Canadian academy.

In many ways, however, institutional diversity initiatives have served only to further alienate the very people they are supposed to benefit. Many have expressed a sense of frustration with the content, approach, and outcomes of these initiatives. There is ample evidence, for example, to suggest that this frustration is rooted in the fact that minoritized populations have not benefited from these initiatives. The experience of historically marginalized groups remains just that, marginal and challenging, in an environment in which institutions are claiming progress on diversity and inclusion (Trehin 2010; James 2012). As Malinda Smith argues, institutions have become increasingly adept at "equity talk" in lieu of "equity practice" (2010, 46). This reflects choices made by universities that focus on diversity management rather than equity as social justice. Diversity management emphasizes the "selling of diversity," a practice that emphasizes the visibility of communities of difference but is largely disconnected from their historical struggles for social justice that demand both institution transformation and redistribution of access and opportunities. Sara Ahmed (2007b) has also described this shift toward a "language of diversity" as a form of marketization of difference. She observes that diversity can be defined in ways that reproduce rather than challenge privilege, and conceal rather than confront unequal power relations. It is little surprise then that diversity programming in many institutions often raises the frustrations of minoritized populations.

The Coalition of Academics of Colour in Canada has identified the persistence of equity-related concerns, including the lack of representation of racialized faculty in most institutions, faculties, and programs, and at the various ranks of academia. It emphasized hostile and alienating work environments and micro-aggressions in everyday interactions, and tracked the ways in which Indigenous and racialized faculty were systematically marginalized and/or excluded from the workplace (Henry and Tator 2009, 52–53). A variety of investigations and task forces have reported similar findings. Numerous studies have examined a broad range of indicators such as representation in the ranks of tenure-track and tenured faculty, the composition of the sessional teaching staff, retention rates for students from historically disadvantaged communities, the breadth of the curriculum, dominant research methodology, what is valued and what is not in terms of knowledge production, and the student experience. When the evidence is amassed, the inescapable conclusion is that, in the words of Frances Henry, post-secondary institutions display a "culture of whiteness" (Henry 2004).

The issue of faculty representation is a key indicator of inequitable access to academic opportunity for Indigenous and racialized scholars. In 1986, the federal government introduced legislation that required employers in its jurisdiction and its contractors to address equity representation for four designated groups (women, Aboriginal, visible minorities, and disabled). Canada's universities have operated under this regulatory regime for close to 30 years. It is now routine for universities to declare that they are equity employers and are committed to diversity and inclusion in their hiring preferences and practices. Recent data on representation in faculties in select universities, however, suggests there has been a loss of momentum. Data shows significant under-representation nationally and in key institutions. Statistics Canada data, for example, indicate that in 2006 (the last available data), 82.7 per cent of Canadian full-time faculty are identified as white, while racialized faculty account for

15 per cent of the full-time appointments. Indigenous peoples account for less than 1 per cent of full-time faculty (Li 2012, 41). While the racialized population in 2006 accounted for 24 per cent of all PhD holders, in most cases they experienced a pay equity gap, with earnings falling below the mean annual rate ($68,906 in 2005). The situation was exacerbated for racialized female faculty, in particular Black women who fell $30,757 below the average, followed by South Asian women (–$29,056), Arab and West Asian women (–$30,119), and minority Latin American women (–$28,991). White women also earned less than the average professorial income but not to the same dramatic extent (–$7,735). Further analysis indicated that these racialized pay gaps were not explained by other relevant factors such as age, length of appointment, immigration status, field of study, or province of residence (Li 2012, 42).

A cursory survey of reports from a number of key institutions, moreover, shows that Indigenous and racialized people repeatedly report in surveys, interviews, and focus groups that the academy remains a hostile environment in which to pursue education, careers, and scholarship. Racialized faculty make specific reference to micro-aggressions that diminish their sense of belonging and their right of place in the academy, hostile and alienating work environments, systematic marginalization and/or exclusion, and chilly climates and vilification when they raised issues of racial oppression.

For the Canadian academy in general, the numerous university reports and initiatives, official and non-official, betray a prevalence of concern about the university as a place where Indigenous and racialized peoples are vulnerable if not at risk. This is consistent with the discourse of disadvantage that accompanies them and ensures the deployment of the social deficit model, which constructs the problem as one of deficiencies as opposed to opportunities. The dream of a place and space of belonging and full membership is fast slipping from the grasp of those who once saw the prospects of transformation as inevitable, especially in light of institutional pronouncements. Marginalized faculty express frustration with what W.E.B. Dubois ([1903] 1994) referred to as a double consciousness. It requires them to cross out of one world into another as an everyday ritual of survival, afraid that the penalty of not passing in a standardized white world will have adverse career consequences. Moreover, the marginalization of their alternative world views means that any related scholarship is subject to devaluation. The scenario requires a performative move that imposes a burden on the mental and emotional health of racialized academics. This is made necessary in part to avert the normative white gaze that appears rooted in condemnation and judgement, precisely the condition that Frantz Fanon spoke so eloquently about in his famous quote from *Black Skin, White Masks*: "And then the occasion arose when I had to meet the white man's eyes.

An unfamiliar weight burdened me. The real world challenged my claims. In the white world the man of colour encounters difficulties in the development of his bodily schema. Consciousness of the body is solely a negating activity. It is a third person consciousness. The body is surrounded by an atmosphere of certain uncertainty" (1986, 110).

Dubois did not focus specifically on the academy, but his insights into the ways in which racial formations organize individual, community, and institutional life provide critical spaces to begin to think about the power of whiteness, colonialism, and capitalism in the academy. The next section draws on critical race theory to provide analytical insights into the Canadian university as a racial institution.

Critical Race Theory, Whiteness, and the Canadian Academy

Critical race theory provides us with an understanding of the prevalence of racialization in key Canadian institutions that help define the Canadian project (Thobani 2007). Critical race theory challenges dominant notions of race and racialization, including concepts such as colour-blindness and meritocracy, and focuses on the lived experiences of Indigenous and racialized people and their capacity to resist and challenge those dominant structures and logics. Universities, similar to all institutions, reproduce social relations that are shaped by broad structural forces that are rarely acknowledged as being biased and exclusionary. As Carl James further explains, "the structures and practices of universities, informed by Western European middle-class, patriarchal ethics, and traditions in combination with the state's discourse of multiculturalism—with notions of cultural democracy, freedom, racelessness and colour-blindness—contribute to a false sense of neutrality, fairness, objectivity, and 'public good'" (2009, 136).

This sense of neutrality and objectivity extends to the idea of whiteness itself, understood here as a subjective condition that is rooted in the assumed supremacy of European civilization, cultural norms, and subjectivities, and held out as a standard for universal conceptions of the "other." Fiona Probyn (2005) has suggested that whiteness refers less to pigmentation than to a set of behaviours that is historically variable, contested, and often invisible to those who are marked by it. It is asserted as a mode of power in a manner that renders its tentacles invisible and banal but not its effects (Razack 1998; Peake and Ray 2001). As Richard Dyer (1988) asserted, whiteness is an expression of control and dominance over racial subjectivities that deflects attention away from its own position and function in the social fabric. Whiteness, in other words, consistently affirms and reinforces its claim to racial centrality and superiority for those it privileges, while insisting on a rhetoric of racial neutrality for its victims (Chidester 2008).

Whiteness and assumptions about white supremacy operate as deep structural foundations that inform the operations and power of the university. Its dominant power relations are reflected in the complex network of relationships and socio-political forces that define the institution. These processes, however, are not totalizing or immune from critique and change. In fact, the academy remains a site of intense political and ideological conflict and struggle, precisely because it routinely exposes its own contradictions—making claims regarding its openness to diversity and inclusion on the one hand and suppressing struggles that seek to make them real on the other. It is possible for us to observe the command and control functions of the institution as well as its mediating functions in these moments of contestation.

Whiteness is implicated in the various stages of development of the university. It provides ideological justifications for the dominant practices and the social psychology of the people who work in it, especially in regard to their understanding of authority and governance. Whiteness also articulates particular relations, norms, values, discourses, and practices that act to reproduce power relations and identities, including racialized identities (Ahmed 2007a). In this way, it functions as an instrument of white unity, supports assumptions of whiteness as natural, and furthers white ideological identity. The boundaries between racially dominant and racially subordinate groups are maintained through processes of entry and exit, rewards and punishment, and the nature of the climate that is nurtured in the institution (Kobayashi, Cameron, and Baldwin 2011).

Whiteness organizes subjective realities in ways that often create a backlash against Indigenous and racialized claims for inclusive curriculum, diverse pedagogical approaches, representation, and cultural space. Often, when demands for curriculum reform are made, the privileges of whiteness are seen as under attack and are defended at the level of "Western civilization." Demands for racial equality are not deemed legitimate by many members of the academy, lip service notwithstanding, because they threaten the social status of the dominant group. A key way in which this delegitimization is achieved is through the assertion of colour-blindness or racelessness as a feature of the university. The concept of colour-blindness literally means the absence of colour or lack of race-consciousness. This applies to the actions of agents as well as systems and outcomes and operates as a form of ideology, framing some realities and erasing others. Colour-blindness is also a highly contested concept because it obscures more than it reveals in terms of the function of race and racialization in society. While the dominant position in Canadian society largely denies the significance of race, this creates key problems for those who are racialized because it eliminates the basis for making claims against the condition they suffer (Bonilla-Silva 2010). This extends to its subjects who consistently challenge claims of oppression and unequal treatment based on race and indigeneity. In fact, the institutional defenders of the academy as a liberal, social mediating institution have tended to defend it precisely on the basis of its "liberal and colour-blind status," choosing to ignore the evidence to the contrary.

Colour-blindness, as Charles Mills has aptly argued, serves to entrench white privilege. He used the metaphor of the fish and water: "The fish does not see the water, and whites do not see the racial nature of a white polity because it is natural to them, the element in which they move" (Mills 1997, 76). Mills, in fact, rejects the notion that the academy is and has ever been raceless, arguing instead that processes of knowledge production, dissemination, and mobilization have characteristically privileged dominant groups to the exclusion of others. On the flip side, the institution articulates subordinate subjectivities that must engage a double consciousness in order to survive in a racially and culturally hostile environment. Many have to accept the norms, values, and affectations of whiteness in order to avoid the penalty that comes from non-conformity in this allegedly race-neutral theatre. The racial climate they encounter has to be negotiated with utmost care in order not to trip the backlash alarm and trigger charges of "double-bind racism." The latter term includes a reluctance to name racial injustices for fear of being accused of pulling the "race card." This reality delegitimizes challenges to practices of whiteness and their racial implications. Those who name the problem, in effect, become the problem.

Carl James (2012) argues that there are three typical responses that racialized university faculty use to deal with these conditions of marginality. He identifies these strategies of engagement as compliance, pragmatism, and critical participation. Based on qualitative research involving faculty members from various universities, he concludes that the *compliant group* accepts the dominant values and norms as fair, viewing discrimination as rare, isolated, or unchangeable. This group tends to accept the idea that one does what is required to get and keep an academic job. Some in the compliant group do not even recognize a racial justice critique of the academy or broader society. The second group, the *pragmatic group*, simply seek to meet the demands of the academy as set out for them without contesting them, although their experience has persuaded them that these demands are exclusionary and inequitable. They learn how to navigate the maze, often overachieving to impress the dominant group members and avoiding being known just for issues of race. Finally, the *critical participation* group addresses issues of inequity and racial injustice within institutions, often at great personal cost to their careers and their emotional and physical health. As one of James's respondents explained, "I feel that I paid a personal price in the academy for actually making a political stand" (James 2012, 148).

In the context of institutions that are key to the formation of the Canadian project such as universities, it is essential to understand the structurally determinative role they play in creating and circulating dominant discourses, myths of nation-making, and ways of knowing about particular groups in society. Racial relations are structural relations with specific operating logics. Over time these logics have become so embedded in everyday norms and values that they are rendered invisible, so much so that demands for racial justice are frequently dismissed as being groundless or self-interested and thus incompatible with pursuits for the greater good. Increasingly there is a tendency to diminish the significance of racialization with the common-sense notions about cultural differences and pathologies, or more typically about the achievement of a post-racial and colour-blind society. The following section turns to this shift.

EDI in Canadian Academy and the Spectre of Colour-Blind Post-Racial Politics

Gramsci used the term "passive revolution" to describe times when insurgent or subaltern forces failed to overcome the dominant order. The concept describes a "revolution without a revolution," when dominant forces use revolutionary rhetoric to consolidate their position and power to maintain the existing social order (1971, 59, 106). A passive revolution leaves an uneasy balance between the old and a potential new order. Gramsci described a possible outcome as the condition of *tranformismo*, whereby the challenging social groups or subordinate classes are incorporated into the existing elite networks and the established order in a manner that effectively aborts the process of change and ensures the restoration of the order under challenge (1971, 58, 110). I want to suggest that this analysis applies to the racial justice challenge to the Canadian academy, and that we are now dealing with a condition of reproduction of dominant relations within the academy because the diversity and inclusion project has floundered as a social justice project.

The counter-hegemonic push for social inclusion for historically marginalized groups and the knowledge systems associated with them in Canadian universities has been aborted through processes of coercion and consent that have largely absorbed these challenges and reasserted the conditions of white privilege using such strategies as normalizing colour-blindness. University EDI initiatives are now underpinned with assumptions about colour-blindness and post-racialism, which, as already discussed, do not reflect the lived experiences of racialized faculty and students. Post-racialism, as Joshua Paul

(2014) suggests, represents discourses and practices that deny that race is not (or is no longer) a relevant reference point for action. More broadly, post-racialism represents a critique of racial discourses, identities, and categorizations, while simultaneously projecting a utopian vision and project of racelessness. According to Paul, the post-racialism project has three primary threads, which involve scientific claims, the political dismantling of the assumptions of race thinking, and an ethical critique of race. Together, these three threads are used to make the case that race thinking and race-based claims ought to be disregarded because race is a false, dangerous, and indefensible category.

Celebrations of colour-blindness and post-racialism in contemporary discourses, however, are not neutral. At the very least, colour-blind discourses serve to narrow the space for articulation of racial injury and exacerbate conditions of disadvantage. Rooted as they are in a condition of whiteness as well as the neoliberal-inspired conceptions of the individual and diversity as a commodity form, they serve to re-entrench racial privilege for the dominant group and intensify disadvantage and marginality among minoritized groups. The invisibility of whiteness is simply taken for granted as a sign that race and racism have been vanquished. Any disparities that coincide with racial categories are explained away with cultural or even biological explanations as opposed to structural impediments (Wise 2010). In the United States, for example, Ward Connerly, a former University of California regent, championed legislation to ban affirmative action in university recruitment on the basis that there were no racially defined injuries that required restitution (Paul 2014). But, as the stories of the experiences of racialized and Indigenous faculty show, colour-blind post-racialism is occurring at the expense of the very groups that are assumed to benefit from the defeat of racism, colonialism, and racialization.

Post-racialism has different ideological nuances on the political left and right. The former sees post-racialism as a necessary step to prevent the cyclical reproduction of the racial category, which it understands to be a prerequisite for racism (Paul 2014). The conservative version argues that race is no longer a significant social and political category. The conservative "end of racism" school points to cultural "deficits" as explanations for persistent racial disparities and dismisses claims of marginalization that are raised by Indigenous and racialized people (Mirza 2010). While the conservative story about the end of racism has become dominant, there appears to be an "ideological" convergence between the left and right on the question of post-racialism. It is as much the post-racial advocates on the right as those on the left that seem engaged in the celebration of the post-racial future. It is this left-right convergence that most concerns the racial and Indigenous advocates of racial justice. The erasure of racial considerations and the resulting normalization of white supremacy as a mode of meritocracy are indicative of the challenges facing Indigenous and racialized peoples in spaces like the academy. In practice, post-racialism takes on an instrumental form that legitimates practices that undermine the ability of racialized and Indigenous students, staff, and faculty to experience a sense of belonging to and full membership in the academy.

Post-racialism is in part a response to (or a cause of) the retreat from the racial justice project by the state and institutions such as the university, in favour of diversity and inclusion as a neoliberal project. This project seeks to commodify and capitalize difference (as a form of human and social capital) without dealing with the underlying inequalities in the relations of power responsible for the historical exclusions. Writing about the American experience, Iverson (2007) has argued that diversity programs set up and use discursive frames that are rooted in neoliberal representations of universities as marketplaces with key actors engaged in transactional relations as opposed to social relations informed by obligations of citizenship. They assume whiteness as a standard against which achievement is measured. This standard tends to reify Eurocentric epistemological perspectives rooted in particular notions of meritocracy, objectivity, and individuality (Iverson 2007). In this context, critiques of diversity projects often represent the discordant voices that are misaligned with both the triumphantalism emanating from university administrations and factions of the white academy that have come to assume a post-racial present as a given. However, what we see juxtaposed against the celebrations of post-racialism and affirmations of colour-blindness are persistent articulations of racial injustice by racialized and Indigenous academics concerned about chilly racial climates, blocked opportunities for progress, racially unequal access to tenure or outcomes of tenure processes, undervalued research projects, and challenges to authority in classrooms (Antone et al. 2010).

The emerging consensus on the question of race, which is seen congealing around the idea of post-racial politics, appears to rest on a fundamental shift in dominant understandings of racism. Using post-racialism as a racial frame, this consensus seeks to reconcile conditions of racial inequity with prevailing market-centred mechanisms of diversity management. Three key factors are an expression of this phenomenon. First, this conception of equity, diversity, and inclusion rejects collective projects and emphasizes individual experiences. This has the potential to erase the political and moral foundations for Indigenous and racially-based demands for redress of historical injustices. Second, the idea of managing diversity through neoliberal logics emphasizes reconciliation, fitting in, mainstreaming, unity, and neutral/neutered conceptions of difference. These changing terms on which the diversity and inclusion project is being undertaken decouples it from the critical discourses of anti-racism, decolonization, and oppression, and from racial justice and decolonial projects more broadly. Third, market logics and the impulse to commodify diversity to increase enrolments deemphasize critical questions of social justice, including the transformation of the very institutions and relations that are responsible for racial disparities and oppression. The changing terms on which the diversity and inclusion project is being undertaken represents a shift away from the critical discourses of anti-racism, decolonization, and oppression to a management regime focused on reconciliation, fitting in, and mainstreaming, which do not significantly disrupt the status quo.

There has also been a fundamental shift within the otherwise empathetic white progressive movement toward an understanding of racism as an individual phenomenon as opposed to a structural or institutional one. In many institutions, this includes feminist faculty who once were instrumental in supporting racial justice action. Here I want to explore some insights from Eduardo Bonilla-Silva (2010) and what he calls "racism without racists," as well as John Powell's (2013) analysis of post-racial politics. They interrogate the ways in which post-racial ideologies decentre structural racism, displacing it in favour of individualist, essentialist, intentionalist, and race-targeted approaches that help refigure the now conventional colour-blind frameworks through which university life is interpreted. Powell (2013) argues that post-racial common sense about the nature of racism has four main themes:

1) Individualist: We associate feelings, beliefs, and behaviours primarily with individuals, such that most accounts imply that racism is first and foremost a matter of individual actions. According to this conception, racism is lodged in the hearts and minds of individuals and manifest in the words they speak, the actions they perform, and the thoughts they harbour.

2) Essentialist: This construction draws on a literal understanding of racialization. Rooted in liberal tradition, it dismisses any claims that do not pass the procedural equality test. Equality is understood as achieved through same treatment regardless of contextual or historical circumstances. In an unnuanced way, it also requires us to assign an identity to the acts of racialization: one is either a racist or not, all the time or never.

3) Intentionalist: As a rule, people's words and actions are interpreted as racist only if they are intentionally enacted to produce outcomes that injure some or benefit others. This ignores the Canadian Supreme Court's position that considers both the intentional and unintentional impacts of laws or actions on individuals or groups.

4) Race-targeted: Here, the designation of racism requires that the offending word or act be race-targeted, as opposed to being systemic and having systemic impacts over time.

These minimalist and literal approaches undermine the ability of administrators, policy-makers, or victims to see racialization from the vantage point of its impacts and outcomes. But they do dovetail with the introduction and normalization of what is referred to as the "new managerialism" or "new public management" (NPM) in post-secondary institutions in that they have had the effect of diminishing social justice rationales for equity, diversity, and inclusion programs and initiatives. NPM injects market logics into the university by prioritizing market discipline, consumer satisfaction, and economic efficiencies, and insists that universities recruit globally to find new revenue streams. NPM empowers particular groups and disempowers others by redefining the public interest to align with commodifiable values. It rejects investments in moral and social justice–related initiatives, unless they can be justified by the market logics. In this context, EDI projects are frequently justified by appealing to the business case. It holds that diversity is a positive value, not because it addresses issues of recognition and inclusion, but rather because it can be used as a form of comparative advantage, including the recruitment of international students who typically pay higher tuition fees than domestic students.

Ahmed has detailed the ways in which the language of diversity strategically accommodates the demands of the establishment in universities. Both the language and the context has shifted from a social justice mission to maximizing the commercial brand value of diversity. "Diversity," she contends, "enters higher education through marketization" (2007b, 236). Reflecting on the Australian case, she argues that universities have branded themselves as diverse even as they demonstrate little institutional commitment to meaningfully addressing demands for equality. As one of her respondents put it, equity concerns "became a bit dated and had actually began to alienate and become marginalized from the business of the university" (2007b, 238). What she refers to as "equity fatigue" opened the door for new diversity frameworks that more closely adhered to the business model of the university. So while diversity was not a new word, it became part of a new language that "secures, rather than threatens the ethos of the university, with its orientation towards education as a form of business" (2007b, 239).

Individual versus Institutional Racism

Increasingly popular definitions of racism refer to common-sense understandings based on individual beliefs and belief systems, feelings, or behaviours as opposed to structures and systems. According to Powell (2013), anti-racism coalitions in the twentieth century focused primarily on structural racism or institutional racism. This perspective recognized that racism need not be accounted for by individual attitudes and behaviours but instead could be embedded in formal rules and organizational cultures. Racialized institutional decisions neither require nor preclude the participation of racist individuals. These institutional and cultural practices generate a dynamic that may or may not be dependent on the racial attitudes of the people engaged in them. An institutional focus thus calls for the transformation of key social, political, and cultural institutions to achieve racial justice. The institutional racism framework reflects a broader recognition of the ways racialized power is deployed, dispersed, and entrenched. Whereas both the individual and institutional racism frameworks emphasize dynamics triggered by race and racism, racial inequalities often originate in treatment inspired by other factors, such as class status, religious belief, and language, which interact with race in patterned ways. According to Powell, this kind of secondary racialization forms the leading edge of structural racism.

Given that understanding, I am suggesting that the shift in focus from institutional to individual explanations of racialization is at the heart of the declining support for anti-racist policy action among Canadian universities. This is perhaps especially notable among white liberals who previously supported systemic racial justice initiatives as moral and political imperatives. The new racial logic, in contrast, contends that we have already built a meritocratic society in which racial disparities can best be explained by cultural pathologies that are internalized by racialized individuals (Bonilla-Silva 2010). Indigenous people and racialized groups are assumed not to be particularly industrious, or are unqualified, or are unduly pliant, or are lacking in requisite human and social capital. The list of stereotypical individual deficiencies is long. The more this racial logic takes hold, however, the more claims for racial justice become as suspect for progressive Canadians as they are for conservatives who have long dismissed the idea of racially determined outcomes. Conservatives have long held that we live in a meritocratic order in which the magic of the market sorts groups and individuals into a socio-economic pecking order in race-neutral ways.

Here, I turn to Bonilla-Silva (2010) who argues that there are four ways in which a structural/institutional racism perspective on racism can disrupt conventional colour-blind frameworks, with important implications for analysis and policy intervention. First, in contrast to the individualist discourse, a structural understanding conceives of racialization as a societal outcome. Second, while emerging conceptualizations of racism present it as a static phenomenon, a structural understanding sees racism as a dynamic force that is recognized more for its effects than for any particular content. Third, while colour-blind approaches identify only race-targeted treatment as possibly racist, a structural understanding underlines the significance of both overt and covert modes of discrimination. Fourth, post-racial understandings of racism conceive of it as a historical phenomenon whose presence in twenty-first century Canada can only be regarded as anomalous, while structural racism recognizes the continuity of racialization as a function of the ongoing mission of a white-identified Canadian project.

Conclusion: Moving Forward

In the face of an atrophied racial justice project in the academy, I suggest that we must return to first principles to recover lost ground and to generate the necessary counter-agencies for a real transformation of the academy. The current moment calls for a profound adjustment in the operating premises of the university, specifically those relating to a liberal education that values knowledge for its own sake, and broadly articulates its mission as creating free, independent, and thoughtful citizens. A starting point is the deconstruction of the underlying logics of the university as a liberal institution and a shift to theorizing and naming its racial and colonial character. Moreover, this decon-struction project must be understood principally as a matter of social justice and as a value that transcends the commodification of diversity and the manage-ment of difference. A shift in assumptions and analysis is essential to get us past the "two steps forward one step back" dance of the existing diversity/inclusion projects. A social justice perspective signals the need to disrupt, not reform, spaces of learning, and to indigenize, rather than reify, Eurocentrism as the normative form of the academy.

The limited progress we see in efforts to diversify (and make inclusive) the academy is rooted in the foundational character of the Canadian univer-sity as a racial institution, in the same way we have come to understand the North American state as a racial state (Goldberg 2001). This understanding has important implications for struggle because it rejects the liberal concep-tions of the university as ideologically malleable and open to new realities of racial, cultural, gender, and sexual difference. A racial institution approach also provides insights into the colonial and racialized nature of dominant social relations that constitute the daily practices of the academy and, in particu-lar, centres on whiteness as a core dynamic of institutional formation and maintenance. It interrogates the colonial and racialized form of the academy and how it generates structures and agencies consistent with white suprem-acy and over-determines racialized identities. It also explains the persistent reports of conditions of an alienating work environment, which is replete with micro-aggressions that diminish the sense of belonging and right of place in the academy for racialized and Indigenous people, even in the face of the various diversity projects undertaken by the universities. New equity prescriptions stand little hope of changing these dynamics unless we first grapple with the constitutive structures of the Canadian academy.

The struggle for racial justice is political and requires racial justice and anti-colonial politics as a basis for deconstructing and reconstituting the dominant structures and logics of the academy as a colonial and racial institution. While increasingly discarded, these basic insights into the nature of the academy represent the essential reboot that we need to effectively disrupt the dominant logics, unsettle dominant orders, and re-establish legitimacy for a racial social justice project.

Because universities are critical sources of societal knowledge and function to legitimate some dominant narratives and silence others, the question of diversifying how we know and what we know is an important part of a process of indigenizing and decolonizing the academy. From an epistemological standpoint, a useful concept to employ here is coloniality, as articulated by Anibal Quijano (2007). He argues that coloniality is a general form of domination that remains in place long after the more explicit forms of colonization are lifted. It still imposes conditions of exploitation and negation of dignity and humanity. "Race" as a category came into being to determine supremacy and inferiority as part of the process of Eurocentrification of the world order. Until these foundations are unsettled, Indigenous and racialized peoples are destined to continue to occupy marginal subject positions in key institutions within that world and institutional order. In the context of demands and aspirations to transform the university as an institution whose logics are embedded in whiteness, it is essential to engage a process of decolonizing structures of knowledge, knowledge production, and dominant narratives that inform common understandings of Indigenous and racialized roles and their place in the academy—however complex, contradictory, and variegated. We have encountered the limits of the equity, diversity, and inclusion model that became popular in the first decade of the twenty-first century. To achieve success, the racial justice and decolonial project has got to be about more that reforming the mechanics of representation and the edges of the curriculum. It must challenge the epistemological dominance of Eurocentrism in the academe, root and branch.

Further Readings

Douglas, Delia D. 2012. "Black/Out: The White Face of Multiculturalism and the Violence of the Canadian Academic Imperial Project." In *Presumed Incompetent: The Intersections of Race and Class for Women in Academia*, edited by Gabriella Gutiérrez y Muhs, Yolanda Flores Niemann, Carmen G. Gonzalez, and Angela P. Harris. Logan: Utah State University.

Henry, Annette. 2015. "'We Especially Welcome Applications from Members of Visible Minority Groups': Reflections on Race, Gender and Life at Three Universities." *Race Ethnicity and Education* 18 (5): 589–610. doi:10.1080/13613324.2015.1023787.

Henry, Frances, Enakshi Dua, Carl E. James, Audrey Kobayashi, Peter Li, Howard Ramos, and Malinda S. Smith. 2017. *The Equity Myth: Racialization and Indigeneity at Canadian Universities.* Vancouver: UBC Press.

Notes

1 See, for instance, McEwen (1995); York University (1984); D. Smith (2002); and Queen's University (1991).

2 A select sample of University reports on diversity include but are not limited to: University of Alberta (2004), U of A Faculty of Education Equity Handbook; McMaster University (2008), Towards a Comprehensive Inclusion Plan for McMaster University: Translating McMaster's Institutional Commitment to Inclusion into Organizational Practices and Policies; McMaster University (2001), Recognizing Sexual Diversity at McMaster University: Experiences of Gay, Lesbian, Bisexual and Queer Students, Staff and Faculty Members; Carleton University (2008), Accessibility for Ontarians with Disabilities Act Accessibility Plan; Lakehead University (1995), Anti-Racism and Ethno-Cultural Equity Policy; Wai (2006), Project Report on Race and Ethnicity Barriers and the Position of Diversity Advisor; University of New Brunswick (2000), President's Taskforce on Creating a Positive Learning and Working Environment: Final Report; University of Toronto Statement on Equity, Diversity and Excellence; University of Toronto (2007), Accessibility of Ontarians with Disabilities Act Plan 2007–2008.

3 See, for example, Corntassel (2013); St. Clair and Kishimoto (2010); and Government of British Columbia (2013).

CHAPTER 6

TREATY MAKING AND BREAKING IN SETTLER COLONIAL CANADA

Hayden King

Introduction

In the beginning there was conflict. In the global accounting of economic activity among diverse peoples, this is generally the case. But it is out of conflict and clashing interests that creative and pragmatic avenues to peace emerge. This was the case with Indigenous peoples before and, for a time, after the first Europeans arrived in North America. When Indigenous people welcomed these newcomers there was an understanding of difference between them, both material and ideational. Indigenous peoples worked on the land and were a part of its very essence; in many ways, they were inseparable. The newcomers embodied a very different orientation to the land. They were, at once, rootless but also attracted to the land as resource ripe for exploitation: fish, fur, soil, minerals. Attempting to assuage these differences were formal agreements— treaties—that actually facilitated peace. But in all cases that peace was short-lived as partnerships broke down, world views and interests clashed, and violence manifest in colonialism with the attendant land theft and ultimately persistent, multi-generational social inequality endured. In the end, there was conflict.

The central purpose of this chapter is to imagine an escape from this trajectory and the endemic inequality that has accrued in the broken treaty relationships between Indigenous peoples and Canadians along the way. The chapter unfolds first by considering Indigenous conceptions of political economy, which historically have nurtured creative and sophisticated relationships with the land while responding to conflicting interests and needs of distinct communities. Second, the chapter argues that Canadian settler colonialism has suppressed these historical conceptions, attempting instead to remove and replace Indigenous presence from the land primarily through a new form of treaty making that commenced during the Canadian Confederation era. Third, the chapter explores the ways in which contemporary forms of land restitution continue to reinforce the dispossession of Indigenous peoples, primarily through the modern land claims system. Finally, the chapter argues that Indigenous resistance to these processes as well as growing disenchantment with settler models of resource extraction and environmental degradation generally reveal an imperfection in settler colonialism and an increasingly precarious form of (mal)governance. In these moments of tension, alternative political economies can offer a discernable path out of the crisis-laden history of land conflict in Canada. This is a path back to the future where Indigenous peoples and Canadians can draw on creative and pragmatic political economies and find a long-suppressed peace, mutual autonomy, and respect.

Eating from the Same Bowl: Indigenous Political Economies

Much of the scholarly and even popular narratives of Indigenous peoples in North America prior to the arrival of Europeans (and during the contact era) pivot on false narratives. The first travellers encountered peoples and societies they could not comprehend, and lacked the conceptual tools to describe them. Fantastic accounts of the supernatural, backward, and unproductive savage quickly emerged, which also served political purposes. As Lumbee legal scholar Robert Williams (1992) describes, such narratives were "discourses of conquest" employed to legitimize colonial policies and practices, promulgating the rightness of colonization as the advance of civilization. They have been applied in various forms to heroic Spanish and Portuguese conquistadors, resilient Jesuits and explorers, earnest American pilgrims, and noble cowboys. It can be seen in contemporary narratives of economic development, which paint Indigenous communities as backwards and as obstacles to development if they refuse such industries as mining and lumbering. For example, opponents of Canada's implementation of the 2007 United Nations Declaration on the Rights of Indigenous Peoples (UNDRIP) argued that it would empower Indigenous peoples to veto critical extraction and infrastructural projects such as the oil sands or pipelines and thus thwart economic development and progress. Then, as now, conquest discourses sanitize and valorize colonization while dehumanizing Indigenous peoples and burying their experiences of contact, conflict, war, peace, and life generally.

More recently, discourses of conquest have been subject to growing waves of critical interrogation. Led by Indigenous historians and scholars, a process of retrieval—an excavation of Indigenous perspectives and a more honest accounting of early colonial history—have reaffirmed the complex, multifaceted, and continuity of Indigenous civilizations and societies. This work, which includes a significant focus on the relationship between Indigenous peoples and the land, reveals new (and yet very old) general principles and practices of an accessible Indigenous theory of political economy. The first of these principles is the common notion among Indigenous peoples of reciprocity: everything taken from the land must be given back, in one form or another. Politically, reciprocity appears as ongoing dialogue and deliberation on the taking and receiving from the land and sharing with each other. Economically, it means the sustainable use of the land (sustainable in this sense means until the end of time). This flows into the second principle, the recognition of the agency of the land and the non-human creatures we share it with. Indigenous political economy privileges the idea that diverse elements of creation, whether human, bear, or muskrat, have distinct legal and economic orders that must be respected. A third principle of Indigenous political economy holds that borders and boundaries that separate distinct political and economic practices are not as rigid as the Westphalian model dictates but, instead, are flexible, dynamic, and overlapping. Autonomous people and creatures can share the same geographic region, making for a terrain mapped by shared jurisdiction.

The following examples represent a brief survey of how Indigenous peoples have cultivated and renewed these complex principles. In this discussion, and as a member of the Beausoleil Anishinaabek Nation, I draw from and reflect on the intellectual, political, and economic traditions of the Eastern Great Lakes Anishinaabek.[1] Despite this, and recognizing the diversity of Indigenous philosophies, many of the principles discussed here are held in common.

Indigenous Treaties as Peace and Friendship

Indigenous principles of political economy flow from relationships with the land, beginning with the very organization of society. In Anishinaabek communities, the social order revolves around the clan system of governance. Each clan—represented by an animal totem—is a collection of related families in a given community or even region (clans ultimately extend across the whole of Anishinaabe territory). Clan representatives speak on behalf of clan members at the council table ensuring democratic decision-making. Individual clan members also serve the community in a specialized way. For instance, Bear Clan members are keepers of community peace (as well as the medicine people), Loon and Crane clan members provide internal and external leadership, Fish Clan members offer education, Eagle Clan members are spiritual advisers, and so on. Each clan receives teachings from their clan animal, observed and distilled over many generations, and, in exchange for these teachings, people are obliged to honour the animal: to acknowledge its contributions, to never hunt or eat it, to advocate on its behalf (Johnston 1982; Benton-Banai 1988). These reciprocal obligations are among the first treaties for the Anishinaabek and illustrate a conception of the land as an economic resource but also as a source of mentorship. The clan system embodies a world view that holds up the land as an entity with agency.

One of the most well-known political and economic agreements with the land echoes the features of the clan system. This is documented in the story of the Treaty with the Deer, a narrative of the breaking and rene-gotiation of an agreement between the deer, moose, and humans that has governed Anishinaabek political economy for centuries. The story goes that one day, very long ago, the people lost track of the deer and the moose. The creatures simply vanished. After searching for many weeks and having their queries rejected by other creatures, the humans discovered that the crows and owls had kidnapped the deer and moose. So the humans embarked on a campaign to free the hooved creatures. After eventually dispersing the birds and reaching the deer and moose, they learned that the latter had not been captured at all, but went voluntarily with the birds because the humans had forgotten their obligations. It was understood that in exchange for sacrificing themselves to feed, clothe, provide tools, and educate the people, the people have obligations to maintain the integrity of the homes of the hooved crea-tures and make space for their societies to thrive into the future (L. Simpson 2008). The people agreed to correct their behaviour as well as make recon-ciliation with the winged creatures and the treaty was renewed. The story underlines the very real consequence for humans who abandon reciprocity and treaty obligations: a potential deprivation of sustenance and life. Whether the treaty is taken literally as an actual event that occurred in our distant past or a device to transmit important teachings about how we relate to the land, the story has proved important enough to be passed on for centuries.

The basic principles of Indigenous political economy also were extended and reproduced in treaties among humans. While the Treaty with the Deer reinforced reciprocity and ultimately sustainability, the first treaty between Haudenosaunee[2] and the Dutch stressed aspects of mutual autonomy common among most Indigenous nations. The Treaty of Tawagonshi, which would become known as the Two Row Wampum, is a part of the Guswenta, the Iroquoian system of treaty making. In the early 1600s the first waves of settlers arrived in Kanien'kehá:ka (or Mohawk) land, the eastern portion of Haudenosaunee territory. Reflecting the pragmatism of Indigenous diplomacy generally, the Mohawk entered into an agreement with these newcomers that they hoped would shape their long-term relationship. Oren Lyons describes the agreement as follows:

This row of purple wampum on the right represents the Ongwahoway
or Indian people, it is their canoe. In the canoe along with the people is
our government, our religion or way of life. The row of purple wampum
on the left is our White brethren, their ship, their government, and their
religions for they have many. The field of white represents peace and the
river of life. We will go down this river in peace and friendship as long
as the grass is green, the water flows, and the sun rises in the east. ...
You will note the two rows do not come together, they are equal in size,
denoting the equality of all life, and one end is not finished, denoting the
ongoing relationship into the future. (1986, 119)

Building on Lyons's interpretation, Michael Mitchell (1989) elaborates on the
parallel lines in the wampum, which signify the mutual sovereignty embedded
in Indigenous treaty making: distinct nations travel the river of peace together
but the vessels are independent, the people from one boat not permitted to steer
the other. While the Two Row Wampum is one agreement connected to many
others in the vast canon of Haudenosaunee diplomacy, it is a powerful and simple
description of an ideal political relationship as it relates to mutual autonomy.

The distinct features of the Two Row Wampum are clearer in the Dish with
One Spoon Treaty, negotiated nearly 100 years later between Indigenous and non-
Indigenous nations in the eastern Great Lakes area. The Dish with One Spoon
followed the French and Indian War (1764) and sought to re-establish peace in
the region. A wampum of nearly all white beads depicts a single purple "lozenge"
in the centre representing a bowl or dish in which the people in the region live
and work. By accepting the treaty, parties have obligations to ensure the dish
never runs empty. This did not entail the surrender of authority or jurisdiction
to one another or any political entity, but instead emphasized mutual obligations
and responsibilities to each other and to the land, a shared jurisdiction. It is also
important to note that on the wampum there are no sharp objects at the table
with which we might stab each other (D. Johnson 2005, 9). In other words, the
Dish with One Spoon recognizes that politically distinct peoples can share
the same territory in peace.

The principles of the Dish with One Spoon Treaty are reproduced in
Anishinaabek relations with other Indigenous nations, especially those on the
western side of our territory. The conflict here was with the Dakota who
the Anishinaabek had been pushing steadily out of their territory since at least
1740, largely under pressure from the American settler expansion. An inter-
esting diplomatic feature of this conflict was the practice of *biindigodaadiwin*,
which translates as "to enter one another's lodges." The practice was to create
temporary truces in the midst of conflict in order to hunt, often together, and
to eat in each other's lodges (Treuer 2011). Neither the Anishinaabek, nor the

Dakota, could condone starvation by limiting access to the land. Allowing the hunting and eating, sustenance, and even economic activity on territory considered "ours" was an important feature of the political economy.

Many enduring themes emerge from this reading of Anishinaabek political economy. The first is reciprocity—the imperative that we have obligations to one another, both human and non-human, as well as responsibility to the land. And if we neglect those obligations or fail to recognize the power and agency of animals, we will suffer greatly or die. The land will hold us accountable. The second and related theme is that the sustainable sharing of the land is an ongoing and permanent condition. It is not a one-time transaction but a never-ending obligation. As Chief Yellowhead, a Great Lakes Anishinaabek leader, said during a recitation of the Dish with One Spoon in 1840, the Council Fires representing peaceful relations between the Anishinaabe and Haudenosaunee shall burn for "as long as the world stood" (Johnston 1982, 11). These obligations of reciprocity and responsibility, as Leanne Simpson puts it, "promote more life" (quoted in Klein 2013, n.p.). Winona LaDuke (2002) makes a similar observation, using the hybrid Anishinaabemowin term *mno bimadiz-iwin* to describe the cyclical and reciprocal reproduction of life or continual rebirth that lies at the core of Anishinaabek political economy. Finally, each of the cases discussed here emphasizes autonomy. In contrast to Canadian notions of demarcated property and exclusive authority over it, Indigenous peoples have practised a political economy emphasizing shared authority and jurisdiction. This latter theme comes up again and again in diplomatic symbols and protocols such as wampum belts, "eating from the same bowl," and "sitting under the shade of the same tree"—metaphors that describe a mutual obligation to each other. We are bound together, to this place, by virtue of our agreement. These principles offer a coherent vision of land management and economic activity. At least, they once did. While still operative in varying degrees in communities today, the core principles of Indigenous political economies have been suppressed and surpassed by radically contrasting visions of economic and political life.

Things Fall Apart: A Brief History of Canadian Settler Colonialism

The long and complex history of Indigenous–settler relations from the era of contact, to trade and reciprocity, to nation to nation, to dispossession and colonization has been expertly detailed in many volumes. But this process of colonization or colonialism itself, at least as it is commonly deployed, does not describe well the experiences of Indigenous people in North America or, for that matter, other white settler British colonies such as New Zealand,

Australia, and the United States. Traditional theories of colonization have generally asserted that imperial powers arrive, exploit the land, resources, and labour for as long as possible, and then when administration of the colonies becomes more expensive than the wealth extracted or colonizers are physically removed, the colonization ends. The process of decolonization begins when the former colonial power leaves (Veracini 2010; Hixson 2013). Such was certainly the case in significant parts of Africa and Asia in the mid-twentieth century when European colonial powers withdrew from their former colonies, often only after years of revolt by the colonized. As a result, the immediate post–World War II period saw the creation of many newly independent states out of the ashes of European imperialism. A few decades later Edward Said had remarked that, "in our time, direct colonialism has largely ended" (1993, 9).

The experiences of Indigenous peoples in North America, however, did not follow a similar contact-exploitation-colonization-decolonization trajectory. Perhaps colonization in the Western Hemisphere initially followed the model, as the first European settlements in North America were set in motion by entities like the fur-seeking Hudson's Bay Company and the tobacco-exporting Virginia Company. But the key difference in the North American context is that colonizers never left. While methods and focus of extraction have changed over time, the colonial presence has endured and multiplied. This is a reflection of the inadequacy of discussions of colonialism in places like North America, where it is ongoing.

Commenting on the permanence of colonialism in contexts such as ours, Patrick Wolfe (2006) describes *settler* colonialism as a structural and permanent phenomenon, as opposed to merely an event or era. Resources and labour are not sufficient in this context. Land and territory are the overriding desire, as settlement and long-term resource exploitation are the fundamental motivations of settler colonialism. In this pursuit, Indigenous political economies present an obstacle and must be liquidated, and replaced with regimes that facilitate a different, contrasting type of economic activity. For Wolfe this "logic of elimination" is undertaken violently or through assimilation, the forced adoption of children, and the breaking down of collective Aboriginal title into fee simple private lands ripe for the selling (2006, 388).

Building on this framework, I argue that the logic of elimination has been clearly articulated in the Canadian settler colonial context. Here, it has been deployed as an alien form of treaty making that privileges European notions of political economy, particularly a transactional model that confers exclusive jurisdiction over land and people. This contrasts with the type of treaty making practised by Indigenous peoples described above. This process began in earnest before Canada came into existence with pre-Confederation treaties, continued with several sweeping post-Confederation-era Numbered

Treaties, and survives in the contemporary era with land claims agreements (so-called modern treaties).

The Sharp Objects of Settler Treaties

The shift from Indigenous political economies to an imposed European control and, ultimately, settler colonization occurred following the Seven Years' War. After the British secured French surrender in 1760, many Indigenous peoples continued to fight against British encroachment. Odawa leader Pontiac gathered nations west of the Great Lakes in an effort to push the invaders out of their country and re-establish Indigenous authority. The negotiations to end the conflict produced the Royal Proclamation of 1763, a policy that stipulated that all territory west of already-existing British colonies would have to be voluntarily shared by Indigenous nations with the colonial power before any settlement proceeded. This shrewd manoeuvre at peace was a simultaneous giving and taking away of what we know today as Aboriginal title, all the while placing the British crown as the arbiter of deliberations on land conflicts. Within a year many Indigenous nations had accepted the Proclamation and worked to reinscribe it in Indigenous terms. This later version is known as the Treaty of Fort Niagara, which espoused a respect for the autonomy of Indigenous nations, a military alliance, free and open trade between the British and Indigenous nations, veto on British expansion, the ongoing provision of gifts, and finally, generally, mutual peace, friendship, and respect (Borrows 1998). The British accepted this vision and enshrined it in the "Twenty-Four Nations" wampum belt, which they gifted to their Indigenous allies.

Unfortunately, in what would become a treaty making trend, these Indigenous terms were rapidly eroded and then conveniently forgotten as British presence and power in the Great Lakes region expanded. A mere 50 years after the Treaty of Fort Niagara, communities were struggling to survive. By the end of the War of 1812, it was clear the settler political economy was ascendant. The pace and the depth of this radical change on Indigenous life was not lost on political leaders. Shingwaukonse ("Little Pine"), an Anishinaabe leader from the Sault Ste. Marie area, lobbied government officials and made numerous speeches about the preservation of Anishinaabek political economy, from the 1820s through the 1840s. The British largely ignored these pleas and frustration mounted. In 1849 he hand-delivered a letter to Governor General James Bruce, the 8th Earl of Elgin, in which he wrote:

> When your white children first came into this country, they did not come shouting the war cry and seeking to wrest this land from us ... they sought our friendship, we became brothers. Their enemies were ours, at the time we were strong and powerful, while they were few and weak. But did we oppress them or wrong them? No! And they did not attempt

to do what is now done, nor did they tell us that at some future day you would. Time wore on and you have become a great people, while we have melted away like snow beneath an April sun; our strength is wasted, our countless warriors dead, our forests laid low; you have hounded us from every place as with a wand, you have swept away all our pleasant land. And like some giant foe you tell us willing or unwilling, you must now go from amid these rocks and wastes, I want them now! I want them to make rich my white children, while you may shrink away to holes and caves like starving dogs to die! (quoted in LaRoque 2010, 78–79)

While Shingwaukonse and his party were well received, his words once again did not compel a substantive response. A year later, in 1850, the aging Ojibwe Elder lost his patience and helped to forcibly retake land at Mica Bay, on the north shore of Lake Huron, which was an active settler-operated mine at the time (Corbiere 2013). He wasn't alone. Indigenous nations consistently protested settler arrogance and designs on land use. Letters from the Ojibwe in northwestern Ontario Treaty #3 area, the Saulteax of Manitoba, through to the West all echoed Shingwaukonse. As the great Cree leader Poundmaker famously told government officials, "This is our land! It isn't a piece of pemmican to be cut off and given in little pieces back to us" (St. Germain 2009, 48).

Responding to this anger, Canadian officials in the era of Confederation embarked on a national treaty making campaign. Eleven Numbered Treaties, stretching across the country between 1870 and 1921, sought to pacify resistance and capture the landmass in legal terms. These treaties were transactional, a simple purchasing of land. The general formula was an exchange, Indigenous land for a number of ill-defined benefits. These included around 600 square metres for each family of five in the community, small amounts of cash (sometimes annuities), an allowance for blankets and hunting and fishing tools, farming assistance, a community school, the right to hunt and fish on all ceded land not used for settlement, and lumbering or mining (this was only promised in writing from Treaty Number #3 onward). Canada was required to build public buildings, roads, and other crucial pieces of infrastructure. Finally, communities were required to keep the peace, maintain law and order, and never possess liquor. Treaties deviated from this formula at times. In Treaty #6, for example, there was the promise of a medicine chest. Indigenous signatories were then expected to "cede, surrender and forever give up title" to their territories. Simply put, Canada believed that through the treaty process it was gaining legal tenure to a country and, in fact, congratulated itself on achieving this goal without the military adventures and mass slaughter that characterized the American experience of dispossession and settlement. It mattered little that they were striving to remove Indigenous presence from the land all the same.

Of course, Indigenous peoples had and continued to have alternative under-standings of these Confederation-era treaties. As Sharon Venne (1998) argues in her study of Treaty #6, Neyihew Elders understood that settlers wanted four things: land for agriculture no deeper than the depth of a plough, timber for homes, grass to feed their animals, and, finally, to live in peace with the Neyihew. In return, it was expected that the newcomers provide services of physicians when required, education, farming assistance, and support in times of need (i.e., famine). There was no discussion of restricting Indigenous access to water or lands. Neither was there agreement on extracting minerals, the imposition of Indian Agents to manage governance, nor interference with Indigenous citizenship and self-determination generally. Even though archival evidence, such as treaty commissioner diaries, confirm Indigenous interpre-tations of the agreements (Long 2010), the written versions of these treaties were privileged by courts in land disputes, used to coerce Indigenous peoples onto reserves and under the Indian Act's jurisdiction.

Complementing the subversion of these agreements has been hundreds of pages of legislation spanning a century and designed to further alienate Indigenous peoples from the land, pacify resistance, and eradicate Indigenous cultures. The focus was on relocating, educating, and converting Indigenous peoples to Christianity. By 1857 a number of Gradual Civilization Acts sought to transform Indigenous men into "bronze White men," and their lands from collective ownership to fee simple land tenure. This trend continued with the 1869 Gradual Enfranchisement Act, which allowed the removal of Indigenous political leaders who were "dishonest, intemperate and immoral." In the process, however, there were attacks of Indigenous women, prohibitions on Indigenous participation in governance, and the erasure of their jurisdiction over lands and water. With the creation of the Indian Act in 1876 and its various subsequent amendments, Indigenous nations would be broken down and band councils established in their place, movement would be restricted by a pass system, and any transaction with settler communi-ties was regulated via a permit system that was managed by the local Indian Agent acting on behalf of the federal Department of Indian Affairs. This was, simply put, a multi-faceted regime of apartheid that separated Indigenous nations from each other, from the land, and from the white settler society emerging as Canada.

Through it all, Indigenous peoples reasserted their interpretation of the treaty relationship and resisted encroachments on progressively diminished Indigenous land. Indigenous leaders, elders, residential school survivors, war veterans, and eventually pan-Indigenous political organizations like the League of Indians (1923) protested in petitions, direct action, and the courts, as their ancestors had before them. Canada responded by outlawing these activities, most notoriously in an amendment to the Indian Act in 1927, which prohibited Indigenous peoples from accessing the courts to reclaim land. The law threatened any Canadian lawyer with a six-month prison term if he or she accepted Indigenous clients. After many years of frustration at the Six Nations of the Grand River in southern Ontario, Cayuga leader Deskaheh (Levi General) travelled to England to appeal to King George V and then the League of Nations for what he saw as Canada's illegal interference in community affairs and encroachments on Six Nations territory. With his efforts eventually stymied by English officials, he returned and made one last plea to ordinary Canadians and Americans for justice before his untimely death: "We have little territory left—just enough to live and die on.... The governments of Washington and Ottawa have a silent partnership of policy. It is aimed to break up every tribe of red men so as to dominate every acre of their territory" (quoted in Monture 2014, 120). Deskaheh's plea is an apt description of logic of elimination, 85 years before the academic field of settler colonial studies emerged.

Reconsidering Restitution in Contemporary Canada

Throughout this history of dispossession, Indigenous peoples have consistently demanded a return to Indigenous political economies that privilege a just and equitable sharing of the land. This loud and focused protest helped shame federal governments into easing some of the most draconian Indian Act laws in 1951, eventually permitting Indigenous political organizing and access to the courts. With legal barriers and penalties removed activism flourished, thus prompting the federal government to shift strategies. In 1973, Indian Affairs drafted and issued the "Statement on Claims of Indian and Inuit people," leading to the establishment of the Office of Native Claims (today known as AANDC's Comprehensive Claims Branch) as well as two channels for land claims: specific and comprehensive. The former addresses violations of pre-existing treaties and obligations, while the latter focuses on communities that have never negotiated treaties with Canada and thus never agreed to share their land. Comprehensive claims have been launched and negotiated in the North, British Columbia, Ontario, and Quebec. While many consider claims to be a positive form of redress and a strategy preferable to conflict, there are reasons to doubt the model. In a liberal rights era violence is less permissible, so new forms of dispossession are crafted and deployed. Given that settler colonialism seeks to eliminate and replace because of its nature as "territorially acquisitive in perpetuity," any recognition of rights in this context is illusionary (Coulthard 2014, 125). Recognition of Aboriginal title, first through the courts, and then negotiated through the land claims processes, may appear as restitution but is ultimately aimed at extinguishing Aboriginal title to lands and allowing for the formal transfer of that land to the Crown.

Modern Treaties and Alternatives

The first successful comprehensive land claim was negotiated between the federal government, the Province of Quebec, the Eeyou Istchee, and the Inuit of northern Quebec. In the 1974 James Bay and Northern Quebec Agreement (JBNQA), the James Bay Cree and the Inuit of Quebec agreed to "cede, release, surrender and convey all their Native claims, rights, titles and interests, whatever they may be, in and to land in the territory and in Quebec" (JBNQA 1974, 2.1). In exchange for transferring almost 90 per cent of their territories (retaining 165,000 of their original one million square kilometres), the Eeyou Istchee and Inuit received $225 million in compensation, local self-government (jurisdiction over health, education, public works) that removed them from the Indian Act, and a consultative stake on lands to which they had extinguished title (Aboriginal Affairs and Northern Development Canada 2014). The JBNQA was contentious from the onset and set in motion a prolonged struggle to address different and often conflicting interpretations of what it actually entailed. Two decades after it was signed, Cree leader Mathew Coon Come exclaimed to the international community that "many important commitments have not been honoured.... Our relationship with Ottawa is filled with difficulty and in need of profound reform" (Coon Come 1996). Since the JBNQA was negotiated there have been at least 24 amendments, and despite the contrary perspective of Canada and Quebec, the Cree insist they have never extinguished title.

In the haze of this ongoing struggle, a second modern treaty was created on the other side of the country. The Nisga'a Final Agreement was compelled by Frank Calder's protracted legal activism and the subsequent decision by the Supreme Court in 1973 that Aboriginal title exists and endures where it has not been extinguished. Two decades later, in the 1994 Nisga'a Final Agreement, the Nisga'a followed the Eeyou and signed a deal that transferred approximately 90 per cent of their territory to the Crown (retaining 1,900 of 22,000 square kilometres). In return they received $196 million in compensation, an escape from the Indian Act with local self-government, and commercial allocations of the timber and salmon harvests. One key difference between the JBNQA and Nisga'a agreements, however, revolved around the notion of extinguishment. Given the backlash to the concept since the JBNQA, the language was changed to "modification" of rights. While softer in tone, modification nonetheless reflected the earlier concept of extinguishment. As Ministry of Aboriginal Affairs' literature on the claim states, "there's no vagueness about the Nisga'a Final Agreement. The Final Agreement is a full and final settlement of Nisga'a Aboriginal rights" (AANDC 2015). The Union of British Columbia Indian Chiefs (UBCIC), representing 118 BC First Nations, rejected the deal and criticized the Nisga'a for having "negotiated into Canada at the status quo" (UBCIC 1998, 17). Ever since, UBCIC communities have refused to submit to the modern treaty process in British Columbia (UBCIC 1998).

Philosophically, modification and extinguishment share their roots in earlier notions of "surrender" found in the text versions of the Numbered Treaties. This is the legal dislocation of Indigenous peoples from their land. In the case of modern treaties, communities have been expected to extinguish rights to nine out of every 10 forests and rivers (or, 90 per cent of their traditional territory). This results in what Mohawk policy analyst Russell Diabo (2012) calls "termination"—the hollowing out of Indigenous rights and title and the reduction of Indigenous nations to municipalities within the Canadian Confederation. Of course, municipalities as creatures of the provinces or subnational governments are subordinate and effectively powerless. This has been borne out in a number of recent conflicts over land use. When modern treaty signatories in the Yukon opposed opening the Peel Watershed to industrial development, the territorial government pointed to provisions in the Yukon Umbrella Final Agreement that permitted them to do so. As the government of the Northwest Territories began the process of devolution,[3] Indigenous nations there rejected a "streamlined" regulatory process that would reduce their input on land management. The territorial government again pointed to modern treaties that transferred ultimate jurisdiction over the regulatory regime to the territory (CBC News North 2015). In these cases, Indigenous peoples find themselves struggling to assert their perspectives, despite the supposedly empowering modern treaties. And in both cases, Indigenous nations have resorted to challenging the interpretations of the Agreements in courts, in streets, and on the land.

Settler Colonialism in Crisis

The claims process and all institutional remedies predating it have been attempts to "perfect" settler colonialism in Canada. In Lisa Ford's formulation (2010), settler state perfection is effective deployment and enforcement of law, which replaces Indigenous models. It is the realization of Wolfe's (2006) logic of elimination. But since the expansion of settler colonialism in Canada there has been Indigenous resistance, or in this context, attempts at sabotaging perfection. These are generally met with state violence or overt political oppression through an intricate legal, military, and penal architecture. Where Indigenous communities have attempted to prevent further incursions on their land or prevent development projects that threaten their way of life, the settler state has frequently intervened to "legally" and coercively neutralize this opposition. These interventions have taken the form of court injunctions, incarceration of Indigenous protesters, state surveillance and the labelling of Indigenous activists as terrorists and threats to national security, and deployment of the military. These are all part of the toolkit of contemporary settler colonial crisis management, which has become more evident as Indigenous resistance grows and industry and governments have increasingly pursued ambitious resource extraction and infrastructural projects near or on Indigenous land, especially in the North. Yet such interventions have failed to "tame" peoples who refuse to be incorporated into an alien political economy that threatens their values and ways of life. The list of projects that have been delayed or halted by Indigenous resistance grows year after year, revealing a growing crisis in the fundamental assumptions and technologies of settler colonialism. In these moments of precarity, settler colonialism is exposed as coercive and dispossessive but also as an unsustainable governing regime.

According to the Ontario Provincial Police, in the decade between 1995 and 2006, there were 100 "Aboriginal critical instances" in that province, most often relating to land claims, resource regulatory regimes, or desecration of burial sites. That number balloons when we look across the country. In many of these critical instances, there is a disproportionate state response. At Gustefsen Lake in British Columbia in 1995, for example, police used armed personal carriers, fired 70,000 rounds of live ammunition, and detonated at least one explosive device (Lambertus 2004). At Oka in 1990, 1,400 troops were deployed in a "military operation" against a few dozen Mohawk men, women, and children (4,000 troops were initially committed by the prime minister) (Lackenbauer 2008). In the more recent protests opposing fracking in Mi'kmaq territory outside Elsipogtog in 2013, Special Forces employed attack dogs, tear gas, and sniper rifles (O'Keefe 2013). In each example police were enforcing injunctions. In other words, judges determined that Indigenous peoples—who still held Aboriginal title under Canadian law in each of these cases—were not lawfully permitted and were impeding access to the rightful owners of the land. The police (or military in some cases) are often successful at dispersing the occupation or protest. But sometimes, like at Oka or Caledonia, a prolonged standoff ensues and the certainty of land tenure becomes questioned in a sustained and very visible way. At the time of writing, the disputed land at these sites remains undeveloped and their future is uncertain. In this sense, the violent confrontation reveals, first, the lengths to which the settler state will go to retain authority, and second, that the uniformity of the state's political economy is actually vulnerable to challenges from Indigenous peoples who insist on asserting their own legal orders and forms of political economy based on their interpretation of treaties or even independent of treaties.

The latter of these strategies, the assertive non-treaty approach, might be considered the greatest current threat to settler colonial perfection, in particular the execution of exclusive jurisdiction. Rejecting the terms of extinguishment in modern treaties, nations like the Tsilhqot'in and Atikamekw, among others, have decided to unilaterally declare sovereignty over their territory. In the case of the Tsilqhot'in, they stated in their Declaration of Sovereignty,

> This has been the territory of the Tsilhqot'in Nation for longer than any man can say and it will always be our country; the outlying parts we have always shared with our neighbours—Nuxalk, Kwakiutl, Lillouet, Carrier and Shuswap—but the heartland belongs to none but the Tsilhqot'in.... We have often declared our willingness to negotiate terms of union with Canada. We repeat that offer now. We make only one condition: the process for negotiation and the final settlement must carry the consent of the Tsilhqot'in Nations. (Tsilhqot'in National Government 1998, 1)

While never wavering from this position, the Tsilhqot'in were emboldened by a 2014 Supreme Court of Canada decision that recognized their title to a portion of their territory that had been staked for gold and copper mining. The Tsilhqot'in subsequently declared the area a park, Dasiqox Tribal Park, and plan to enforce their jurisdiction (M. Anderson 2014).

Similarly, after 35 years of fruitless negotiations, the Atikamekw have declared sovereignty over 80,000 square kilometers of Algonquin territory in central Quebec. Sovereignty for them includes approving any and all development within their territory. Speaking to the United Nations soon after the Declaration of Sovereignty, Chief Awashish announced, "We are determined to vigorously defend our rights with governments and private corporations that want to continue to develop our Nitaskinan without negotiating with our people with dignity and in good faith. The time of colonialism must end" (Atikamekw Nation 2015, n.p.).

The Tsilhqot'in and Atikamekw are not suggesting that Canada (the province, industry, individuals, and families) does not have the right to exist but that many others have the right to a good life. This includes Indigenous peoples, the waters, and the land. These examples represent an attempted return to Indigenous political economies. While distinct from the Great Lakes Anishinaabek mentioned at the outset of this chapter, the Tsilhqot'in and Atikamekw, nonetheless, amply illustrate notions of shared jurisdiction and signal a direction forward that involves looking backward. While it may be unreasonable to suggest a settler colonial state premised on the replacement of the Indigenous population is open to this offer being made, there are really no alternatives but more conflict. The imperfection of settler colonialism is likely to continue to strain under increasing resistance. Unwilling to negotiate (or renegotiate) the terms of the relationship, Indigenous nations will simply force their jurisdictional claims outside formal legal and political channels and in spite of violence or intimidation.

Conclusion

While Indigenous peoples and communities have always imagined alternatives, they are increasingly being acted upon, and Canadians now have an opportunity to reflect on the future of the relationship, or put another way by Michael Asch (2014), to consider how Canadian legal orders and political economy can be reconciled with Indigenous sovereignty, not the other way around. In real terms, this would hopefully lead to an undoing of settler colonialism and notions of exclusive jurisdiction. This is not a demand for non-Indigenous Canadians to leave Indigenous territories or submit to Indigenous demands. We have models that we can draw from to help shape our shared future. What would a modern-day Dish with One Spoon look like, for instance? Can we move toward principles of reciprocity, sustainability, and mutual autonomy? In the case of the Confederation-era treaties, perhaps reserve borders could be blended with provincial or federal Crown lands. In these enlarged areas of shared jurisdiction the appropriate Indigenous nations would shape the "management" of these lands. Provincial, territorial, and federal authority would not disappear; these governments would contribute to policy and administration. Though mining, forestry, and hunting might take place, land use generally would conform to principles that respect Indigenous community desires as well the rights of the land, as was originally intended. In areas where there are no treaties, Indigenous title to land would be recognized outright and jurisdiction honoured. All provincial and territorial plans on lands where title exists would seek approval and be harmonized with pre-established Indigenous land and resource priorities. This proposal would also have implications for provincial and territorial authority generally. In these zones of shared sovereignty, all law and policy would require collaboration and hopefully consensus. There would be sacrifice, and conflict, too. But as our ancestors did, for a time at least, we can learn from it.

Among all the challenges and inequities described in this book, there are few as persistent and chronic as the disparity in social welfare, justice, and prosperity between Indigenous peoples and Canadians generally. While this is obvious to most readers, as a country we have been paralyzed by the scope and

complexity of the challenge. Our prescriptions favour the simple and conve-
nient. Abrogating treaties instead of honouring them is a common suggestion,
for instance, refusing to engage fundamentally with the source of the problem: divergent understandings of the land, and our relationship with it and to
each other. Yet as the multi-generational Indigenous resistance grows more
organized, vocal, and insistent, as reflected in the Idle No More movement,
the justice for missing and murdered Indigenous women campaign, and the
findings of the Truth and Reconciliation Commission, the damage of centuries of settler colonialism is coming into focus. It is no longer the precarity or
vulnerability of Indigenous peoples and communities that requires attention
but the fragility of a settler political economy premised on theft and deceit.
Indigenous peoples can and will continue to offer alternatives, away from
exploitation and toward obligation, to one another and to the land.

Further Readings

Borrows, John, and Michael Coyle, eds. 2017. *The Right Relationship: Reimag-
    ining the Implementation of Historic Treaties.* Toronto: University of Toronto
    Press.
Kanahsatake: 270 Years of Resistance. 1993. Documentary by Alanis Obam-
    sawin. Ontario: National Film Board of Canada.
Manuel, Arthur, and Grand Chief Ronald Derrickson. 2016. *Unsettling
    Canada: A National Wake-Up Call.* Toronto: Between the Lines Press.

Notes

1   The Anishinaabek are a broad and flexible confederation of three nations, the
    Ojibwe, Odawa, and Pottowatomi, who have lived and worked, historically and in
    the present, across the Great Lakes basin or Anishinaabe Aki.
2   The Haudenosaunee, sometimes referred to as the Iroquois, are a confederacy of six
    nations made up of the Mohawk, Seneca, Onondaga, Cayuga, Oneida, and Tuscor-
    ara. They have been the long-time neighbours of the Anishinaabek to the southeast
    of the Great Lakes.
3   Devolution is a process that has been occurring slowly in both the Yukon and
    the NWT, whereby the territories assume elements of jurisdiction over land and
    resources from the federal government.

PART III

Activism and Alternative Futures

CHAPTER 7

PERILS OF PETROCULTURE IN A NEOLIBERAL RESOURCE ECONOMY

Meenal Shrivastava

Introduction

Canada's rise to the club of top 10 oil producers and exporters in the world in the early twenty-first century coincided with a number of alarming trends; among them, the erosion of redistributive policies and programs, and the multiplication of policies that have effectively removed resource rents from the control of the state, workers, and resource-dependent communities. In this milieu, and despite the change in the federal government and in the provincial government of petro-province Alberta, popular demands for social justice and policies promoting economic and environmental sustainability continue to be displaced by the language of "economic efficiencies" and "international competitiveness." While questioning the focus of oil and democracy studies on countries in the global South, this chapter argues that the resultant increase in economic and political inequality is eroding democracy and is a manifestation of the tightening stronghold of petroculture in Canada.

Amitav Ghosh's (1992) term "petrofiction" sets the foundation for a field of global study that explores the representational and critical domains within which oil is framed and imagined in popular culture. The past few decades have also seen the evolution of the concept of "petroculture" as a marker of the contemporary era. Imre Szeman used the term petroculture, for example, to denote the role of oil as the "central protagonist directing and organizing human life activity" in the past century (2012, 3). Coinciding with the notion of the Anthropocene Era,[1] the breadth of petroculture as a field of inquiry is evident in its overview of a broad spectrum of cultural forms as aesthetic, sensory, and emotional legacies of petroleum (LeMenager 2014) and its description of various forms of violence, intrusions, and disruptions that flow from oil extraction (Aghoghovwia 2014). Adding to the growing literature, this chapter focuses on specific political aspects of petroculture, drawing from studies that explore the relationship between the reliance on oil revenue and its impact on institutions of democracy.

Despite some arguments to the contrary (Haber and Menaldo 2011), the overwhelming majority of oil and democracy studies conclude that there is a strong and negative relationship between dependence on oil revenue and transitions to democracy (Ross 2001, 2009; Tsui 2011; Wantchekon 2002). A survey of the literature on oil and democracy, however, reveals two recurring limitations: first, studies exploring the intersection of oil and democracy focus almost exclusively on democratic transitions in countries in the global South; second, these studies typically use minimalistic interpretations of liberal democratic theory and measures of democracy that are too crude to account for changes in established democracies (Shrivastava and Stefanick 2012). As examined elsewhere (Shrivastava 2015a), this is problematic not only because of the vast diversity of democracies in the world, but also because the list of the top 20 oil-exporting countries of the world includes eight OECD countries.

In the twenty-first century, it is important to question the exclusive focus of oil and democracy studies on the global South, as concerns are also rising about a growing democratic deficit in the United States, Canada, and Europe (Norris 2011). In addition, a marked shift in global oil markets is evident with the United States overtaking Saudi Arabia and Russia as the world's leading producer of oil and natural gas liquids, on the back of soaring oil extraction from shale formations in Texas and North Dakota and the fracking of sweet oil wells[2] (International Energy Agency [IEA] 2014). These two trends are fundamentally altering the political economy of oil-exporting nations, including countries that are regarded as established democracies.

Canada entered the list of top 10 oil-exporting countries at number eight in 2007, and by 2014, it was the fifth largest crude oil producer in the world, 82 per cent of which came from bitumen oil (Eurasia Review 2015). Canada has had a long tradition of questioning reliance on natural resources. The idea of the so-called resource-curse, for example, is at least as old as the writings of Harold Innis ([1930] 1977), who, in the 1930s, developed a devastating critique of the long-term negative consequences of staple/resource-led development in Canada. While scholarly advances in staples theory continue to evolve, the vast literature on oil and democracy continues to regard the dynamics of the resource-curse as a problem that is exclusive to the global South. Thus, the focus of this chapter is to combine the two theoretical strands to analyse the shrinking of redistributive policies and programs accompanying the rise of Canada as a major global oil-exporting country. This chapter examines whether these trends are indicators of the weakening of institutions of democracy in

Canada. It begins by defining the framework and context of liberal democracy as a conceptual tool.

Liberal Democracy in Oil-Exporting Countries

In retrospect, it is clear that the liberal triumphalist celebration of markets and democracy at the end of the Cold War exaggerated the coherence of the processes of democratization around the world (Huntington 1991). The collapse of communism did not necessarily lead to more democracy, while liberal democracies themselves differ widely in terms of institutional structures, political culture, and even the fundamental principles that inform them (Ware 1992; Offe 2011). Invariably, in a liberal democracy, the state is assigned a crucial role in establishing institutional changes, exercising organizational capacity, and instituting and enforcing rules that underpin a free market economy (Streeck 1995).

For the purposes of this chapter, then, liberal democracy will be broadly defined as a mode of governing that is based on the twin core assumptions of "capitalist market relations" and "developmental liberalism." Arguably, these two assumptions of liberal democracy provide important checks and balances for a sustainable and well-functioning system. In particular, the financial crisis of 2008–09 brought into sharp relief the role of the state beyond managing market relations. In addition, the economic growth of emerging economies, the deceleration of economic growth in the global North, and the role of inequality in economic stability further compels us to pay heed to the scholarship on developmental liberalism as a core aspect of liberal democracy.

Calmers Johnson (1982) defined developmental liberalism in the Japanese context as state-led interventions by bureaucrats, particularly those in the Ministry of International Trade and Industry (MITI), to design and implement macroeconomic regulations for economic development. Subsequently, the notion of a developmental state has been widely used in international political economy as the most compelling explanation for the economic successes of East Asian countries. The argument is that this approach worked because East Asian states had effective control over a variety of factors critical to economic growth; among them, capital, national economic planning, social policies, industrial policies, and political insulation. As Sylvia Chan (2002) highlights, however, the role of the state in providing the conditions and possibilities of economic development, or "developmental liberalism," underlies liberal democratic frameworks in a variety of contexts, not just in East Asia. After all, most industrialized democracies have applied various degrees and forms of Keynesianism, social policies, inflation control, corporate protection, and export promotion, which are essentially state intervention policies for achieving economic and social goals.

Despite this overlap, the significance of developmental liberalism continues to be studied either in the Asian and African contexts or within the scholarship on liberal democratic theory. For instance, many critical International Political Economy (IPE) scholars have criticized representations of the free market as an apolitical economic realm that is self-regulating and immune from (indeed, harmed by) the state interventions of politics (Polanyi 2001; Teivainen 2002; Lavelle 2013). These studies point out that the dichotomous separation of economic and political spheres is not natural but, instead, is socially constructed and could well be seen as producing limits on democracy domestically and internationally. Furthermore, this separation is seen as contributing to the failure of the liberal economic models of democracy to do justice to the core ideals of democracy, such as legitimacy, social justice, and equality. For instance, Peter Hall (2015) argues that neoliberal policies that promote privatization, deregulation, and contracting-out have undermined the authority of the liberal democratic state, not the least by constraining their fiscal capacities and opportunities for intervention. Combined with new forms of finance, which have raised the risks of financial crises, the altered operation of the state has limited its capacities to engage in public investment in education, research, and infrastructure that are crucial to long-term economic success. Ignoring this substantial scholarship, however, an economistic application of liberal democracy informed by a neoliberal framework continues to dominate much of the world in the contemporary era.

Neoliberalism is a confusing and contested term because it is used in several ways to describe an ideology, economic theory, development theory, or economic policy (see Boas and Gans-Morse 2009). This chapter applies neoliberalism as the discourse of governance that offers a particular economic and governmental order for society. In this usage, by representing key institutions operating in the economic sphere as non-political or beyond politics, neoliberalism transforms public and political activities into a private and apolitical realm (Plattner 2013). As argued elsewhere in some detail (Shrivastava 2015a, 2015b), such a conception of the polity and the economy only allows for a minimalistic application of liberal democratic theory, leading to widespread social-economic-political inequality, and indeed a loss of economic growth (Cingano 2014).

While retaining its focus on countries in the global South, the oil and democracy literature has clearly incorporated core concerns of developmental liberalism, highlighting the erosion of principles and institutions of liberal democracy in the wake of the vast wealth generated in a short span in oil-exporting countries. For instance, many studies have emphasized the role of economic and political institutions as critical determinants of the rents gained from resource exploitation (Ross 2009; T. Mitchell 2011). Nevertheless, despite a growing number of studies exploring the perceived democratic deficit in OECD countries, neither the oil and democracy literature nor comparative studies on democratization adequately include oil-exporting OECD countries in their analysis. In part, this omission reflects the dominant binaries of North/South silos within which global patterns continue to be analysed. More importantly, the omission in these studies of certain countries where democracy is assumed to be healthy ignores an important paradox of the practice of liberal democracy in the neoliberal context, whereby it is shorn of its core principles such as social justice and equality. Nevertheless, valuable insights from the oil and democracy literature regarding the political and economic outcomes of resource dependence can easily be applied to oil-exporting OECD countries, such as Canada (Nikiforuk 2010; Homer-Dixon 2013) or even oil-producing countries such as the United States (Relly and Schwalbe 2016; Gilens and Page 2014; Scott 2014).

While the insights of the oil and democracy literature can be used to track economic distortions, such as the so-called Dutch Disease and resource-curse[3] in oil-exporting economies, it is equally important to investigate the sources, dynamics, and effects of economic and political inequality, relations of power, and social upheavals and struggles that characterize the processes and outcomes of petroculture. In this context, by focusing on institutional changes and policy mechanisms to avoid the resource-curse, staples theory rather neatly complements the oil and democracy literature, while also overlapping with the realm of development liberalism (Watkins 2007). Staples theory focuses on developmental questions, linking them to policy, infrastructure, and redistribution capacity, thereby providing a policy-oriented approach to examining the political economy of a resource-exporting country. Noting the recent retreat of the regulatory role of the state (Drache 2013) and rising income inequality (Yalnizyan 2013), which restrict Canada's ability to retain a socially, economically, and environmentally sustainable trajectory, some theorists have asserted a regression into a neo-staples economy for Canada in the wake of the bitumen boom (Mills and Sweeney 2013). Essentially, these authors are pointing to the entrenchment of the staples economy and exacerbation of the staples trap, because oil has weak linkages to other sectors of the economy, such as manufacturing, and a negative impact on social and economic policies (Watkins 2013).

Although Canada fares fairly highly in terms of the attributes of liberal democracy measured by indices such as the Democracy Index or Polity IV, a critical exploration of the *practice* of liberal democracy and its impact on institutions of democracy is warranted in the wake of rising inequalities in Canada.

The Canadian case study is likely to be relevant not only in examining the political economy of an oil-exporting country, but also as a study of the impact of neoliberal political ideology on the liberal democratic mode of governing.

Neoliberalism and Petroculture in Canada: A Crude Alliance

The concept of "petroculture" describes the ways in which oil and energy production shape the political, social, cultural, and economic life of a petroleum-exporting country. A great number of case studies have established that large and persistent economic and political inequalities, often foster-ing democratic deficits, are the common denominators of a petroculture. A petro-state is defined as an oil-rich country with weak political institutions and a concentration of wealth and power in the hands of the few. The mini-mum threshold for a petro-state qualification is dependence on petroleum for 50 per cent or more of export revenues, 25 per cent or more of GDP, and 25 per cent or more of government revenues (Karl 1997).

Within Canada, only the Province of Alberta qualifies as a "petro-prov-ince" by exceeding these critical thresholds, where oil and gas account for 70 per cent of its exports, 27 per cent of its GDP, and 28 per cent of government revenues (Alberta Energy 2014). For Canada as a whole, oil and gas account for only 6 per cent of Canada's GDP and 16.5 per cent of Canada's merchan-dise exports, while oil rent as a percentage of Canada's GDP has ranged from 2.4 in 2010 to 3.2 in 2014 (World Bank 2015). Therefore, not only has the oil and gas industry not been the engine of economic growth as touted by the official rhetoric, but even its contribution to the Canadian tax revenue fell from 9.4 per cent in 2006 to 4.3 per cent in 2011; while in Alberta, during the same period, it fell from 40 per cent to 30 per cent (Leach 2013). Since the collapse of the world oil prices in June 2014, the contribution of this sector to the whole economy has only dropped further, and governments have begun to search for new ways of diversifying economic activity.

Moreover, there are other factors that make the situation in Canada unique among the major oil-exporting countries. For instance, Canada is also a major importer of oil, with Quebec and the Atlantic provinces dependent on foreign oil for more than 80 per cent of their fuel needs (Campbell 2012). Additionally, Canadian heavy crude, which already has the highest cost of production in the world, also has the lowest selling price, fetching US$27.88 a barrel, compared to the global benchmark oil price of US$41.13 in March 2016 (Government of Alberta 2016). In addition, Canadian heavy crude has to contend with trans-portation, trading, and storage in US facilities, which are already facing the challenges of oversupply in the wake of a massive oil boom due to shale oil and hydraulic fracturing activities (Maugeri 2013).

Particularities aside, the rise of Canada as one of the top 10 oil-exporting countries in the world has been accompanied by increasing income inequality nationally and a backward slide on social-political goals on many indices (OECD 2014). While the causal links between oil dependence and democratic malaise are not always direct, a number of studies confirm that governance processes and policy in Canada are creating a democratic deficit through declining democratic accountability and increasing economic, political, and social inequality, which are also unmistakable features of petroculture. This chapter contends that the entrenchment of the neoliberal state has facilitated the institutionalization of petroculture in Canada.

The Rise of Neoliberalism and Inequality

A staples exporting economy since its inception as a modern state, Canada's reliance on trade in fish, fur, lumber, agricultural products, and now energy has deeply affected Canadian political economy in terms of the relationship between the centre and the regions, as well as links with Europe and the United States (Innis [1930] 1977; Watkins 1977, 2007, 2013). While fiscal consolidation and austerity are not new in the staples economy of Canada (Heylen and Everaert 2000), the election of the federal Conservative Party in 2006 saw a decided shift away from social citizenship rights and social solidarity policies to the wholesale embrace of market values, norms, and ideals, and an intensified focus on the resource sector, especially oil. Moreover, the Conservative government's responses to the 2008–09 financial crisis only served to increase inequities, while ignoring the role of neoliberal policies in the creation and the amelioration of the crisis (Brodie 2014). The new political regimes in Canada and Alberta may be seen as a public indictment of the effects of these policies on the Canadian state and the economy. Nevertheless, the changes instituted over the past two decades are not likely to disappear quickly or significantly with the changes in government. Rather, we need both a critical understanding of neoliberalism and conscious efforts to address the democratic deficits in Canada.

Neoliberalism as a program of state reform essentially redefined what states should and can do, displacing state-led development and redistribution policies with structures of incentives and competitive pressures of "efficiency" provided by the market. The disastrous economic and political consequences of neoliberalism on developing countries in the 1980s and 1990s are well documented, whereby international and bilateral debt programs were used to forcibly reduce the role of the state in providing public investment, employment, and public goods. However, few studies consider these trends in parallel with the creation of major welfare gaps and the retrenchment of the welfare state during the same period in the global North. In particular, the losses in formal employment, decline in full-time jobs in sectors such as manufacturing, deteriorating provision of strategic public goods such as health care and education, and regulatory and institutional changes to decrease the protection of jobs and wages are some of the trends in OECD countries since the 1980s that have been recently linked to the unprecedented and growing gap between the rich and everyone else in these countries (OECD 2008, 2011).

The OECD reports (2008, 2011) also note the role of the tax and benefit systems that have become less redistributive in many countries since the 1990s, and the social, economic, and political challenges posed by rising income inequality (Cingano 2014). Despite the existence of strong philosophical and economic arguments that greatly expand the notions of distributive justice beyond provisions of welfare, policy trends continue to be confined to considerations of equality of welfare. For instance, Rawlsian "resourcism" has focused on the fair distribution of a broad array of resources defined as primary goods, including access to education and influence over political decisions (E. Kelly 2001). Amartya Sen's (1999) "capability approach" brings in considerations of variability in the ability of individuals to convert resources into valuable outcomes, which is particularly relevant for gendered, ethnic, and other minorities. These debates are particularly salient because income inequality reinforces political and legal inequalities, which in turn affect average levels of health, life expectancy, and educational outcomes (Kawachi and Subramanian 2014; Wilkinson and Pickett 2009). It is also the case, however, that countries that have seen the largest increases in inequality are also those that have provided the largest tax cuts to the top income earners. The United States, for instance, is often regarded as the poster-child of income inequality, where the income of the top 0.01 per cent grew by 76.2 per cent between 2002 and 2012, while the income of the bottom 90 per cent fell by 10.7 per cent during the same period. This has made inequality climb to the highest levels on record since the government first instituted income tax in 1913 (Saez 2013). Although economic inequality has become a volatile political issue in the United States, the 2016 American presidential campaign resulted in the election of a billionaire outsider, Donald Trump, who promised to further lower taxes on the very rich and on corporations.

While still below the American levels, inequality in Canada has been rising at a faster rate than in many other OECD countries (OECD 2014). Andrew Jackson (2013) argues that this disturbing trend raises important questions about whether the market is distributing wealth fairly, or is adequately reflecting the productive contribution of individuals. For example, a good part of the wealth gap in contemporary Canada can be attributed to intergenerational income sources, which are not earned in the same sense as income from wages and salaries. This inequality of financial wealth is further reinforced by tax policies that favour those with high levels of financial wealth, and at the same time erode the state's capacity to fund critical public goods, such as health care and education for the majority of the population. Thus, driven by a neoliberal focus on capitalist market relations at the cost of developmental liberalism, inequalities are growing and the middle class is shrinking.

Undoubtedly, a robust middle class is a critical driver for economic growth, social cohesion, and trust in economic and political institutions. A shrinking middle class signifies reduction in economic and social upward mobility, and a shift from an inclusive to an extractive society (Acemoglu and Robinson 2012; Beach 2014). Moreover, the conceptual framework of neoliberalism goes beyond capital and class, reproducing a complex set of power relations that encompasses global capitalism and the neoliberal state, as well as the patriarchal family (Hubbard 2004). Neoliberalism thus also contains within it a gendered dimension to the processes of the exclusion of marginalized groups from political and economic spaces. Many studies have shown the role of neoliberal policy in recentring masculinity and producing inequality, where women and visible minorities disproportionately bear the social and economic burdens of gendered and racialized structures (Fuller and Vosko 2008; Green and Kesselman 2011). Even the more critical studies of inequality, however, often do not sufficiently factor in the increasing economic and political marginalization of the Indigenous populations of Canada, considering them as a category on their own "outside" the mainstream inquiry.

While historic dispossession, persecution, and discrimination have led to much higher levels of poverty and exclusion among Indigenous peoples than any other group in Canada, the structure of domination that frames Indigenous–state relations in Canada are exacerbated further by neoliberal governing practices (Coulthard 2007). Recent studies have shown that despite the dramatic increase in Indigenous peoples' engagement in extractive industries over the past 30 years, in the neoliberal context of declining union power, and an increasingly internationalized Canadian resource sector, the downloading of local costs, such as environmental degradation and pollution, is further disempowering Indigenous communities (Mills and Sweeney 2013; MacDonald 2011). Policies such as Impact and Benefit Agreements (IBA) are functioning as tools to privatize traditional lands and to bypass the federal duty to consult Indigenous peoples about resource development on their lands (Cameron and Levitan 2014). The shifting relations between Indigenous peoples, mining corporations, and the state are indicative of a larger trend, enriching any exam-ination of the impact of neoliberal processes on democracy in Canada.

The State of Democracy in a Qualified Petro-State

In Canada's decentralized federal political system, energy resources are controlled, for the most part, by provincial governments. As already noted, Alberta as the home of bitumen oil reserves is the only province in Canada that can be considered a "petro-state or sub-state," not only due to its economic reliance on oil, but also because of a number of political attributes that are often the characteristic markers of a petro-state. These include a history of one party rule,[4] strong executives facing minimal opposition from weak legislatures, and significant involvement of the oil industry in the regulatory functions of the government and in political processes more generally (Shrivastava and Stefanick 2012). Moreover, the disciplinary role of the government favouring capital interests over the provision of social and economic justice in Alberta has effectively limited opportunities for public engagement with issues that relate to resource development, shrinking the public space for discussion and contestation of public policy, limiting local influence over resource develop-ment, redistributive policies, and employment. The neoliberal dismantling of the welfare state and the classic instability of a staple economy in Alberta has meant that the richest province as measured by per capita income also has the largest gap between the rich and the rest of the population. During the 44-year reign of the Alberta Progressive Conservative Party, predictable plunges in the international price of oil always disproportionately impacted those at the bottom of the economic ladder, who have repeatedly faced the duel impact of job losses and austerity measures aimed at social programs and public goods.

Far from being a provincial phenomenon, the impact of these trends on democratic accountability and developmental liberalism are indeed signifi-cant for the whole country. "Albertization" of the Canadian political system is evident in policies that facilitate the regulatory capture of labour, influxes of temporary workers to supply precarious labour, lax environmental laws that mask the costs of resource exploitation (Barnetson and Foster 2015), and inter-national trade agreements that constrain governments to pursue developmental projects (Gill and Cutler 2014). A few other manifestations of the tightening hold of petroculture and neoliberalism in Canada during the Conservative regime included centralization of power in the Prime Minister's Office and unelected officials; arbitrary prorogation of Parliament for partisan ends; limit-ing parliamentary debate on sweeping legislations; undermining of unionized public service employers, such as educational and medical institutions, and postal services; sustained attacks on scientific and research facilities, and data collection; and the revolving door between powerful industrial and mining sectors and high-ranking political officials.

While there is a discernable pattern of erosion of the practice of democracy in Canada, its relationship with oil-exporting status is often brushed aside, despite the overlaps with attributes of petroculture. It is clear, however, that a neoliberal governance model provides the fertile ground that allows for the flourishing of petroculture. The penetration of market values and instruments into the democratic apparatus redefined public roles, compromised the institutional integrity of the public sector, and created problems of transparency and democratic accountability (Bexell and Morth 2010). The resultant decline in democratic accountability has removed the causes of inequality from the realm of democratic debate or contestation, leaving it in the hands of a hamstrung technocratic public service at best, or the market forces at worst. In the case of Canada, the entrenchment of neoliberal ideology is indeed prompting a country that is statistically not a "petro-state" to behave like one in terms of its disregard for the basic tenets of liberal democracy, such as social justice and developmental liberalism, while conflating the best interests of the oil and gas sector with "national interest."

The Harper era exhibited many of the behaviours that are typically associated with petro-states, including inaction on climate change; revisions to Canadian environmental law to suit the short-term needs of the oil industry; use of provincial and federal government officials as lobbyists for the Alberta oil industry; sacrificing broad-based public interest and sustainable economic goals at the altar of the short-term growth of the energy sector (Hoberg 2014); and curtaining public and parliamentary debates on matters of significant public policy. The Harper government used its majority to push such draconian legislation as Bill c-51 through Parliament. It has been widely criticized for enabling deep and broad intrusions into privacy, criminalizing expression of dissent, and further weakening of accountability processes and mechanisms (Various Authors 2015). Specifically, the bill enables the criminalization of critics of the oil and gas industry in Canada. It strengthens the disruptive role of the Canadian Security Intelligence Service (CSIS), which already considers various environmental and Indigenous activist groups as targets. This abuse of privacy rights, surveillance, and unaccountable state policing (though ostensibly against "terrorists") redefines democratic protest and mobilization as a threat to the petro-state. Bill c-51 certainly fits within the pattern of ongoing erosion of civil liberties on the pretext of the "war on terror" and dilution of the apparatus of democratic accountability in Canada (Stefanick 2015). At the same time, the bill can also be seen as yet another attempt by the neoliberal state to preserve a minimal definition of liberal democratic citizenship.

While the unexpected political regime changes in Canada and Alberta may be interpreted as a reflection of growing public impatience with the political and economic manifestations of neoliberal strategies, structural and institutional changes will require more than just the electoral defeat of specific political parties, such as Stephen Harper's Conservative Party. Moreover, what would it take to fundamentally alter the political terrain of natural resource management in Canada? Not only oil and gas in Alberta, but much of Canada's natural resources are in areas that are governed by First Nations Treaties. Indigenous peoples are thus the front-line demographic bearing the impact of changes in the environment and the political economy that are driven by the extractive sector. This is significant not only in revealing the multiple axes of inequality and injustice in an oil-exporting country, but also because it is an important intersectional dimension that has often been sidelined in conventional studies about democracy and inequality. Nevertheless, new coalitions and alliances involving Indigenous peoples are increasingly evident in the crises and contradictions of oil extraction in Alberta and beyond, potentially signalling the emergence of a new kind of politics crystalizing out of a lengthy series of political blockages, compromises, and co-optations (Haluza-DeLay and Carter 2014).

Over 30 distinct First Nation communities live in the oil sands region of northern Alberta. As with many resource extraction industries, the oil industry has been a mixed blessing for these communities. While mining activities in the region have indeed provided more employment and business opportunities to communities in the area (Canadian Association of Petroleum Producers [CAPP] 2015), these economic benefits are often outweighed by the negative impacts on water quality and watersheds, the environment, community health (Kelly et al. 2010), and wildlife habitat (Canadian Parks and Wilderness Society and David Suzuki Foundation 2013). Various social movements have arisen to oppose tar sands development, which have included a variety of environmental organizations and activists from the First Nations of Athabasca Chipewyan, Chipewyan Prairie, Fort McKay, Fort McMurray, Mikisew Cree, as well as the Alberta Federation of Labour and the Council of Canadians, to name several. Public campaigns have coalesced into oppositional mobilizations in the form of National Energy Board hearings of the Northern Gateway Pipeline proposal, and opposition to the broad legislative sweeps of the Harper government's omnibus bills, as well as the Idle No More movement.

Public mobilization has not necessarily halted the expansion of the extractive project. Alberta, for example, sold endangered caribou habitat to energy developers despite widespread opposition and against its own policy, following the recommendation of a panel of federal scientists that all Alberta's mountain caribou herds should be elevated to endangered status. All the same, a new social and political pattern is clearly emerging where the response of the government, particularly toward environmental and Indigenous rights advocates, can be simultaneously seen as a pertinent manifestation of the tightening stronghold of "petropolitics" in Canada, and the possibility of new political spaces for contestation and alliance. If Bill C-51 can be seen as a reaction to the growing environmental, Indigenous, and social justice critics of petroculture, perhaps the electoral victory of the NDP in Alberta that dislodged the several-decades-old conservative rule in the province, or the victory of the federal Liberals on a progressive platform, might be seen as the manifestation of the pushback generated by these new alliances. The recently elected Liberal government of Justin Trudeau's rejection of the Northern Gateway pipeline project in late 2016 also reflects the growing political heft of these new alliances. However, for pipeline opponents, this apparent victory was only partial as two other pipeline projects were approved. It is simply too early to predict the impact of either regime changes or oppositional forces on the defining features of petroculture in Alberta or in Canada.

Conclusion

In a critical review of research on the impact of inequality on democratic and economic institutions, Savoia, Easaw, and McKay conclude that high levels of inequality harm both political and economic institutions in a country. Their study notes that market-economy institutions have failed to provide access to resources for a broad base of the population, and that inequality limits effective democracy since redistribution is too costly for the elite in such a scenario (2010, 143). Like most oil and democracy studies, though, this study also focuses on institutional quality only in developing countries. However, most of the trends related to inequality and its impact on political and economic institutions are increasingly evident in a number of OECD countries, and Canada is not immune to this trend. The analysis provided by staples theory surely confirms the negative impact of resource reliance on attributes of liberal democracy in Canada. The selective forgetting of this rich tradition of questioning reliance on resources in Canada perpetuates the idea that the resource-curse is exclusively a problem of developing countries.

Despite adhering to the theoretical assumptions of liberal democracy—concern for political legitimacy and broad-based economic development—most studies of oil and democracy use measures and indicators that provide only a minimalistic interpretation of democracy. While these measures of democracy provide valuable insights into a democratic transition of oil-exporting countries, the use of such standardized measures falls short in accounting for a discernable democratic deficit in oil-exporting OECD countries such as Canada, the United Sates, and even Norway. As Amitav Ghosh has argued, "In several instances ... oil and the developments it has brought in its wake have been directly responsible for the suppression of whatever democratic aspirations and tendencies there were within the region" (1992, 32). Trends in the oil-exporting OECD countries are highlighting that the negative impact of oil dependence on institutions of liberal democracy is not just a malady unique to the oil rich regions of the Middle East. The Canadian case study certainly highlights the disjuncture between the principles and the practice of liberal democracy in an oil-exporting country, where the fundamental assumptions of liberal democracy are being compromised under a neoliberal model of governance. It is therefore important to look beyond the apparent functionality of the democratic apparatus and use alternative conceptual tools to understand the political economy of oil-exporting countries around the world, beyond the North and South silos.

Finally, while the interconnection of petroculture and neoliberalism is increasing political and economic inequality, and creating a democratic deficit in Canada for all population groups, Indigenous peoples are emerging at the forefront of resistance to the expansion of extractive projects in Canada, especially in the resource rich northern parts of the country, not unlike the ongoing resistance by Indigenous peoples in the Amazon region and the Niger Delta. Indigenous sovereignty initiatives to regain control over their ancestral lands are proving to be a potent environmental strategy for opposing the relentless push to expand extractive projects in the Canadian North. In a period marked by volatile global oil markets, unconventional oil booms, shifting economic geographies, and catastrophic signs of climate change, containing these incredibly destructive extractive projects by supporting Indigenous land rights claims is likely to benefit both the environment and the institutions of liberal democracy in Canada.

Further Readings

Adkin, Laurie, ed. 2016. *First World Petro-Politics: The Political Ecology and Governance of Alberta*. Toronto: University of Toronto Press.

Laxer, Gordon. 2015. *After the Sands: Energy and Ecological Security for Canadians*. Madeira Park, BC: Douglas & McIntyre.

Shrivastava, Meenal, and Lorna Stefanick, eds. 2015. *Alberta Oil and the Decline of Democracy in Canada*. Athabasca, AB: Athabasca University Press.

Notes

1 The Anthropocene Era is defined as a new geological epoch of geological and morphological modification of the planet by the growth of the human population and its activities (Crutzen and Stoermer 2002).

2 The petroleum industry generally classifies crude oil by the geographic location, its measure of density, and its sulphur content, which is then used to determine the price per barrel. Crude oil is considered "sweet" if it contains relatively little sulphur, or "sour" if it contains substantial amounts of sulphur. Sweet oil commands a higher price and has lower production costs. As the world's reserves of light and medium sweet oil are depleted, oil refineries are increasingly processing heavy oil, bitumen, and tight oil, which use more complex and expensive methods to produce the required products.

3 Resource-curse refers to the phenomenon of dependence on resource extraction leading to weak economic growth and lack of broad-based development. It is related to the concept of Dutch Disease, which explains the role of volatile prices and financial flows in depressing manufacturing and other sectors in a resource dependent economy.

4 In May 2015, in a dramatic upset, the PC Party rule ended with the electoral victory of the left-leaning New Democratic Party (NDP). Although this regime change signifies an interruption to the 44 years of conservative rule in Alberta, the length of this interruption and the policy implications of this change remain to be seen.

CHAPTER 8

ON ANGER AND ITS USES
FOR ACTIVISM

Alexa DeGagné

Introduction

This chapter examines the role of anger in social justice activism, focusing specifically on contemporary lesbian, gay, and bisexual (LGB), queer, and trans politics in Canada. Anger has many synonyms, among them acrimony, exasperation, furry, and petulance. Anger is also one of the many emotions associated with social and political activism. Anger often erupts in the face of complacency, exclusions, perceived injustices, inequalities, and outright discrimination and violence, emanating from the state and from civil society. However, anger is often dismissed in formal political settings as being irrational, inappropriate, unproductive, and a violation of both familiar political protocols and established channels of claims-making. It is commonly argued that governments are more receptive to hearing and addressing the grievances of marginalized citizens when they follow formal institutional channels and conduct themselves with "rationality" and "civility."

Anger is also identified as a reason to dismiss, deny, and undermine those who are speaking out against their marginality and inequality. Historically and currently, particular members of society have been cast as irrationally and unreasonably angry, not the least those who identify as people of colour, Indigenous, women, LGB, trans, gender-non-conforming, queer, mentally ill, disabled, or poor. The calling-out of injustices through anger is a challenge to existing and normalized power relations. Accordingly, those who express anger are deemed irrational, uncooperative, uncivilized, inflexible, and even juvenile. The dismissal of what I term "anger activism" both delegitimizes marginalized individuals and their claims, and reinforces the power relations that sustain the status quo.

Women of colour feminist activists and scholars, such as Audre Lorde, Patricia Hill Collins, and Sara Ahmed, have long applauded anger and its uses in activism. They have argued that anger is an understandable and legitimate emotion in the face of injustices (Lorde 1984). Although anger is differently defined and regulated based on one's marginality and/or privileges, it can and does create solidarity within social justice communities (Collins 2000). These scholars point out, however, that anger can also challenge, transform, or unravel social movements when it is directed inward—for example, when racism, classism, and other exclusions were challenged within the feminist movement itself (Ahmed 2004b, 2010).

Although there is a deep and nuanced scholarship on the role and power of anger in feminist activism, there remains a stark lack of scholarship on the role of anger within LGB, trans, and queer activism, and even less so in the Canadian context. Canadian LGB, trans, and queer activists, nevertheless, have expressed anger and used it to motivate their activism since the emergence of the LGB liberationist activism of the 1960s and 1970s. Accordingly, in this chapter, I use anger as a case study to investigate how LGB, trans, and queer activists in Canada have articulated and fought for social justice issues, asking whether LGB, trans, and queer activists favoured more tempered, "rational" assimilationist strategies, or whether they used anger to articulate and motivate vocal challenging and radical strategies in their social justice projects. In what follows, I trace how anger has been taken up during several activist moments in Canadian LGB, trans, and queer politics since the 1960s. These activist moments include the gay bar raids and riots of the 1970s and 1980s, the HIV/AIDS crisis, and the fight for same-sex marriage in the early 2000s.

Many influential activists and governments, I argue, viewed same-sex marriage as the most important and even final goal of mainstream LGB campaigns for human rights, citizenship equality, and social justice. In contrast to the United States where same-sex marriage has been a bitterly contested social division, the fight for same-sex marriage in Canada was resolved relatively quietly by litigation through the courts as a logical extension of existing minority rights protections. As this chapter explains, however, the moments and events that preceded the court victories in Canada were fuelled by anger over injustices, discrimination, and violence. The fight for same-sex marriage thus marked a decided shift from anger activism to an assimilationist and "tempered" strategy that emphasized loving emotions and positive outcomes. This shift, however, distanced the mainstream of the movement from more radical LGB, trans, and queer activism. Finally, this chapter examines three contemporary moments of social justice activism in which anger plays important, revealing, and varied roles: first, campaigns that problematize and challenge the priorities and tactics of the mainstream LGB movement in

Canada; second, Black Lives Matter Toronto's involvement and protests during Pride Toronto's 2016 festival and parade; and third, the ongoing campaign to have gender identity added to the Human Rights Act and the Criminal Code of Canada. Based on these cases, I argue that anger can be productive as it can galvanize marginalized citizens to challenge normalized power relations within and outside the LGB, trans, and queer community, and forge new alliances that push back against silences, exclusions, and social injustice.

Anger, Transgression, and Social Justice

Many theories in the social sciences have explored the complex interplay between emotions, activism, and social movements. Early theories viewed social movements as predominantly irrational and deviant expressions of emotion. Resource mobilization and rational choices theories, in turn, downplayed the role of emotions in motivating social activism, arguing instead social movements arise when resources are available and individuals rationally calculate that rewards outweigh the risks of joining a movement. Contemporary social construction theories have focused on the cultural and discursive contexts of social movements. Specifically, social construction theories argue that society's understandings and valuations of emotions can influence movements' formation, focus, longevity, and impact (Beyerlein and Ward 2007; Goodwin, Jasper, and Polletta 2001; Elbaz 1995). Emotions are differently understood and valued; for example, happiness is usually cast as positive and productive, while anger is cast as negative and destructive. The varied valuations of the emotions are thought to determine both how a social movement characterizes itself and how society interprets and reacts to it.

Social movement theorists have argued that the relationship between emotions and activism cannot be fully explained by looking at one level of analysis; rather, a combination of individual biology and psychology, group identities and dynamics, structural power relations, and cultural norms, values, and roles explain what prompts emotion—and if and how emotion is politically motivating (Goodwin, Jasper, and Polletta 2001). In what follows, I am less concerned with psychological dispositions and group identities that prompt individual engagement in social movements than with the ways in which anger is discursively defined, valorized, and attached to particular marginalized populations and used by activists when making social justice claims.

Discourses can be oppressive or transgressive. Judith Butler argues that discourse becomes oppressive "when it requires that the speaking subject, in order to speak, participate in the very terms of that oppression" (2006, 175). Particular populations, therefore, reproduce their own oppression when they identify with or embrace constructs that normalize and marginalize their identities, roles, and actions. In contrast, discourses that challenge the terms of oppression, refusing to replicate them, are transgressive. As Christina Foust explains, "Transgressive actions incite reactions due to their relationship to norms: Transgressions violate unspoken or explicit rules that maintain a particular social order" (2010, 3–4). When violating the rules of social order, transgressive discourses can expose power relations and the limits of normality (Foust 2010), rendering them open to further scrutiny and dismantlement.

I argue that anger, directed at discourses that demonize, ridicule, and silence particular populations, can both inspire transgressive discourses and fuel social justice activism. Simon Thompson argues that anger is connected to activism in at least two respects. "One idea is *mobilization:* here the implication is that anger is the emotion which is capable of motivating people to engage in political action. The other idea is *injustice*: here it is implied that the reason why people mobilize is in order to overcome such perceived injustice" (2006, 124, italics in original). Anger is a dominant and active emotion that mobilizes people to take political action. Other emotions, such as sadness, fear, and anxiety, may be caused by political relations and events, but they may simply generate passivity, alienation, and resignation to the status quo (Farinas 2012; Beyerlein and Ward 2007). In contrast, anger is, in many respects, an "essential political emotion," representing a response to perceived violations of self and status as well as expressing expectations about what they deserve (Beyerlein and Ward 2007; Zembylas 2007; Thompson 2006). Therefore, anger can be transgressive, not just because it galvanizes and motivates political action and activism but because the political action it motivates is focused on calling out and challenging normalized, oppressive power relations. Moreover, as Thompson argues, "If [anger] is regarded as the emotion which people feel when they express injustice, then understanding anger may offer us insights into the nature of justice itself" (2006, 124).

Thompson (2006) refers to justice broadly, but it is equally applicable to social justice concerns. While the focus of social justice activism has shifted across time and place, two common and interconnected themes have consistently informed social justice movements, notably political recognition and economic redistribution. Iris Marion Young describes the contours and importance of recognition: "I have defined justice as the institutionalized conditions that make it possible for all to learn and use satisfying skills in socially recognized settings, to participate in decision-making, and to express their feelings, experience, and perspectives on social life in contexts where others can listen" (1990, 91).

Recognition, thus, is vital for people to voice their opinions and concerns, and to expose and challenge injustices, inequalities, discrimination, and violence.

As Nancy Fraser argues, however, recognition cannot be contingent on people's assimilation to the terms or discourses of oppression (1996, 14). Such assimilation does not fundamentally challenge but actually reinforces the relations of oppression. Recognition can lead to redistribution when the voices of the marginalized are heard, respected, and addressed, at least in part, by the redistribution of capital and resources through social services, education, and employment opportunities. Mary Holmes underlines this point: "Anger can call attention to a group's demand for respect and recognition, but also highlight inequalities more generally. Demands for respect can be expressed through anger, which can performatively reorient relations with others" (2004, 222). Through anger, marginalized people are making claims to legitimacy as speaking people with concerns and needs. Recognizing people's anger, as opposed to dismissing it as irrational and destructive, legitimizes the voices and the demands of those who experience injustice, discrimination, and violence. "The benefit of taking anger seriously," as Peter Lyman explains, "is that listening to those who feel they have lost their right to be heard reduces social suffering, enriches political dialogue, and enhances the ability of politics to redress injustice" (2004, 133–34).

Speaking with anger, however, is threatening to power relations that are often premised on the silence and complacency of particular kinds of people. Anger, then, becomes a challenge to normal power relations as marginalized people make claims to better access to both decision-making processes and social equality. Transgressions against norms and hierarchies expose the fluidity and fragility of a system of power, ultimately weakening the legitimacy of authority structures (Foust 2010). Accordingly, using anger to dismantle social injustices and inequalities can be met with backlash from those who stand to lose dominance through shifting power relations.

Normative discourses regulate anger to mediate its potentially threatening effects. The acceptability of anger depends, to a degree, on who is expressing the anger. Throughout history there have been people and groups that are empowered through their expressions of anger, not denigrated. "Anger privilege" refers to instances when anger expressed by already privileged people is seen as justified and thus is indulged (Taylor 2004). The "angry white men," who were a major force in the ascension of conservatism and neoliberalism in the 1980s and iconic figures in the 2016 election of US President Donald Trump, stand as an example of anger privilege. The common interpretation was that this amorphous group of voters were legitimately angry because their social status and privilege had eroded. The Trump campaign's promise to "make America great again" corresponds to abundant research demonstrating that conservative politicians and organizations have successfully provoked and used emotions, including anger, to galvanize electoral support (Frank 2005;

Kintz 1997). Channelling anger can be an important political tool and not only for those in marginalized positions.

The anger of marginalized people is generally met with particular kinds of normative regulation because it violates the rules of who can be indignant and who can speak (Collins 2000). In order to undermine and delegitimize the anger of those who seek to disrupt political relations and social order, the anger of particular people is often dismissed as irrational and uncivilized (Holmes 2004). As Linklater points out, the binary of emotion and rationality is racialized. For example, European colonial forces distinguished between "advanced," "civilized" and "rational," and "savage," "uncivilized," and "emotional" peoples (2014, 576). The binary is also gendered. Emotion is associated with the body, nature, and the private, and thus with femininity (Ost 2004). White women are expected to be emotional but passive rather than angry. Conversely, women of colour are expected to be emotional and aggressive, and they are consequently defined as angry (Logie and Rwigema 2014). Carmen H. Logie and Marie-Jolie Rwigema's study of lesbian, bisexual, and queer women of colour in Toronto and their experiences with white privilege found that "LBQ women of color were further marginalized by constructions of (real) women as passive, feminine and white, and conversely perceptions of women of color as fierce (aggressive), emotional, and hypersexualized" (2014, 180–81). The binary is also sexualized as non-heteronormal people, specifically queer men, are characterized as juvenile, impulsive, and irresponsible, and thus unable to control their own sexuality, much less their emotions. Thus, emotions are differently constructed and valued in order to regulate who can speak and who is heard, and what language and what emotions they can use to effect change.

Anger is also often used as justification for exclusion from recognition and representation in the public. If someone reacts in anger to particularly egregious situations, their anger is seen as a temporary state that can and should be surmounted by reason and rationality. Failing to silently self-regulate one's emotions demonstrates both an inability to rationally participate in public life, and a refusal to take responsibility for one's position in society (Lyman 2004). In a neoliberal regime, where individualism and self-sufficiency are crucial for survival, expressions of anger in reaction to supposed inequality and injustice are characterized as lazy excuses and attempts to reassign blame for failing to succeed in a "fair" economy. This dismissal of anger simultaneously blames the marginalized for their marginalization, and silences critiques of the system (Lyman 2004).

Faced with such regulation of anger, many marginalized groups have been compelled to deny, suppress, and abandon anger as a motivation and means of activism, choosing instead to conform to the language and means of "proper" rational political engagement in order to stand a chance of being recognized within the public. As Audre Lorde argues, expressing anger can potentially lead to vulnerability, but denying, suppressing, or silencing one's anger is more detrimental. Lorde offers this reflection in *Sister Outsider:* "My response to racism is anger. I have lived with that anger, ignoring it, feeding upon it, learning to use it before it laid my visions to waste, for most of my life. Once I did it in silence, afraid of the weight. My fear of anger taught me nothing. Your fear of anger will teach you nothing, also" (1984, 124). bell hooks also warns against the silencing of anger and outrage in *Killing Rage: Ending Racism*: "All our silences in the face of racist assault are acts of complicity. What does our rage at injustice mean if it can be silenced, erased by individual material comfort?" (1996, 19).

Silencing one's own anger reinforces the oppressive power relations that are the source of the anger in the first place. Taylor further argues that the suppression of anger among feminists leads to "hampered communication, visibility, and empowerment for self-definition" (2004, 4). This silence means that angry subjects cannot name, much less challenge, the injustices they face, rendering them complicit in their own oppression.

With this complex and challenging construction of anger, activist communities and social movements are left with several questions: How can anger be used as motivation for political action against injustice and inequality? How can communities and movements move beyond the frustration of being ignored, delegitimized, and silenced when showing anger? How can anger be uniting, as opposed to destructive, for communities and movements? In response to such questions, Sara Ahmed (2004b) suggests that anger can be productive when anger is used in reaction to collective problems or injustices. Expressing anger, Ahmed emphasizes, should not be seen as the driving purpose of a social movement (2010, 4). Instead, anger should be used for exposing, criticizing, and dismantling structural and institutional power relations. This shift in focus enables activists to unite around shared injustices, to offer solidarity to those who experience injustice, and to ask broader questions about the foundations of justice and equality (2004b, 175–76). Accordingly, I trace the historical and current relationship between anger and LGB, trans, and queer activist communities in Canada in order to understand the changing ways in which social justice has been understood, articulated, and fought for in these communities.

Historical Moments of Anger in Canada's LGB, Trans, and Queer Activism

In this section of the chapter I examine three moments in the history of LGB, trans, and queer activism in Canada when anger galvanized activists—the bathhouse raids and anti-police riots of the 1970s and 1980s, the HIV/AIDS crisis of the 1980s and 1990s, and the fight for same-sex marriage in the 2000s. Of course, there were moments of political protest and action before the 1970s that were motivated by anger. Charles Hill, the founder of the first gay rights group in the country (the U of T Homophile Association), stated that he found the courage to start the organization as he was motivated by "anger and irritation" over his arrest, and eventual acquittal, for dancing at a gay club. Hill added, "We were an invisible minority and as long as we were invisible, people could create their own theories about us" (quoted in Perdue 2009, n.p.). Many homophile groups in Canada and the United States were founded to dispel negative characterizations of homosexuals, making the case that homosexuals were not sick, deviant, criminal, or threatening. While many people joined homophile organizations out of anger, outrage, irritation, and fear, the groups largely redirected their anger, sought positive attention, and pursued assimilationist tactics as they sought social acceptance, or at the very least, an end to outright targeting and violence at the hands of the government, police, and fellow citizens (Warner 2002).

The end of the 1960s and beginning of the 1970s saw a shift in the tone, tactics, and goals of LGB and trans activism in Canada and the United States with the birth of the gay liberation movement. As Tom Warner states, in Canada, the gay liberation movement and its ideology were "the products of anger and outrage channelled into collective action" (2002, 7). He continues: "[LGBT] history is one of resistance and astonishing perseverance, textured with the exuberance of outlaw sexuality" (2002, 7). The activists were angry, outraged, and fed up, and exuberant, bold, militant, assertive, daring, noisy, and defiant. Moreover, the activists' pride in their outlaw sexuality enabled them to express anger, and other aggressive and confrontational emotions, because they were not seeking tolerance, acceptance, or approval, but instead recognition on their own terms (2002, 7). Thus, in contrast to the homophiles, the liberationists recognized the power of anger, channelling it toward collective action and ends, which included achieving visibility and recognition in order to challenge discrimination and violence.

In Canada and the United States, anger set the tone for many liberationist marches, protests, and riots that were triggered by police raids of clubs, bars, bathhouses, and meeting areas that were frequented by LGB and gender-non-conforming people. Speaking about the American police raids and liberationist riots, John D'Emilio observed that: "The bars proved themselves to be repositories of political consciousness and a place from which gay anger erupts" (2013, 93). Although highly celebrated and mythologized as the beginning of the gay liberation movement, the Stonewall riots of 1969 were not the first or last moments of angry rebellion and protest against police brutality toward LGB and gender-non-conforming people (D'Emilio 2002). Beginning in early 1975, police in Montreal began raiding gay establishments in an attempt to "clean up" the city for the 1976 Olympic games. Over the next year, a series of high profile raids were conducted in bars and bathhouses, using bawdy-house and indecency laws, which resulted in hundreds of arrests and convictions of homosexual men and women. These raids angered and galvanized Montreal's gay and lesbian communities into action. New alliances were formed between French and English gay and lesbian groups, and, on 19 June 1976, more than 300 gay rights activists protested the police targeting, surveillance, raids, and violence, as they chanted "Down with police repression!" (Kinsman and Gentile 2010).

Raids also had been taking place in Toronto. In 1981, during the biggest raid, targeting four bathhouses, the police inflicted violence, verbal abuse, and property damage, and arrested 304 men (Guidotto 2011). The next day more than 2,000 people took to the streets and chanted "Fuck you 52" as they headed to police Division 52 headquarters. The Coalition for Gay Rights in Ontario was a main organizer of the protest. At the time, one of its members, Christine Donald, stated: "I was actually quite frightened on that demo. The anger was enormous, just enormous" (quoted in Warner 2002, 111). Another activist who was involved, Chris Bearchell, interpreted the anger of the protests differently, saying that the shock of the raids "gave way to fury; women and men in the community went from disbelief to just rage. Rather than letting that anger weigh us down—debilitate and demobilize us—we were able to channel it into a collective statement." Bearchell added that the angry reaction to the raids also created public space for people to voice their frustration with police violence and homophobic discrimination (quoted in Jennex 2015; Sutherland 1982).

Thus channelling anger was productive in these cases as it led to united and forceful protest actions, and created space and opportunity for marginalized people to voice their concerns in the face of intimidating police interventions. Nadia Guidotto points out, for example, that gay and straight women were not at the bathhouse raids, but they had experienced state regulation of their bodies and sexualities by other means. Accordingly, gay and straight women channelled their anger and acted in solidarity by joining the protests against the police (2011, 70). In Toronto, during the protests and the years that followed, the critiques of police injustices spanned from the bar raids to the relationship between the police and a broad spectrum of marginalized communities (Guidotto 2011).

Craig Jennex identifies several hand-bills, flyers, and posters that were made for the 1981 rallies and the 10th anniversary 1991 rallies, which connected police violence to many marginalized communities. One flyer said "Now is the time to unite with minority communities to call for an end to police

harassment!" (Jennex 2015, n.p.). Another flyer asked: "What has changed in
10 years? The police continue to harass and attack people of colour, women,
Native peoples and lesbians and gay men in this city" (2015, n.p.). A poster
argued: "Over the last years, it hasn't just been gays who have felt the brunt
of police violence. Blacks and other visible minorities face racist and sexist
police and street harassment. It was only last year that Albert Johnson, a Black
man, was murdered by police. And it is women who daily face sexism and
harassment on this city's streets. The raids on the gay community are a threat
to everyone's civil and human rights. We cannot let Toronto become a city
where police are free to trample on the rights of any community or group"
(2015, n.p.). The flyers and poster were themselves angry public statements
and rallying cries drawing on the anger of oppressed minority groups in reaction to police violence and street harassment. Here, anger was identified and
used to attempt to galvanize and unite various marginalized communities in
demanding the end of violence, the protection of rights, and the building of
social justice. These calls for reflection and action on the ways in which police
violence and public harassment are experienced by marginalized communities
on the basis of sexuality, race, and gender demonstrate that anger can be used
to offer meaningful critiques to and challenges of multiple systems of power.

That said, the posters' messages were also problematic. Some failed to grasp
the intersectionality of police violence (that which was experienced by gay
Black men and trans women), while others presented gay people as experiencing the worst of police and public discrimination: "[The protest] will call
for an end to police harassment against all minorities. But we must realize that
right now gays are on the front-line of attack, as Blacks have been in the past"
(Jennex 2015, n.p.). The implication that people of colour experienced violence
only in the past is striking, especially in light of the ongoing killing of people
of colour and Indigenous people, including Two-Spirited people, by police
and individuals across Canada and the United States. Thus, despite attempts
to unite in anger across marginalized communities, there remained exclusions.

Still, the first half of the 1980s was characterized by community and organization building in order to secure safe spaces in the face of police and public
harassment. The anger generated by the raids led, in part, to the creation of
new LGB organizations, the building and/or expansion of gay neighbourhoods in Montreal, Toronto, and Vancouver, and the initiation of Toronto's
first Pride march in 1981, as well as other Pride parades across the country
(Connor 2014; Warner 2002). By the mid-1980s, however, the HIV/AIDS
crisis evoked another surge in anger-based activism. This moment of anger has
been the main focus of many academic pieces on the role of anger in LGB,
trans, and queer activism. Deborah Gould, for example, argues that initially
the response to the HIV/AIDS crisis was steeped in grief and shame, focused

on caring for people living with HIV/AIDS (2002), and tempered, stoic, non-aggressive lobbying of government bodies for better, or at least non-hostile, hospital and end-of-life care. While this type of tempered lobbying persisted throughout the HIV/AIDS crisis, formidable, anti-assimilationist organizations also emerged in the face of the epidemic. These organizations were motivated by anger over the lack of government response to the HIV/AIDS crisis; the seemingly unjustifiable delays in medical and pharmaceutical research and production; the discrimination within and abandonment by medical systems; the denial of job and housing protections for people living with HIV/AIDS; and the social discrimination against people living with HIV/AIDS, and all marginalized communities that were associated with the disease at the time (Chvasta 2006; Gould 2002; Shepard 2002).

This shift to anger activism in response to the HIV/AIDS crisis was best exemplified by the AIDS Coalition to Unleash Power (ACT UP), which was founded in the United States in 1987, with chapters forming across the United States, and in Vancouver, Montreal, and Toronto, and by Toronto's AIDS Action Now (AAN) (AIDS Action Now n.d.; M. Brown 1997). These organizations were grassroots, community-based, and radical coalitions of activists who coupled anger and frustration with direct action tactics, including street protests, disruptions and civil disobedience, dramatic, satiric, and campy performances, and die-ins. The protests used emotions of sadness, fear, and anger, and emphasized pride in overt-sexuality and promiscuity. For example, AAN and ACT UP, including its Vancouver, Toronto, and Montreal members, protested and delayed Prime Minister Brian Mulroney's speech at the International AIDS Conference in Montreal in June 1989 (M. Brown 1997). Afterward, the organizations published the *Montreal Manifesto*, an international bill of rights for people living with HIV/AIDS (AIDS Action Now n.d.). These direct-action tactics were designed to gain public and political recognition in order to confront and hold accountable government bodies, the scientific-medical establishment, pharmaceutical corporations, the media, and broader society (Chvasta 2006; Gould 2002).

The grief did not lessen within these activist communities, but as Gould argues, grief was attached to anger and pride, while they redirected shame onto governments. Anger also transgressed discourses, within and outside LGB communities, which maintained that the only form of legitimate political activity takes place through traditional and formal systems (2002, 182). As Gould states: "Given our grief and under these dire circumstances where we and our loved ones are being murdered by our government, anger and confrontational activism targeting state and society are legitimate, justifiable, rational, righteous, and necessary. ACT UP offered an emotional and political sensibility that simultaneously acknowledged, evoked, endorsed, and bolstered lesbians' and gay men's anger" (2002, 182). HIV/AIDS activists were ignored, denigrated, and silenced by those in positions of formal power, rendering emotional grass-roots, street-based actions as attractive means to achieve recognition and social justice. The rejection and silencing, in combination with strength through anger, also led to the creation of communities of care in which people living with HIV/AIDS could depend on wide networks of people to provide medical, financial, and child care—all elements of social justice that were not being provided by governments. This embrace of anger and confrontational activism was also coupled with unapologetic sex radicalism and disinterest in social acceptance, thus establishing the foundations for queer theory, activism, and community, which continues to engender radical, anti-assimilationist activism in both Canada and the United States.

During the HIV/AIDS activist campaigns of the 1980s and 1990s, LGB activists and organizations continued to focus on formal avenues of political action and communication, including lobbying and litigation. These activists were seeking equality. They fought for liberal rights, freedoms, and protections. They began speaking in "rights talk," which Mariam Smith defines as a type of political discourse that prioritizes the law and courts as a mechanism to resolve political issues, particularly those pertaining to different social groups' interests in relation to other social groups and/or the state (1999, 75). The incorporation of sexual orientation under section 15 of the Canadian Charter of Rights and Freedoms became a major focus of equality seekers, as did other rights-based initiatives, such as same-sex marriage and adoption. In seeking these ends, activists expressed frustration and anger in reaction to the anti-homosexual discourse of many politicians, public figures, citizens, and activist organizations.

Equality-seeking required a degree of assimilation to the discourses, precedents, and procedures of legal and legislative institutions. Expressions of anger, frustration, hostility, and transgression were not well entertained within these institutions. Accordingly, activists tempered their emotions and adopted rights talk, making the case that homosexuals could be granted various rights without fundamentally disrupting public norms, practices, or institutions. These tactics of assimilation are best exemplified in the fights for same-sex marriage across advanced democracies. Same-sex marriage campaigns in Canada, the United States, and Australia harnessed emotion-based discourses, specifically the emotion of love because it was seen as positive and non-aggressive. It was hoped that governments would be more amenable to listening to the activists if they evoked love (DeGagné 2015). This self-regulation downplayed the negative, overly emotional, irresponsible characterization of homosexuality that liberationist and radical HIV/AIDS activists had harnessed. Instead, love was used to make the case that particular kinds of homosexual citizens were fit for marriage because they replicated the heteronormal family structure and function, including monogamous love, procreation, and economic self-sufficiency. Speaking to the Australian case, Renata Grossi (2012) maintains that discourses of homosexual love and marriage can be used to transgress the heteronormativity family and marriage laws. Regarding Canadian same-sex marriage campaigns, Suzanne Lenon counters: "The legal arena requires comparison to others in a relevant category (in this case, heterosexual conjugal couples) in a way that tends to suppress differences and emphasize similarities, and to coalesce around the most normative construction of that identity. In this sense, law demands assimilation. Discursive representations of 'ordinary' lives and 'ordinary' love thus require un-marking sexual orientation as a sign of 'difference,' one that should not matter or at the least be considered contingent by judges and politicians" (2011, 366).

While anger was used to lend confidence to queer activists' sex radicalism and anti-assimilationism, love was used to prove that some homosexuals' sexuality was normal and non-threatening to established social hierarchies and institutions. Therefore, they argued, heteronormal homosexual sexuality should not impede access to certain rights and protections.

Love evoked in this way was problematic because it addressed equality on an individual basis, and sought privatized solutions to inequality. Equality was individualized as people fought to gain rights and protections on the basis of their private heteronormative relationships. Marriage reinforced a "private zone" for two people free from state intervention. Although, as Lenon argues, the private is a privilege for those who assimilate to the economic, racial, and sexual norms of the state. One such norm includes economic self-sufficiency. The discourse of love was used to evoke homosexual couples' commitment, dependency, and self-sufficiency (2011, 363). Same-sex marriage, therefore, would facilitate same-sex couples' self-sufficiency and thus absolved the state of social justice responsibility.

The deployment of the idea of love to gain recognition and acceptance in the broader public undercut critiques of systemic inequalities experienced by those who could not marry and those whose social justice problems—such as poverty, police and public violence, over-criminalization, and discrimination in health services—could not be solved by entering into a private relationship. In effect, the appeal to love and marriage splintered the movement and elevated autonomous couples in private relationships as those worthy of rights and protections. In contrast, the anger of the liberationists and radical HIV/AIDS activists led to the building of organizations, neighbourhoods, and communities of care. In the decade since the legalization of same-sex marriage in Canada, LGB, trans, and queer activism has followed different paths as some organizations continue to pursue formal, assimilationist, tempered, and individualized political action, while others draw on anger to transgress norms and fight for social justice on a systemic level. The next section offers a snap-shot of how anger is currently being evoked in Canadian LGB, trans, and queer activism.

The Current State of Anger in Canada's LGB, Trans, and Queer Activism

In the wake of the fight for same-sex marriage, anger has continued to motivate LGB, trans, and queer activism in new and important ways. Campaigns problematize and challenge the priorities and tactics of the mainstream LGB movement in Canada, the Black Lives Matter protests during Toronto's 2016 Pride festival, as well as the ongoing campaign to have gender identity added to the Human Rights Act and the Criminal Code of Canada are three prominent examples. These three moments of anger are unique in their goals, strategies, and avenues for activism. Each directs anger toward a different community and outcome, be it anger within the LGB, trans, and queer communities or anger in reaction to repeated denials of rights protections by federal legislators. Accordingly, these moments offer different possibilities for solidarity, community building, and social justice within and beyond Canada's LGB, trans, and queer communities.

Ahmed (2004b) argues that those marginalized and unrecognized within a social movement often direct their anger toward those who are privileged and dominant within that movement. The prioritization of equality and rights-based issues and goals within mainstream LGB organizations has sparked such anger. Equality and rights were largely prioritized by elite members of Canada's LGBT communities, and by mainstream organizations (Mariam Smith 2010; Rayside 2009), thereby silencing the voices of marginalized members of the community. Organizations such as Against Equality (United States and Canada), various Dyke Marches (Toronto, Ottawa, Vancouver), Queers Against Israeli Apartheid (Toronto), and the Community Response Project (Edmonton) have often expressed anger and frustration over both the dominance of elites within mainstream organizations, and their prioritization of rights-based issues, which do not address the many pressing social justice issues that affect the daily lives of many LGB, trans, and queer people in Canada. They argued that despite the incorporation of sexual orientation into section 15 of the Charter, the legalization of same-sex marriage, and the strengthening of hate-crime laws, LGB, trans, and queer populations still experienced disproportionate rates of poverty and homelessness, under-representation in governments, overrepresentation in prison and justice systems, neglect in immigration and refugee policies, and daily discrimination, bullying, harassment, and violence (Crawford and Nichols 2012; Malinda Smith 2012). Therefore, it has been argued that the focus on equality and rights has only benefited the already privileged within the movement. Anger arises, then, as the momentum of the movement has been used to gain rights and equality for a select few, effectively sidelining critical social justice issues. The prioritization of rights-based issues, they have argued, compromised avenues for recognition and social equality as the voices and needs of the most marginalized within the community are silenced and neglected by mainstream LGB organizations, and by the state.

The anger of marginalized people toward others within the social movement is often met with defensiveness, dismissal, or exclusion. For example, while first initiated as angry, politically radical protests and marches, Pride parades and festivals across the country increasingly have become corporate, "family friendly," pro-police, and liberal rights celebrations. The defiant and boisterous displays of "deviant" sexualities that once characterized Pride parades have been replaced with de-sexualized and "respectable" imagery. Moreover, Pride parade organizations have tried to censor and ban many radical, angry queer and trans political activist organizations from participating, including the attempted exclusion of the Queers Against Israeli Apartheid group from Pride Toronto's 2010 parade (Kouri-Towe 2011). More tempered, assimilationist liberal rights issues of same-sex marriage and adoption, and Gay-Straight Alliances, were welcomed in the parades, as were major political parties and elected officials. Examples such as this further marginalize those whose exclusion from representation and decision-making sparked their anger in the first place. Thus expressions of anger both by social movements and within social movements are met with regulation, exclusion, and dismissal because in both cases unjust power relations are being challenged. Yet if the anger of these radical, angry queer and trans political activist organizations is acknowledged and respected, it could be used to produce new understandings of diverse experiences, perspectives and needs; to challenge power relations within the movement; and to engage in social justice work for those who are marginalized in the community (Holmes 2004).

In 2016, Pride Toronto invited Black Lives Matter (BLM) Toronto to be an honoured group for the year's festival and parade, potentially signalling a shift in Pride Toronto's politics, image, and solidarities. BLM Toronto accepted the invitation with hesitation, however, given Pride Toronto's historical and ongoing exclusion of Black, Lantinx, and Indigenous queer and trans people. In an interview with *Daily Xtra,* BLM Toronto co-founder Janaya Khan stated: "We also know that historically Pride has not been about our pride.... Not just about our black pride, but our pride as black queer and trans people" (quoted in Mann 2016a, n.p.). BLM Toronto was also concerned that they were being included as a token group (Mann 2016b), which would allow Pride Toronto to claim that they were inclusive without fundamentally changing the festival's focus, policies, or goals. To these ends, Khan said, "We want to hold Pride accountable and take up space in a particular way that shifts those narratives and makes people uncomfortable, that makes Pride political again" (quoted in Mann 2016b, n.p.). BLM Toronto saw their participation in the festival and parade as an opportunity to shift the narratives of pride by returning the Pride parade to its rebellious and political roots; by creating space for Black, Lantinx, and Indigenous queer and trans people; and by calling on the festival to be accountable for how police involvement in the festival and parade affects racialized queer and trans people who are targeted, abused, criminalized, and killed by police organizations in Canada.

During BLM Toronto's participation in Toronto's 2016 Trans March, Dyke March, and Pride parade, anger was used as a tool for activism to shift the festival and community's narratives, to carve out space for excluded communities, to make people uncomfortable and unsettled, to have their demands heard, to hold the festival and community accountable, and to motivate intersectional solidarity. After leading a die-in during the Dyke March, members of BLM Toronto spoke to march participants, community members, and onlookers. Their speeches evoked many emotions—sadness, excitement, frustration, joy, and anger. The anger was used to express resistance, as a BLM Toronto member said to the crowd:

> The first pride was a riot! Don't get it twisted ... I want to live in a time where black lives matter, and sex workers' lives matter, disabled lives matter, and Muslim lives matter, and dykes' lives matter! ... The world is rising and we can rise with it. What will they say about us in 10 years, in 20 years? Will the story of the Dyke March of 2016 prove to be a catalyst? That we took back the streets? That we took back this city? That we decolonized or recolonized? That we fought for all oppressed people, or just some? ... We have one thing over the state—the state with its infinite resources, its military powers, its capitalism—we have us! We are the majority! I believe that we will win! (DeGagné, 2 July 2016, personal recording)

This BLM Toronto member's impassioned speech galvanized the crowd, calling for intersectional solidarity among all oppressed people, and calling on Dyke March participants and supporters to honour the momentum of the day by continuing to fight the state for social justice.

Anger was also used to call out members of the Dyke March, and onlookers, who were not fully inclusive and supportive of justice for Black people, and who refused, for example, to say the words "Black Lives Matter" (Black Lives Matter 2016a). Anger was deployed by BLM Toronto members to make particular people uncomfortable and unsettled, asking them to acknowledge their privilege and their role in perpetuating racism within and outside the

LGB, trans, and queer community. Once people were uncomfortable with their role in perpetuating exclusions and were unsettled from their positions of privilege, power relations could shift and space could be carved out for those who were excluded from the LGB, trans, and queer community, enabling different voices and narratives to exist within the Dyke March and larger community.

BLM Toronto walked in Pride Toronto's 2016 parade as an honoured group. After a parade-wide moment of silence for those who died in the Orlando shootings at a gay night club, the BLM Toronto group engaged in direct action by initiating a sit-in. BLM Toronto members, Indigenous Two-Spirit groups, Latinx groups, and allies sat down in the street, halting the parade, and began drumming, singing, chanting, and making speeches. With indignation, a BLM Toronto member said to fellow protestors and parade onlookers: "Are we proud? I don't think we have much to be proud about! I don't think this is a cause for celebration when there are Black people dying, when there are queer and trans people dying! We are constantly under attack. Our spaces are under attack. Pride Toronto: We are calling you out. For your anti-Blackness. Your anti-Indigeneity. Everyone in this space sit down. This is your space!" (Black Lives Matter 2016a, n.p.). The sit-in protest, which was an act of non-violent direct action, was inspired and maintained through passion, frustration, determination, and anger over the deaths of Black, Lantinx, and Indigenous queer and trans people, largely at the hands of police officers. Anger infused the protestors with strength, resolution, and unity, enabling them to hold ground in the face of jeers from many onlookers, sitting down and maintaining their space on the street as part of the parade and within the LGB, queer, and trans community. Speaking of the power of BLM Toronto's protest, Al Donato states: "It's impossible to deny the tactical brilliance behind a peaceful civil act that makes multiple politicians and powerful corporations stop dead in their tracks. When else has the head of anyone's country been physically immobilized by a movement led by Black queer and trans locals? The usual run-arounds, email chains, and responsibility ducking that executives do when faced with large-scale organizational reform is impossible in a standstill watched by hundreds of thousands" (2016, n.p.).

BLM Toronto carved out (and continue to maintain) their own space through physically stopping their bodies, and stopping the bodies of provincial and federal leaders, corporations, police and corrections organizations, and LGB, trans, and queer organizations. In that moment, the influential, powerful decision-making bodies could not ignore BLM Toronto or dismiss their actions or demands as irrational and uncivilized expressions of anger, though such undercutting came later. With the parade halted, BLM Toronto presented a list of demands to Pride Toronto's executive director, which included increased funding and support for Black spaces and events during Pride Toronto; increased American

Sign Language interpretation during Pride Toronto events; increased representation of Black trans women, Black queer people, and Indigenous folks among
Pride Toronto's staff; "removal of police floats/booths in all Pride marches/
parades/community spaces"; and a public town hall between marginalized
communities and Pride Toronto to discuss the implementation of the demands
(Black Lives Matter 2016b). The BLM Toronto group resumed marching in
the parade, chanting in celebration "we won" after Pride Toronto's executive
director agreed to their demands (CBC News 2016).

Angry backlash was hurled at BLM Toronto during their sit-in and in
the following days. During the sit-in, onlookers booed, jeered, insulted, and
threatened BLM Toronto for stopping "their" parade, many claiming that the
Pride parade was not a time for Black people to fight for justice. In the days
that followed, BLM Toronto was subjected to hate-mail, online harassment,
media criticism, and condemnation by various LGB organizations, including Pride Toronto, which rescinded its support for BLM Toronto's demands
(Mann 2016b). Much of the angry backlash focused on the tactics of BLM
Toronto and their demand that police floats and booths be removed from
Pride Toronto marches/parades/community spaces. Regarding BLM Toronto's
tactics, LGB and trans community members argued that the parade should be
a celebratory, positive, inclusive space for all, while hypocritically calling for
the exclusion of protests concerning Black, Lantinx, and Indigenous queer and
trans people. Here, Pride was held to be a supposedly neutral, liberal rights,
positive space, which largely represented white LGB people, despite the fact
that Pride marches were initially led and maintained by Black and Latinx trans
and gender-non-conforming people. Thus while white LGB people exercised
their anger privilege via hate mail, online posts, mainstream media, and LGB
organizations, anger was illegitimate when expressed by Black, Lantinx, or
Indigenous queer and trans people during a Pride march.

This division was further marked as Pride Toronto's executive director
stated "[BLM Toronto] could have sent me an email and I would have agreed
to all these things" (Wilson 2016, n.p.), implying that had the protestors used
appropriate channels of communication, wherein anger and frustration is
not easily communicated, then Pride Toronto would have complied with
their demands. This statement negated past and ongoing exclusions of Black,
Lantinx, and Indigenous queer and trans people who repeatedly attempted to
engage on the "civil" terms of LGB and trans organizations, communities, and
spaces. Instead, by mounting an indignant act of direct action, BLM Toronto
succeeded in unsettling LGB, trans, and queer people and organizations; BLM
Toronto shifted the narrative about the role of police in queer and trans spaces,
the racism within LGB, trans, and queer communities, and the future direction of Pride events in the country.

In contrast to this anger within the movement, made manifest by BLM Toronto, some trans activists expressed anger in reaction to repeated rejections of proposed legislation to add gender identity to the Human Rights Act and the Criminal Code of Canada. In 2005, NDP Member of Parliament Bill Siksay introduced a bill that proposed the additions of gender identity and gender expression to the Human Rights Act. Siksay introduced the bill again in 2009, this time seeking to also include gender identity and gender expression to the hate crimes provision of the Criminal Code. The 2009 version made it past a third reading in the House of Commons but failed to be considered in the Senate before the dissolution of Parliament for the 2011 federal election. These trans rights bills, like those for same-sex marriage, were attempts to attain rights for particular groups of people based on their shared identity. In both cases, a degree of assimilation was required of those who wanted rights: trans people had to define themselves according to a state definition of "gender identity" much like same-sex couples had to define their relationship according to the state definition of marriage.

There certainly was anger among same-sex marriage advocates during the fight for same-sex marriage in the early 2000s, but public expression of such anger was seen as damaging to the claim that homosexuals were civilized, loving, grateful, and normal citizens, and thus worthy of rights. The anger in relation to the denial of trans rights was different from that which was expressed in previous LGB, trans, and queer campaigns because trans advocates and activists publicly expressed anger in reaction to the multiple rejections of the various bills, and to the discriminatory, hostile, and abusive arguments that were used by Members of Parliament and political organizations who were against the bills. Ultimately, this anger points to increasing disillusionment with formal institutional channels and potential abandonment of seeking rights and protections as a route toward equality and social justice.

In this case, anger was expressed from within the formal institutional channels. Expressing anger in this environment was possible because it was expressed by a Member of Parliament, and it was an expression of anger in reaction to being denied inclusion into the human rights system as opposed to anger at the system itself. Both of these conditions rendered the anger relatively acceptable as the anger actually shored up the formal institutional channels rather than challenging them. Speaking in the House of Commons to the merits of the bill in 2011, MP Siksay stated:

> As a gay man, I know that the battle for my equality in our society
> was often led, often championed, by members of the transgender
> and transsexual community. I know that it was the drag queens who
> helped us fight back, and perhaps taught us to fight back, against
> the oppression, discrimination, prejudice and violence that we faced.

At Stonewall, but also long before and long after Stonewall, it was members of the trans community who helped lead and motivate our fight, and who stood in solidarity with us time and time again. That is one reason why I am proud to stand in solidarity with the transgender and transsexual community, as we finally seek their full equality and seek to establish their full human rights in law in Canada.... I have seen and sometimes shared the frustration, the anger, the tears and the deep sadness of people who are not yet equal, who too often face violence, sometimes to the point of death, and who mourn the loss of friends and family for whom the pain was more than they could bear. I have been strengthened by their resolve to claim their true identity and their place in our society, to live full lives and to be fully human. (2011, n.p.)

Siksay's (2011) references to the riots and rebellions which came before, during, and after Stonewall drew a connection between the anger felt during the rebellions of the liberationists, and the anger felt in reaction to the denial of gender identity rights. In this moment, Siksay attempted to use anger to unite portions of the LGB, trans, and queer community, arguing that the factions of the community have long come together and fought back in moments of oppression, discrimination, prejudice, and violence. Moreover, Siksay acknowledged that trans and gender-non-conforming people were crucial in the liberationist rebellions. Yet the public and political condemnation of liberationists' anger and aggression was erased as Siksay used the comparison to justify his support of trans rights. Trans people's use of anger was legitimate in this contemporary moment, according to Siksay, because it was in reaction to years of denied rights, "full equality," and "their place in society" as opposed to the anger-fuelled anti-police and anti-government activism of their predecessors.

At the same time, this case produced organized campaigns motivated by anger and frustration with formal institutional channels. The latest iteration, Bill C-279, was introduced to the House of Commons by NDP Member of Parliament Randall Garrison. Over the 10-year fight, trans activists expressed anger not only at the series of delays, but also the years of particularly bigoted and hateful debates that surrounded the bills, and the continuing and daily discrimination, violence, and injustice that trans people face in Canada. In reaction to 2015 Senate delays, which proposed amending the bill to exclude trans rights in relation to sex-specific space, such as crisis centres, washrooms, change rooms, and prisons, the head of the Trans Rights Lobby Group in Toronto, Susan Gapka, stated: "I feel angry about this injustice. When I feel angry I become defiant. Subsequently, today and everyday afterwards I will boldly go into public washrooms and change rooms to use them for my own use. I will perform this act of defiance every day" (quoted in Gothoskar 2015, n.p.).

As part of this protest, trans activists across Canada used social media to post pictures of themselves in both the gender-segregated facilities of their choice, and in the gender-segregated facilities that they would be relegated to with the proposed amendments (Page 2015). These acts of direct action and public defiance compare to the tactics of the liberationists, radical HIV/AIDS activists, and Black Lives Matter Toronto.

In July 2015, Bill C-279 was permitted to die on the order paper when government Senate leader Claude Carignan deliberately delayed debate on its passage (Baglow 2015), amounting to nearly 10 years of attempts to attain these rights for trans people.[1] This case revealed the negative impacts of attempting to gain inclusion through formal institutional channels, which required assimilation, made marginalized people vulnerable to increased public abuse, ridicule, and violence, and reproduced exclusions. Attempting to fight for social justice through formal institutional channels, the supposed arena of civility and rationality, actually produced emotionally negative reactions among those who went through the "appropriate" formal channels and were still mistreated and rejected by the institution. Anger was used to express frustration with the political system, to demonstrate the absurdity of unjust government laws, to garner public attention, to make claim to space and safety, and to fortify the movement's resolve. Trans activists' anger and frustration with formal political channels was well expressed in these protests, but it remains to be seen whether these activists will choose to channel their anger into pursuing social justice goals outside of the exclusionary, regulatory, and angering formal institutional channels.

Conclusion

American trans activist, and star of the Netflix series *Orange Is the New Black,* Laverne Cox, has often quoted Cornel West's statement "Justice is what love looks like in public" (Z. Ford 2014, n.p.). Here, love refers to mutual and collective respect, advocacy, and support that can foster social justice for all members of a community. The use of love in the LGB movement's same-sex marriage campaigns was individualized and privatized. As I have argued in this chapter, anger has been formidable and productive in community building and social justice campaigns for Canadian LGB, trans, and queer activists. Governments and the mainstream LGB communities have both tried to temper and silence anger for fear of its transformative potential. In the case of BLM Toronto, mainstream LGB communities used their anger privilege to attempt to silence and exclude Black, Lantinx, and Indigenous queer and trans people from participating in, holding accountable, and transforming Pride Toronto's parade and festival. Ahmed says that people cannot control if and how their anger will be interpreted and regulated (2004b, 177). What is important, however, is how we react to anger (in ourselves and others), and the ways in which we channel our anger. While the deployment of anger is not without its own problems, exclusions, or resistance, anger can advance social justice activism in several ways. It can unite marginalized people who share anger in reaction to injustices, discrimination, and violence. It can forge new alliances and build community. It can be used to deny assimilation and embrace difference. It can empower silenced voices and challenge normalized power relations. Anger is an integral part of the toolkit of social justice activism both within and outside LGB, trans, and queer communities.

Further Readings

Cohen, Peter F. 2014. *Love and Anger: Essays on AIDS, Activism, and Politics.* New York: Routledge.

Maynard, Robyn. 2016. *Policing Black Lives: State Violence in Canada from Slavery to the Present.* Winnipeg: Fernwood Publishing.

McCaskell, Tim. 2016. *Queer Progress: From Homophobia to Homonationalism.* Toronto: Between the Lines.

Note

1 In 2016, the federal Liberal government introduced Bill C-16, which added both gender identity and gender expression to the Canadian Human Rights Act's and the Criminal Code's hate crime sections (Government of Canada 2016).

CHAPTER 9

SOCIAL MOVEMENTS ON THE PATH TO ECONOMIC AND SOCIAL EQUALITY

Judy Rebick

Introduction

My book *Transforming Power: From the Personal to the Political* described a new politics emerging in Latin America and at a grassroots level in the United States and Europe in the early twenty-first century (Rebick 2009). This new political approach was built from the bottom up, led by those most oppressed, and was inclusive and intersectional, often combining growing concerns about environmental sustainability with old and new social justice issues. Since then, new social movements have sprung up around the world. Similar to the New Left of the 1960s, these movements are telling us that the old ways, structured around the right, left, and centre, are not working anymore. Despite increasing inequality and the rise of new social movements fighting for the poorest and most marginalized, the political left has largely failed to develop new paths to political and social change. This concluding chapter thus looks at some key ideas that the new social movements of the twenty-first century are raising through their practices and discussions in an attempt to further develop our understanding of how to emerge from contemporary environmental, democratic, and economic crises with a society that better serves us all.

In the wake of the 2008 financial crisis, many new movements, including the Arab Spring, Occupy Wall Street, the Maple Spring, Idle No More, and Black Lives Matter, have developed novel ideas about and approaches to the problems posed by the decline of neoliberal capitalism; among them, growing income inequality and precarity, the thinning of democratic participation, the disproportionate power of corporations and the ultra-rich, and inadequate responses to climate change. When we look back, I have no doubt we will see the second decade of the twenty-first century as a decade of people power. I believe this decade is as, or more, important than the 1960s were to my generation. Yet many commentators fail to see the significance of these movements because they look different. They don't always have clear demands and they rarely focus on electoral politics. Sometimes they appear ephemeral, here today and gone tomorrow. They are easily crushed, as in Egypt, or sidelined, as in Hong Kong, or drowned out, however momentarily, by right-wing populist and xenophobic appeals to pervasive insecurity. Twenty-first century social movements have not yet built institutions that reflect and advance their values. Even when they produce an electoral voice, as in Greece or Spain, they have not yet achieved the necessary power to affect real change.

Indeed, twenty-first century social movements do look different, but I would argue they are just as powerful and significant as the peace, student, anti-war, environmental, women's, LGBTQ, and anti-racist movements of previous generations; and the task of transformation before them is even greater. Similar to earlier movements, they have emerged spontaneously, organizing through diverse networks rather than around a specific platform the way that political parties characteristically do. Unlike the social movements arising in the 1960s, however, these new movements are more diverse, more focused on process and class issues, and more aware of the barriers facing them.

The Arab Spring protests in 2011 inspired a generation of young people to rally against sometimes brutal and soul-destroying oppression. Soon after, the youth of Europe began a rebellion against draconian austerity measures that followed in the wake of the 2010 European financial crisis. Scarcely reported in North America, the 15 May movement began in Madrid in the spring of 2011 with a massive protest against European government cuts and spread to more than 700 locations across Europe. In 2015, we saw a reflection of those movements at the electoral level with the victory of the anti-austerity Syriza Party in Greece and the meteoric rise of Podemos in Spain. Both newly minted parties emerged out of the new social movements of the twenty-first century.

Commentators have called 2011 the year of global uprisings. Protests spread across North Africa and the Middle East to Europe and then to the belly of the beast—the financial district of New York City. The Occupy Wall Street (OWS) movement took some cues from the Egyptian 6 April movement, which used social media to invite tens of thousands of citizens to occupy Cairo's Tahrir Square to demand democratic reform (Harris 2011). While also protesting the erosion of democracy, the OWS movement focused its message on economic inequality, which had reached historic proportions in the United States in the wake of the 2008 financial crisis. Similar to the anti-austerity protests across Europe, OWS quickly spread across North America and around the world to an estimated 1,500 locations, prompting *Time* magazine to name the protester as the 2011 "person of the year." As Amy Goodman of *Democracy Now!* summed up, "From the Arab Spring to Occupy Wall Street, millions of people took to the streets to oppose repressive regimes and an unjust economic system" (quoted in Democracy Now! 2012).

In 2012, it was Canada's turn. What has been called "the Maple Spring" began with a massive and prolonged strike by Quebec students against an intransigent government and ended with a historic uprising of Indigenous peoples across the country who declared that they would be "Idle No More." Two years later, the feminist movement had a resurgence in reaction to sexual assault charges against two celebrities, one in Canada and one in the US Under the Twitter hashtag #beenrapedneverreported, thousands of women told their stories, many for the first time, revealing the appalling lack of justice for women who have been sexually assaulted. And, beginning in the unlikely place of Ferguson, Missouri, Black youth rose up across the United States against police violence with the slogan "Black Lives Matter."

Twenty-First Century Social Movements

Twenty-first century social movements are decentralized and deeply democratic in the sense that much of the initiative belongs to the grassroots. Occupy Wall Street had no visible leadership and spread mostly through social media, but it managed within a few weeks to make the question of economic inequality central to public debate. Public opinion polls showed that three months after the occupation began on Wall Street in October 2011, fully three-quarters of Americans agreed with OWS's core message that the rich and corporations had too much power (Pew Research Center 2011). Identifying and popularizing an issue is a central task of a social movement. OWS identified income inequality as the elephant in the room of American society and politics. They named a central problem that most people experienced but few in the mainstream acknowledged. The chant "We are the 99%" popularized the feeling of unease that many people had with the growing inequality they themselves were experiencing or saw around them in their families and on the streets. OWS gave people a metaphor to help understand their daily lives and struggles.

Critics have claimed that OWS and similar new movements were ineffective because they did not congeal into formal organizations with a fixed leadership and policy agenda. My response to such criticisms is that they have already been effective. For years, left-wing think tanks and agencies serving the poor had been publishing data showing the growing gap between the rich and the rest of us, but it wasn't until Occupy Wall Street that the issue moved to the front pages and the centre of public debate. Moreover, in 2016, economic inequality and its deleterious influence on democracy were core themes in Senator Bernie Sanders's campaign for the Democratic Party's presidential nomination. His message, which mobilized millions of primary voters, campaign workers, and small-scale campaign donations, is a powerful legacy of OWS that remains in play in American politics.

The same can be said about the key role of new movements in making visible many other injustices, including sexual assault and police violence against racial minorities. Within days of the Jian Ghomeshi scandal in Canada, for example, women from around the world spoke out about having been raped or sexually harassed, creating a virtual movement that instantly exposed the failure of institutions from legislatures to universities to provide clear penalties or even procedures to stop sexual violence and harassment. Similarly, Idle No More mobilized Indigenous people, systemically dispossessed and oppressed since contact, by showing them that they could organize and make change and that many non-Native people would join them in their struggle for recognition, voice, dignity, and social justice. The Idle No More movement helped mobilize Indigenous voters in the 2015 federal election to demand a new relationship with the Canadian government and was instrumental in compelling the federal government to establish an official inquiry into missing and murdered Indigenous women.

Standing up against internalized oppression is a key feature of social movements, especially those that mobilize marginalized groups. This was what the Black liberation movement, including both the Civil Rights movement and the Black Power movement of the 1960s, did for African Americans. These earlier movements did not eliminate systemic racism or achieve full equality for African Americans, but they did change the political landscape through such concrete measures as voting rights, affirmative action, and anti-discrimination and anti-hate laws, and thus set the foundations for ongoing struggles for social justice. Systemic racism takes on many different forms, creating and recreating new expressions of internalized oppression. The war on drugs, as many Black activists have argued, has resulted in growing police violence and the disproportionate criminalization and incarceration of young Black men. It is no accident that the main slogan of the resistance to police violence beginning in Ferguson, Missouri, was "Black Lives Matter." Similar to the women's movement of my generation, the most important achievement was not the rights that we won or the laws we changed, however important these are, but, instead, changing how women thought about themselves. When I was young, women didn't think they could be politicians, journalists, musicians, artists, carpenters, lawyers, doctors, and professors. We were supposed to support men to do all those things. It was only when the women's movement started organizing and demanding equal rights that our consciousness was changed. The consciousness-raising groups of the late 1960s and early 1970s, much ridiculed in the media at the time, showed us that what we thought were personal problems were really shared political and social issues, and that women were capable of solving them collectively. The lesson of yesterday and today is that oppression only works when the oppressed internalize the idea that they are inferior to the dominant group. Breaking out of that paralyzing internalized oppression is the core task of all social movements.

Bottom-Up Democracy

All of the new social movements mentioned above have several features in common. The first and most important element is the absence of centralized and hierarchical leadership. Most new movements, starting with the anti-globalization movement that emerged from the mass demonstrations in Seattle and Quebec City at the turn of the twenty-first century, challenged the top-down structures of society, including those within the traditional left and in trade unions. The problem of hierarchy goes beyond what the feminist movement saw as the prevailing patriarchal order to our very notions of power itself. We have always seen power as being located in the state and in the corporations. It thus followed that the way to change the world was to get state power and make changes to state and economic structures. Then, the women's movement, anti-racist groups, and the environmental movement introduced the idea that we must also change our personal behaviour if we want to change the world. Power was understood as something each of us exercises in our everyday lives, including our domination over nature. These ideas were influential, but somehow didn't alter our views on how political change could be achieved.

A second key feature of contemporary social movements is their commitment to the voices of ordinary people and the principle that knowledge should come from the bottom up, not from the top down. I have been part of and have studied social movements all of my life and, for most of that time, I firmly believed that democracy was about the conflict of ideas. In almost every arena of decision-making, we are presented with opposing ideas. At most conventions, for example, there is a pro and con microphone. We are presented with a proposal and you are either for or against it. The new social movements of the twenty-first century are experimenting with different approaches to collective decision-making. Instead of deciding through the *opposition of positions*, the general assembly (GA) of OWS, for example, sought to make decisions through sharing of information and experience. The GAs worked on the principle of consensus. At their best, they were not about debating an issue with polarized positions, but rather about hearing all voices. Instead of presenting proposals to be debated, the GAs went around the circle and heard from every person about their view on the issue under discussion. Then a moderator tried to identify what was common and the discussion continued from there. Of course, this approach does not always work perfectly, but these practices point toward more inclusive ways of developing policies and a new direction in democratic processes.

The GAs of Occupy were an example of participatory democracy. There are other examples that could be more easily scaled to citywide or even country-wide levels. One I have studied is the participatory budget in Brazil. When the Workers' Party was first elected in Porto Alegre, a city of 1.5 million, they established a participatory budget for citizens to decide how to spend new monies in the city budget. The city was divided into neighbourhoods. Each discussed its priority for the budget and then elected individuals to participate in citywide budget-making. This experiment in expanding democracy has been copied by hundreds of cities in Latin America and Europe. The key feature of the participatory budget is that citizens decide upon priorities not as a consultation process, but as a decision-making process. The impact has been extraordinary—it has engaged those who felt marginalized by representative democracy, cut down on corruption, and created social solidarity. Participatory budgets, however, have rarely been used beyond the municipal level. At the provincial and national levels, entrenched interests have a stronger grasp on the reins of power, making participatory government much more difficult.

Other examples of the power of social solidarity come from countries that have been ravaged by government austerity measures, which have rapidly dismantled social infrastructures and social safety nets in the wake of the 2008 financial crisis. Citizens in Greece and Spain responded to government cuts by setting up their own medical clinics, residences for the elderly, and other services, which were run by volunteers. There are numerous examples around the world from the protest spaces of OWS to climate disasters such as Hurricane Sandy where ordinary citizens have stepped in where state agencies have failed to adequately provide for the needs of citizens. New technological developments mean that these experiences can be shared at a profound level, so that ordinary citizens can show each other what to do. Experts become less necessary. We begin to have a vision of a community organized at a local level through democratic neighbourhoods, schools, and workplaces. It is no accident that it is in Greece and Spain that new political parties on the Left have emerged challenging the old top-down Socialist and Communist parties for power.

In recent Spanish municipal elections, activists from the Indignado movement have taken the idea of using technology to combine electoral and participatory democracy to a new level. The candidate from Barcelona en Comú (Barcelona in Common), a coalition of activists, founded just a year before, won as mayor of Barcelona in the summer of 2015. Their strategy was (and still is) what campaigners call "municipalismo," or municipalism, an attempt to democratize local politics by making government institutions responsive and accountable to citizen participation. They are using a crowd-sourced electoral platform, which includes ending the privatization of health services, tackling high utility bills, controlling mass tourism, creating a renewable energy operation, and improving municipal democracy, with a portion of the city budget allocation decided directly by citizens. They are allied with the anti-austerity Unidos Podemos (United We Can) Party, which placed third in the 2016 Spanish election.

The victory of Syriza, a new type of left-wing party, in Greece in early 2015 quickly led to disappointment when they were forced to accept the vicious austerity measures that they had campaigned against. Andreas Karitzis, a key strategist for Syriza, said that "the Greek experience teaches us that we need to go beyond electoral politics.... We experienced a strategic defeat. Now we need to set up processes that will empower people—for example, by advancing social economy and cooperative initiatives or community control over functions such as infrastructure facilities, energy systems, and distribution networks. These are ways of gaining a degree of autonomy" (quoted in Rozworski 2015, n.p.).

The astonishing victory of Jeremy Corbyn in the leadership race of the British Labour Party is another example of how young activists are seizing whatever tools they can find to upset the neoliberal status quo. It remains to be seen whether this old-time socialist will adopt some of the new ideas emerging from twenty-first century social movements. Even the strength of Bernie Sanders in the Democratic Party primaries in the run-up to the 2016 American presidential election is a reflection of the continuing power of the social movements in the United States. The translation of ideas from social movements to political parties is never perfect nor complete. Justin Trudeau's rise to power in Canada's 2015 federal election came, in part, because of his promises to tax the rich, create jobs, build infrastructure, and to pursue nation-to-nation relationships with Canada's Indigenous peoples. The Occupy Wall Street and Idle No More movements, in part, had already laid the groundwork for the success of this political agenda.

Networked Politics

Networks are the preferred method of organizing among contemporary social movements. The use of the Internet makes participatory democracy more possible, while networking brings together movements that often have worked separately in the past, whether because of national or political divisions or because of colonialism. Networks foster a great potential for social movements to work together and support each other, educating, organizing, and mobilizing at the same time. In the age of information technology, networks are also transformative. In my generation, coalitions were built among different sectors, for example, Quebec/Canada or women's movement/unions, through long and careful negotiation. Representatives from key movement organizations would meet and develop a manifesto or a plan of action. Each representative would then go back to their group and get approval or changes to negotiate for another day. Today, generations of division can be surpassed in moments. A recent example is the astonishing turnaround in public opinion created by the movement against Bill C-51, an anti-democratic bill passed by the Harper government in its dying days, despite robust public opposition. A massive network of opponents of the bill, from civil liberties groups to open democracy groups, from Indigenous groups to unions, from Muslim groups to environmental groups, immediately saw the danger in expanding the power of CSIS, Canada's security and intelligence agency. Within a couple of weeks, rallies were organized across the country, online petitions amassed thousands of signatures, and devastating legal critiques were posted online and published in major dailies. All this work would have taken months in the past, but today it happens almost instantaneously. The Toronto demonstration against C-51 was more diverse than I have ever seen, organized by people I had never met—and I thought I knew all the activists in the city. In a couple of weeks, public opinion shifted against the bill and it became a core issue in the 2015 federal election campaign.

The power of networked politics was also clearly visible in the eruption of the so-called Maple Spring in early 2012. This movement began as a massive and prolonged student strike against the provincial government's proposed tuition increases, but soon evolved into a broad coalition of opponents to austerity. Hundreds of thousands of students hit Montreal streets in mass demonstrations in late March, but the nightly "Casseroles" were critical in building social solidarity for the student movement. Night after night, residents were invited to stand on their porches or join in marches in support of the anti-austerity protests. In more than 35 cities and towns across Canada, people went out into the streets clanging pots and pans to demonstrate their solidarity with the students of Quebec and their battle against austerity. The media coverage of the student strike hit a new low outside of Quebec. It was one-sided and biased, reporting only from the perspective of the government and focusing on the isolated incidents of vandalism. But this time, we had an alternative to the mainstream media in online independent media, such as rabble.ca, and social media. What's more, student activists in Quebec understood the need to communicate with English Canada for support.

I remember sitting in a Calgary cafe in 2012, crying, while I watched another joyous and beautiful video of the pots and pans marches in Quebec. I don't know if it was the inspiring music of ordinary people coming into the streets to defy an unjust law or the awesome courage and determination of the Quebec students or the shifting sands of the global youth uprising, but for the first time in my lifetime there appeared to be a solidarity movement growing in Canada for the people of Quebec. This possibility resonated with me because I have worked to bridge the divide between Canada and Quebec my whole adult life. It started in the 1970s when a few of us, including the brave NDP under the leadership of Tommy Douglas, stood up against the imposition of the War Measures Act in the midst of the FLQ crisis. This was a turning point in my politics because I realized that the Canadian government was just as capable of repression and violence as the American government. To see Montreal occupied by the Canadian army and people rounded up and jailed for their politics was a deeply radicalizing experience for me. A decade later, during the first Quebec referendum in 1980, I worked with a group of about 30 people in Toronto on the Committee to Defend the Right of Quebec to Self-Determination. Most of us didn't want to see Quebec leave Confederation, but we deeply believed that it was the right of Quebecers to make that decision. We also thought that the English media and the federal government were distorting the issues and creating hysteria, which we sought to counter. We were isolated, but we stood up for what we thought was right.

Just before I became president of the National Action Committee on the Status of Women (NAC) in 1990, the FFQ (Quebec Federation of Women) left NAC, primarily because most women's groups in English Canada opposed the Meech Lake Accord and its "distinct society" clause. A few of us fought that position unsuccessfully at first, but when I became president we were successful in developing a different vision of Canada as a nation of nations containing Quebec, First Nations, and the rest of Canada, each with the right to self-determination. When we had a chance to talk to Canadians about this kind of solution during the Charlottetown Accord debate, there was a lot of support, but not among the premiers who came up with the final version of the Accord. This version gathered opposition from a variety of quarters and was defeated in a national referendum in 1992. Then came the second Quebec sovereignty referendum in 1995, and whatever progress we had made in building bridges with people in Quebec was once again torn apart by the federalist hysteria.

Almost everyone I knew in Quebec—unionists, feminists, radicals, social democrats—was a sovereigntist. They taught me about the history of Quebec, the oppression of the Québécois by the Anglos and the Church, the heroic struggle of union activists against Duplessis, and their strongly held values of social justice and equality. They felt that the only way to build the society they wanted was to have their own country. We don't really learn that history outside of Quebec. A central weakness of the Left in Canada, in my view, has been its failure to understand the fact that Canada is in practice a nation of nations. While there have been moments where that understanding was expressed, it was never central to our politics. However, for a moment, the Maple Spring bridged that gap with a new consciousness around colonialism and the rise of Indigenous peoples through Idle No More (INM). Here again, not only is INM willing to embrace allies, but through networking it is possible for allies to join in. This is because the issues raised are not only Indigenous rights (although that should always have been enough), they are also the key issues of democracy and survival of the planet. As Pam Palmater, one of the spokespeople for Idle No More, has pointed out, "First Nations are the last best hope that Canadians have of protecting lands for food and clean water for the future—not just for our people but for Canadians as well" (quoted in LaDuke 2013, n.p.).

In British Columbia, the always strong environmental movement has become stronger by building networks with groups, often led by First Nations, opposed to pipelines and tankers. The leadership of Indigenous activists is also helping to build a pan-Canadian movement that links climate and justice. Naomi Klein's book *This Changes Everything* (2015) is being translated into movements in Quebec and the rest of Canada in ways that would be hard to imagine before the days of networked politics. I went to a national meeting in Toronto called by Klein and organized by 350.org, a U.S.-based group that works entirely by networks, to prepare the ground for the Leap Manifesto (2015), "A Call for a Canada Based on Caring for the Earth and One Another." Klein's idea of linking environmental and social justice issues is certainly a challenge for networked politics, given the different culture and politics of the environmental movements and trade unions, but the leading role of Indigenous activists is helping to bridge that divide.

Conclusion: Building Alternatives

Corporate globalization was the first feature of the transformation of this stage of capitalism, which, social movements rightly contend, has deepened inequality and eroded democracy. Canada was in the forefront of the movement against corporate globalization through the free trade fight of the 1980s. A broad coalition of unions, churches, women's groups, and environmental groups managed to convince the majority of Canadians to oppose free trade with the United States. Unfortunately, because of the distortions of our first-past-the-post electoral system, Brian Mulroney's Conservatives won the 1988 election and signed the Free Trade Agreement. The youth uprising, called the anti-globalization movement, that emerged late in the 1990s identified multinational corporations as the enemy. Free trade agreements and binding international economic agreements promoted by the World Trade Organization (WTO) and the International Monetary Fund (IMF) have effectively forced governments to restructure their economies through a variety of means, resulting in an unprecedented redistribution of wealth from the poor and working classes to the rich. Policy measures to reverse this inequality are well known: progressive taxes, a living wage or minimum annual income, reducing the wage gap between men and women, and social services, such as universal child care. The problem is that there is little political will to achieve these changes. Thanks to Occupy, the anti-austerity movements in Europe and Latin America, and now the beginnings of their expression in political parties, such as Syriza and Podemos, there is at least a discussion of the problem. In many ways, the election of the Trudeau government, which presented itself as progressive, is another sign of a desire to break with the austerity politics of neoliberalism. Although losing the popular vote by nearly three million votes, the 2016 election of Donald Trump as President of the United States demonstrates that the struggle against austerity politics is both challenging and relentless.

What's needed is at least as radical a restructuring and transformation of the economic, social, and political systems as was achieved by the neoliberal ideologues and their political leaders, such as Margaret Thatcher and Ronald Reagan. A guaranteed annual income, for example, seems to me to be an essential policy for overcoming inequality in a world of increasing technology and precarious work. This policy challenges the status quo not only of old-line parties but of unions as well. At the political level, parties in Canada are hanging on to old ideas and are, if anything, less democratic than they have ever been. New political parties like Syriza have come smack up against the centralized power of neoliberal capitalism; while others like the Alberta NDP are trying to make small, less threatening steps toward change on economic, social, and environmental levels. There is little question that neoliberal ideas are losing their grip on the population, as evidenced by sudden shifts: for example, the election of the NDP in Alberta, the election of Jeremy Corbyn as leader of the British Labour Party in Britain, and the rejection of Stephen Harper's Conservative Party. At the same time, the growing popularity of right-wing populist leaders across Europe, rising xenophobic sentiments and violence, Brexit, and the election of Donald Trump all demonstrate that precarious electorates are vulnerable to pernicious appeals that preserve or intensify neoliberal governing practices.

Some argue that real changes can only happen from the bottom up, decentralizing energy, organizing at the local level, and mobilizing citizens to make decisions and solve problems in their own communities. But ideas, processes, and policies generated from below also spread rapidly across national frontiers and through levels of government to transform what citizens demand of their leaders and governments. Many argue that political parties, competing in national elections, remain critical vehicles for achieving more equality and improving democracy. Others, however, stress the importance of new technologies in transforming both the economy and the political system. Each of these perspectives has merit. From my perspective, the contemporary social movements that are emerging around the globe are the forces most likely to find the directions, policies, and political will we need to make the transformations necessary to save the planet and most of us living upon it. We can already see their imprint on local, national, and international political terrains and, perhaps most important, on how we think about and engage in social justice activism.

Further Readings

Conway, Janet. 2013. *Edges of Global Justice: The World Social Forum and Its "Others."* London: Routledge.

The Kino-nda-niimi Collective. 2014. *The Winter We Danced: Voices from the Past, the Future, and the Idle No More Movement.* Winnipeg: ARP Books.

Klein, Naomi. 2015. *This Changes Everything: Capitalism vs. the Climate.* Toronto: Knopf Canada.

BIBLIOGRAPHY

Aboriginal Affairs and Northern Development Canada (AANDC). 2015.
"Comprehensive Claims." https://www.aadnc-aandc.gc.ca/eng/1100100030577/
1100100030578 (accessed 9 October 2017).

Aboriginal Affairs and Northern Development Canada (AANDC). 2014. "General
Briefing Note on Canada's Self-Government and Comprehensive Land Claims
Policies and the Status of Negotiations." https://www.aadnc-aandc.gc.ca/eng/1373
385502190/1373385561540#s2-1 (accessed 9 October 2017).

Accessibility for Ontarians with Disabilities Act (AODA). 2007. *Accessibility of Ontarians
with Disabilities Act: University of Toronto Accessibility Plan, 2007–08*. Accessibility
Planning Committee, University of Toronto. http://dlrssywz8ozqw.cloudfront.net/
wp-content/uploads/sites/12/2016/05/AODA-2007-08.pdf (accessed 9 October
2017).

Acemoglu, Daron, and James A. Robinson. 2012. *Why Nations Fail: The Origins of Power,
Prosperity, and Poverty*. New York: Crown Business.

Aghoghovwia, Philip Onoriode. 2014. "Ecocriticism and the Oil Encounter: Readings
from the Niger Delta." PhD diss., Stellenbosch University. http://scholar.sun.ac.za/
handle/10019.1/86488.

Agrawal, A.J. 2016. "Why Diverse Teams Win: Companies that Employ a More
Diversified Team Oftentimes Perform Better than Others." Inc. http://www.inc.
com/aj-agrawal/why-diverse-teams-win.html (accessed 9 October 2017).

Aguirre, Adalberto, Jr. 2010. "Diversity as Interest-Convergence in Academia: A Critical
Race Theory Story." *Social Identities* 16 (6): 763–74. doi:10.1080/13504630.2010.524
782.

Ahmed, Sara. 2012. *On Being Included: Racism and Diversity in Institutional Life*. Durham,
NC: Duke University Press.

Ahmed, Sara. 2010. "Feminist Killjoys (And Other Willful Subjects)." *The Scholar and
Feminist Online* 8 (3). http://sfonline.barnard.edu/polyphonic/print_ahmed.htm
(accessed 9 October 2017).

Ahmed, Sara. 2007a. "A Phenomenology of Whiteness." *Feminist Theory* 8 (2): 149–68.
doi:10.1177/1464700107078139.

Ahmed, Sara. 2007b. "The Language of Diversity." *Ethnic and Racial Studies* 30 (2):
235–56. doi:10.1080/01419870601143927.

Ahmed, Sara. 2007c. "'You End Up Doing the Document Rather than Doing the Doing': Diversity, Race Equality and the Politics of Documentation." *Ethnic and Racial Studies* 30 (4): 590–609. doi:10.1080/01419870701356015.

Ahmed, Sara. 2004a. "Declarations of Whiteness: The Non-Performativity of Anti-Racism." *Borderlands* 3 (2). http://www.borderlands.net.au/vol3no2_2004/ahmed_declarations.htm (accessed 7 October 2017).

Ahmed, Sara. 2004b. *The Cultural Politics of Emotion.* New York: Routledge.

AIDS Action Now. n.d. "History." http://www.aidsactionnow.org/?page_id=38 (accessed 7 October 2017).

Alberta Energy. 2014. "Oil Sands: Facts and Statistics." Government of Alberta. http://www.energy.alberta.ca/oilsands/791.asp (accessed 7 October 2017).

Alboim, Naomi. 2009. "Adjusting the Balance: Fixing Canada's Economic Immigration Policies." MayTree Foundation. http://wiki.settlementatwork.org/index.php/Adjusting_the_Balance:_Fixing_Canada's_Economic_Immigration_Policies (accessed 7 October 2017).

Alfred, Taiaiake. 2004. "Warrior Scholarship: Seeing the University as a Ground of Contention." In *Indigenizing the Academy: Transforming Scholarship and Empowering Communities,* edited by Devon Abbott Mihesuah and Angela Cavender Wilson, 88–99. Lincoln: University of Nebraska Press.

Anderson, Bridget. 2013. *Us & Them: The Dangerous Politics of Immigration Control.* Oxford: Oxford University Press. doi:10.1093/acprof:oso/9780199691593.001.0001.

Anderson, Kirk, and Maura Hanrahan. 2013. "Four Decades of *Morning Watch*: Moving to Indigenizing the Academy." *Morning Watch* 40 (3): 1–3.

Anderson, Mitchell. 2014. "Fresh Off Title Victory, Tsilhqot'in Unveil Tribal Park." *The Tyee,* 3 November. http://thetyee.ca/Opinion/2014/11/03/Tsilhqotin-Tribal-Park/ (accessed 7 October 2017).

Andrees, Beate, and Patrick Belser, eds. 2009. *Forced Labour: Coercion and Exploitation in the Private Economy.* Boulder, CO: Lynne Rienner Publisher.

Angenendt, Steffen. 2014. "Triple Win Migration—Challenges and Opportunities. Migrant Strategy Group." The German Marshal Fund of the United States. http://www.gmfus.org/publications/triple-win-migration-challenges-and-opportunities (accessed 7 October 2017).

Antone, Eileen, Grace-Edward Galabuzi, Cyesha Forde, Salmaan Khan, Carlos Flores, Mandissa Arlain, Olivene Green, Ruth Koleszar-Green, Lynn Lavalee, John Miller, et al. 2010. *Final Report of the Ryerson University on Anti-Racism.* Toronto: Ryerson University.

Anwar, Shamina, Patrick Bayer, and Randi Hjalmarsson. 2012. "The Impact of Jury Race in Criminal Trials." *Quarterly Journal of Economics* 127 (2): 1017–55. doi:10.1093/qje/qjs014.

Asch, Michael. 2014. *On Being Here to Stay: Treaties and Aboriginal Rights in Canada.* Toronto: University of Toronto Press.

Atikamekw Nation. 2015. "Affirmation of Sovereignty and Socioeconomic Development: Atikamekw Nation Makes its Mark at the UN." *Cision,* 23 April. http://www.newswire.ca/news-releases/affirmation-of-sovereignty-and-socioeconomic-development-atikamekw-nation-makes-its-mark-at-the-un (accessed 7 October 2017).

Baglow, John. 2015. "Senate Tramples Transgender Rights." *Toronto Star,* 7 July. http://www.thestar.com/opinion/commentary/2015/07/07/senate-tramples-transgender-rights.html (accessed 7 October 2017).

Bailey, Deborah Smith. 2006. "Diversity's Dividend: Diversity Enhances Group Decision-Making in Unexpected Ways, Study Finds." *American Psychological Association* 37 (5): 18. http://www2.apa.org/monitor/may06/dividends.aspx.

Bannerji, Himani, Linda Carty, Kari Dehli, Susan Heald, and Kate McKenna. 1991. *Unsettling Relations: The University as a Site of Feminist Struggles.* Toronto: Women's Press.

Banting, Keith. 2010. "Is There a Progressive's Dilemma in Canada? Immigration, Multiculturalism, and the Welfare State." *Canadian Journal of Political Science* 43 (4): 797–820. doi:10.1017/S0008423910000983.

Barnetson, Bob, and Jason Foster. 2015. "Exporting Oil, Importing Labour and Weakening Democracy: The Use of Foreign Migrant Workers in Alberta." In *Alberta Oil and the Decline of Democracy in Canada,* edited by Meenal Shrivastava and Lorna Stefanick, 249–73. Edmonton: Athabasca University Press.

Barnsley, Roger H., and A.H. Thompson. 1988. "Birthdate and Success in Minor Hockey: The Key to the NHL." *Canadian Journal of Behavioural Science* 20 (2): 167–76. doi:10.1037/h0079927.

Barry, Brian. 2005. *Why Social Justice Matters.* Cambridge, MA: Polity Press.

Bauder, Harald. 2006. *Labor Movement: How Migration Regulates Labor Markets.* New York: Oxford University Press.

Bauman, Zygmunt. 2002. *Society under Siege.* London: Polity Press.

Bauman, Zygmunt, and Leonidas Donskis. 2016. *Liquid Evil.* Cambridge, UK: Polity Press.

Bauman, Zygmunt, and Carlo Bordoni. 2014. *State of Crisis.* Cambridge, UK: Polity Press.

Baumgartner, Jeffrey. 2010. "Why Diversity Is the Mother of Creativity." *Innovation Management,* 24 November. http://www.innovationmanagement.se/imtool-articles/why-diversity-is-the-mother-of-creativity/ (accessed 7 October 2017).

BBC News. 2004. "Queen's Speech: The Full Text of the Queen's Christmas Broadcast." 25 December. http://news.bbc.co.uk/2/hi/uk_news/4125229.stm (accessed 7 October 2017).

BC Federation of Labour. 2013. "BC Unions Take Aim at Foreign Worker Program with Hard Hitting Radio Ad." News Release, 18 February. http://bcfed.ca/news/releases/bc-unions-take-aim-temporary-foreign-worker-program-hard-hitting-radio-ad (accessed 7 October 2017).

Beach, Charles. 2014. "What Has Happened to Middle-Class Earnings? Distributional Shifts in Earnings in Canada 1970–2005." Canadian Labour Market and Skills Researcher Network: Working Paper No. 131 (March). http://www.clsrn.econ.ubc.ca/workingpapers/CLSRN%20Working%20Paper%20no.%20131%20-%20Beach.pdf (accessed 7 October 2017).

Beck, Ulrich, and Elizabeth Beck-Gernsheim. 2002. *Individualization: Institutionalized Individualism and Its Social and Political Consequences.* London: Sage.

Bedard, Kelly, and Elizabeth Dhuey. 2006. "The Persistence of Early Childhood Maturity: International Evidence of Long-Run Age Effects." *Quarterly Journal of Economics* 121 (4): 1437–72.

Benjamin, Rich. 2009. *Searching for Whitopia: An Improbable Journey to the Heart of White America.* Toronto: Hachette Books.

Benton-Banai, Edward. 1988. *The Mishomis Book: The Voice of the Ojibway.* Harvard, WI: Indian Country Communications.

Bexell, Magdalena, and Ulricha Morth, eds. 2010. *Democracy and Public Private Partnerships in Global Governance.* Basingstoke, UK: Palgrave MacMillan. doi:10.1057/9780230283237.

Beyerlein, Kraig, and Matthew Ward. 2007. "The Importance of Anger for Explaining Participation in Various Types of Activism." Presentation at the American Sociological Association Annual Conference, New York, NY, 11 August.

Black, Jerome H.A. 2013. "Racial Diversity in the 2011 Federal Election: Visible Minority Candidates and MPs." *Canadian Parliamentary Review* 36 (3): 21–26. http://www.revparl.ca/36/3/36n3e_13_Black.pdf.

Black Lives Matter. 2016a. "Dyke March Speech." Facebook, 3 July. https://www.facebook.com/blacklivesmatterTO/videos/519986288196866/?autoplay_reason=all_page_organic_allowed&video_container_type=0&video_creator_product_type=0&app_id=6628568379 (accessed 7 October 2017).

Black Lives Matter. 2016b. "Black Lives Matter – Toronto, Along with Various Community Groups, Including BQY and Blackness Yes Have the Following Demands." Facebook, 3 July. https://www.facebook.com/blacklivesmatterTO/photos/a.319994704862693.1073741829.313499695512194/519230751605753/?type=3&theater (accessed 7 October 2017).

Blyth, Mark. 2010. *Austerity: The History of a Dangerous Idea.* London: Oxford University Press.

Boas, Taylor C., and Jordan Gans-Morse. 2009. "Neoliberalism: From New Liberal Philosophy to Anti-Liberal Slogan." *Studies in Comparative International Development* 44 (2): 137–61. doi:10.1007/s12116-009-9040-5.

Bohnet, Iris. 2016. *What Works: Gender Equality by Design.* Cambridge, MA: Belknap Press.

Bonilla-Silva, Eduardo. 2010. *Racism without Racists: Colour-Blind Racism and Racial Inequality in Contemporary America.* New York: Roman & Littlefield.

Borrows, John. 1998. "Wampum at Niagara: The Royal Proclamation, Canadian Legal History and Self-Government." In *Aboriginal and Treaty Rights in Canada: Essays on Law, Equity, and Respect for Difference,* edited by Michael Asch, 155–72. Vancouver: UBC Press.

Brenner, Neil, Jamie Peck, and Nik Theodore. 2010. "After Neoliberalization?" *Globalizations* 7 (3): 327–45. doi:10.1080/14747731003669669.

Brodie, Janine. 2014. "Elusive Equalities and the Great Recession: Restoration, Retrenchment and Redistribution." *International Journal of Law in Context* 10 (4): 427–41. doi:10.1017/S1744552314000202.

Brodie, Janine. 2012. "Social Literacy and Social Justice in Times of Crisis." *The Trudeau Papers* 4 (1): 114–46. http://www.trudeaufoundation.ca/sites/default/files/u5/social_literacy_and_social_justice_in_times_of_crisis_-_janine_brodie.pdf.

Brodie, Janine. 2010a. "The Social in Social Citizenship." In *Recasting the Social in Citizenship*, edited by Engin Isin, 20–43. Toronto: University of Toronto Press.

Brodie, Janine. 2010b. "The 3Ds of the Canadian Women's Movement: Delegitimization, Dismantling, Disappeared." *Equity Matters*. Federation of the Humanities and Social Sciences (29 January). http://www.ideas-idees.ca/blog/3ds-canadian-womens-movement-delegitimization-dismantling-and-disappearance.

Brodie, Janine. 2007. "Reforming Social Justice in Neoliberal Times." *Studies in Social Justice* 1 (2): 93–107. doi:10.26522/ssj.v1i2.972.

Brown, Michael P. 1997. *Replacing Citizenship: AIDS Activism and Radical Democracy*. New York: Guilford Press.

Brown, Wendy. 2015. *Undoing the Demos: Neoliberalism's Stealth Revolution*. New York: Zone Books.

Bryan, Christopher J., Carol S. Dweck, Lee Ross, Aaron C. Kay, and Natalia O. Mislavsky. 2009. "Political Mindset: Effects of Schema Priming on Liberal-Conservative Political Positions." *Journal of Experimental Social Psychology* 45 (4): 890–95. doi:10.1016/j.jesp.2009.04.007.

Butler, Judith. 2006. *Gender Trouble: Feminism and the Subversion of Identity*. New York: Routledge.

Cameron, Emilie, and Tyler Levitan. 2014. "Impact and Benefit Agreements and the Neoliberalization of Resource Governance and Indigenous-State Relations in Northern Canada." *Studies in Political Economy* 93 (1): 25–52. doi:10.1080/19187033.2014.11674963.

Campbell, Bruce. 2012. "A Tale of Two Petro-States (Part I of III): Norway Manages Its Oil Wealth Much Better than Canada Does." Canadian Centre for Policy Alternatives (1 November). http://www.policyalternatives.ca/publications/monitor/tale-two-petro-states-part-i-iii (accessed 7 October 2017).

Canada News Centre. 2012. "Connecting Canadians with Available Jobs." Government of Canada News Release, 24 May. https://www.canada.ca/en/news/archive/2012/12/connecting-canadians-available-jobs.html?=undefined&wbdisable=true (accessed 7 October 2017).

Canadian Association of Petroleum Producers (CAPP). 2015. "Aboriginal Affairs: Industry Works with Potentially Affected Aboriginal Groups to Seek Ways to Mitigate the Impacts of Oil Sands Development." *Oil Sands Today*. http://www.canadasoilsands.ca/en/explore-topics/aboriginal-affairs?utm_source=oil_sands&utm_medium=other&utm_campaign=Page+Sharing#.WeuADjXXmow.email (accessed 7 October 2017).

Canadian Association of University Teachers (CAUT). 2007. "A Partial Picture: The Representation of Equity Seeking Groups in Canada's Universities and Colleges." *CAUT Equity Review* 1: 1–5.

Canadian Board Diversity Council (CBDC). n.d. http://www.boarddiversity.ca/en/ (accessed 15 December 2016).

Canadian Centre for Diversity and Inclusion (CCDI). 2016a. "Diversity by the Numbers: The Legal Profession." Toronto: Canadian Centre for Diversity and Inclusion. http://www.ccdi.ca/attachments/DBTN_TLP_2016.pdf (accessed 7 October 2017).

Canadian Centre for Diversity and Inclusion (CCDI). 2016b. "What Gets Measured Gets Done: Measuring the Return on Investment of Diversity and Inclusion." Toronto: Canadian Centre for Diversity and Inclusion. http://ccdi.ca/wp-content/uploads/2016/06/CCDI-Report-What-Gets-Measured-Gets-Done.pdf (accessed 7 October 2017).

Canadian Federation of Independent Business (CFIB). 2014. "Taking the Temporary out of the TFW Program: Breaking Myths About the Shortage of Labour and the Temporary Foreign Worker Program." *Research* (December). http://www.cfib-fcei.ca/cfib-documents/rr3341.pdf (accessed 7 October 2017).

Canadian Parks and Wilderness Society (CPAWS) and David Suzuki Foundation. 2013. Population Critical: How are Caribou Faring? Annual Report (December). http://cpaws.org/uploads/BorealCaribouReport-CPAWS_DSF.pdf (accessed 7 October 2017).

Canadian Press. 2017. "Kevin O'Leary: Justin Trudeau Valued Diversity More Than Competence in His Cabinet." *Huffington Post* (9 March). http://www.huffingtonpost.ca/2017/03/08/kevin-oleary-trudaeu-cabinet_n_15241804.html (accessed 7 October 2017).

Catalyst. 2013. "Why Diversity Matters." Catalyst Information Centre (July). http://www.catalyst.org/system/files/why_diversity_matters_catalyst_0.pdf (accessed 7 October 2017).

CBC News. 2016. "Black Lives Matter Toronto Stalls Pride Parade." *CBC News*, 3 July. http://www.cbc.ca/news/canada/toronto/pride-parade-toronto-1.3662823 (accessed 7 October 2017).

CBC News North. 2015. "Delay to N.W.T Land and Water Superboard Brings Mixed Reactions." 2 March. http://www.cbc.ca/news/canada/north/delay-to-n-w-t-land-and-water-superboard-brings-mixed-reactions-1.2979324 (accessed 7 October 2017).

Chan, Sylvia. 2002. *Liberalism, Democracy and Development*. Cambridge: Cambridge University Press. doi:10.1017/CBO9780511491818.

Chevreau, Jonathan. 2016. "Nearly Half of Canadians are Living Paycheque to Paycheque – and That Has Big Consequences for Retirement Security." *Financial Post*, 7 September. http://business.financialpost.com/personal-finance/retirement/nearly-half-of-canadians-living-paycheque-to-paycheque-and-that-has-big-consequences-for-retirement-security/wcm/31330057-2e5c-434c-b572-2268537e62e1 (accessed 7 October 2017).

Chidester, Phil. 2008. "May the Circle Stay Unbroken: Friends, the Presence of Absences and the Rhetorical Reinforcement of Whiteness." *Critical Studies in Media Communication* 25 (2): 157–74. doi.org:10.1080/15295030802031772.

Chvasta, Marcyrose. 2006. "Anger, Irony, and Protest: Confronting the Issue of Efficacy, Again." *Text and Performance Quarterly* 26 (1): 5–16. doi:10.1080/10462930500382278.

Cingano, Federico. 2014. "Trends in Income Inequality and its Impact on Economic Growth." Organization for Economic Cooperation and Development (OECD): Social, Employment, and Migration Working Papers, no. 163. Paris: OECD Publishing. doi:10.1787/1815199X.

Clarke, John. 2012. "What Crisis Is This?" In *Soundings on the Neoliberal Crisis*, edited by Jonathan Rutherford and Sally Davidson, 44–54. London: Soundings.

Clegg, Alicia. 2017. "Unconscious Bias Hinders Diversity Recruitment: Training Has Proved Inadequate at Removing Innate Prejudices." *Financial Times*, 27 February. https://www.ft.com/content/b6065b00-d340-11e6-b06b-680c49b4b4c0.

Cole, Desmond. 2015. "The Skin I'm In: I've Been Interrogated by Police More than 50 Times—All Because I'm Black." *Toronto Life*, 21 April. http://torontolife.com/city/life/skin-im-ive-interrogated-police-50-times-im-black/ (accessed 7 October 2017).

Collins, Patricia Hill. 2000. *Black Feminist Thought: Knowledge, Consciousness, and the Politics of Empowerment*. New York: Routledge.

Connor, Kevin. 2014. "From Adversaries to Allies on Gay Rights in Toronto." *Toronto Sun*, 14 June. http://www.torontosun.com/2014/06/14/from-adversaries-to-allies-on-gay-rights-in-toronto (accessed 7 October 2017).

Coon Come, Matthew. 1996. "Remarks of Grand Chief Matthew Coon Come." Presentation at the Harvard Center for International Affairs and Kennedy School of Government, Cambridge, MA, 28 October.

Corbiere, Alan Ojiig. 2013. "Ojibwe Chief Shingwaukonse: One Who Was Not Idle." *Muskrat Magazine*, 6 June. http://muskratmagazine.com/ojibwe-chief-shingwaukonse-one-who-was-not-idleojibwe-chief-shingwaukonse-one-who-was-not-idle/ (accessed 7 October 2017).

Corntassel, Jeff. 2013. "Indigenizing the Academy: Insurgent Education and the Roles of Indigenous Intellectuals." Presentation at the Federation for the Humanities and Social Sciences. http://www.ideas-idees.ca/blog/indigenizing-academy-insurgent-education-and-roles-indigenous-intellectuals (accessed 7 October 2017) .

Coulthard, Glen. 2014. *Red Skin, White Masks: Rejecting the Colonial Politics of Recognition*. Minneapolis: Minnesota University Press. doi:10.5749/minnesota/9780816679645.001.0001.

Coulthard, Glen S. 2007. "Subjects of Empire: Indigenous People and the 'Politics of Recognition' in Canada." *Contemporary Political Theory* 6 (4): 437–60. doi:10.1057/palgrave.cpt.9300307.

Coyne, Andrew. 2015. "Trudeau Cabinet Should Be Based on Merit, Not Gender." *National Post*, 2 November. http://news.nationalpost.com/full-comment/andrew-coyne-trudeau-cabinet-should-be-built-on-merit-not-gender (accessed 7 October 2017).

Crawford, Lucas, and Robert Nichols. 2012. "Rethinking Hate Crimes: The Hard Work of Creating Social Equity." In *Beyond the Queer Alphabet: Conversations in Gender, Sexuality and Intersectionality*, edited by Malinda S. Smith and Fatima Jaffer, 57–59. Ottawa: Canadian Federation for the Humanities and Social Sciences.

Crenshaw, Kimberlé. 2016. "The Urgency of Intersectionality." TED Women (October). https://www.ted.com/talks/kimberle_crenshaw_the_urgency_of_intersectionality (accessed 7 October 2017).

Crozier, Michael, Samuel Huntington, and Joji Watanuki. 1975. *The Crisis of Democracy: Report on the Governability of Democracies to the Trilateral Commission*. New York: New York University Press.

Crul, Maurice. 2016. "Super-diversity vs assimilation: how complex diversity in majority-minority cities challenges the assumptions of assimilation." *Journal of Ethnic and Migration Studies*, 42 (1) : 54–68.

Crutzen, Paul J., and Eugene F. Stoermer. 2002. "The Anthropocene." *Global Change Magazine* 41: 17–8.

Curry, Bill. 2014. "Low-Wage Foreign Worker Program Faces Elimination: Kenney." *The Globe and Mail*, 25 June. https://beta.theglobeandmail.com/news/politics/ elimination-of-foreign-worker-program-will-be-on-the-table-in-2016/ article19322845/?ref=http://www.theglobeandmail.com& (accessed 7 October 2017).

Davidson, Julia O'Connell. 2010. "New Slavery, Old Binaries: Human Trafficking and the Borders of Freedom." *Global Networks* 10 (2): 244–61. doi:10.1111/j.1471-0374.2010.00284.x.

DeGagné, Alexa. 2015. "Investigating Citizenship, Sexuality, and the Same-Sex Marriage Fight in California's Proposition 8." PhD diss., University of Alberta.

Dei, George, and Agnes Calliste. 2000. "Introduction. Mapping the Terrain: Power, Knowledge and Anti-Racism Education." In *Power, Knowledge and Anti-Racism Education: A Critical Reader*, edited by George Dei, Agnes Calliste, and Margarida Aguiar, 11–22. Halifax: Fernwood.

D'Emilio, John. 2013. *Making Trouble: Essays on Gay History, Politics, and the University*. New York: Routledge.

D'Emilio, John. 2002. *The World Turned: Essays on Gay History, Politics, and Culture*. Durham, NC: Duke University Press. doi:10.1215/9780822383925.

Democracy Now! 2012. "Year of the Global Uprisings, from the Arab Spring to Occupy Wall Street: A Special Look Back at 2011." *Democracy Now!*, 2 January. https://www.democracynow.org/2012/1/2/year_of_global_uprisings_from_the (accessed 11 January 2016).

Dhir, Aaron. 2015. *Challenging Boardroom Homogeneity: Corporate Law, Governance, and Diversity*. New York: Cambridge University Press. doi:10.1017/ CBO9781139053327.

Diabo, Russell. 2012. "Harper Launches Major First Nations Termination Plan: As Negotiating Tables Legitimize Canada's Colonialism." *Intercontinental Cry*, 9 November. https://intercontinentalcry.org/harper-launches-major-first-nations- termination-plan-as-negotiating-tables-legitimize-canadas-colonialism (accessed 20 January 2016).

Donato, Al. 2016. "Black Lives Matter Held Pride Accountable—and Toronto Should Too." *The Torontoist*, 6 July. http://torontoist.com/2016/07/black-lives-matter-held- pride-accountable-toronto-should-too/ (accessed 20 December 2016)

Drache, Daniel. 2013. "'Rowing and Steering' Our Way out of the Staples Trap." *The Progressive Economics Forum: The Staples Theory @ 50*. http://www.progressive- economics.ca/2013/10/30/staple-theory-50-daniel-drache/ (accessed 14 January 2016).

Dreher, Rod. 2016. "What If Diversity Is Our Weakness?" *The American Conservative*, 25 March. http://www.theamericanconservative.com/dreher/diversity-weakness- utah/ (accessed 12 November 2016).

Dua, Enakshi. 2009. "On Effectiveness of Anti-Racist Policies in Canadian Universities: Issues of Implementation of Policies by Senior Administration." In *Racism in the Canadian University: Demanding Social Justice, Inclusion and Equity*, edited by Frances Henry and Carol Tator, 160–95. Toronto: University of Toronto Press.

Dubois, W.E.B. [1903] 1994. *The Souls of Black Folk*. New York: Dover Publications.

Dworkin, Ronald. 1977. *Taking Rights Seriously*. Cambridge, MA: Harvard University Press.

Dyer, Richard. 1988. *White: Essays on Race and Culture*. New York: Routledge.

The Economist. 2014. "Buttonwood: Secular Stagnation: The Long View." *The Economist*, 3 November. https://www.economist.com/blogs/buttonwood/2014/11/secular-stagnation (accessed 3 April 2016).

Elbaz, Gilbert. 1995. "Beyond Anger: The Activist Construction of the AIDS Crisis." *Social Justice* 22 (44): 43–76.

Employment and Social Development Canada (ESDC). 2014. "Temporary Foreign Worker Program - Moratorium on the Food Services Sector." http://www.cic.gc.ca/english/resources/manuals/bulletins/2014/ob574.asp (accessed 7 October 2017).

Essed, Philomena. 2004. "Cloning Amongst Professors: Normativities and Imagined Homogeneities." *NORA* 12 (2): 113–22. doi:10.1080/08038740410004588.

Essed, Philomena, and Gabriele Schwab. 2012. *Clones, Fakes and Posthumans: Cultures of Replication*. Leiden, The Netherlands: Brill.

Essed, Philomena, and David Theo Goldberg. 2002. "Cloning Cultures: The Social Injustice of Sameness." *Ethnic and Racial Studies* 25 (6): 1066–82. doi:10.1080/01419 87022000009430.

Eurasia Review. 2015. "Canada Energy Profile: One of World's Five Largest Energy Producers and Principal Source of US Energy Imports – Analysis." *Eurasia Review*, 13 November. http://www.eurasiareview.com/13112015-canada-energy-profile-one-of-worlds-five-largest-energy-producers-and-principal-source-of-us-energy-imports-analysis/ (accessed on 6 October 2017).

Fan, Donald. 2011. "Proof that Diversity Drives Innovation: Do Diverse Teams Solve More Problems Creatively than Homogenous Teams?" *DiversityInc*, 31 August. http://www.diversityinc.com/diversity-management/proof-that-diversity-drives-innovation/ (accessed 15 January 2017).

Fanon, Frantz. 1986. *Black Skin, White Masks*. London: Pluto Press.

Faraday, Fay. 2012. *Made in Canada: How the Law Constructs Migrant Workers' Insecurity*. Toronto: Metcalf Foundation. http://metcalffoundation.com/wp-content/uploads/2012/09/Made-in-Canada-Full-Report.pdf (accessed 12 January 2016).

Farinas, Richard. 2012. "Political Discontent, Anger, and Support for Social Movements: Analyzing Support for the Tea Party and Occupy Wall Street Movement." Presentation at the Southern Political Science Association Annual Conference, New Orleans, LA, 12–24 January.

Ford, Lisa. 2010. *Settler Sovereignty: Jurisdiction and Indigenous Peoples in America and Australia, 1788–1836*. Cambridge, MA: Harvard University Press.

Ford, Zack. 2014. "Laverne Cox: Loving Trans People Is a Revolutionary Act." *Think Progress*, 31 January. https://thinkprogress.org/lgbt/2014/01/31/3235351/laverne-cox-loving-trans-people-revolutionary-act/ (accessed 19 January 2016).

Foster, Jason. 2014. "From 'Canadian First' to 'Workers Unite': Evolving Union Narratives of Migrant Workers." *Relations Industrielles* 69 (2): 241–65. https://doi.org/10.7202/1025028ar.

Foster, Jason. 2012. "Making Temporary Permanent." *Just Labour: A Canadian Journal of Work and Society* 19: 22–46.

Foust, Christina R. 2010. *Transgression as a Mode of Resistance: Rethinking Social Movement in the Era of Corporate Globalization.* Lanham, MD: Lexington Books.

Frank, Thomas. 2005. *What's the Matter with Kansas? How Conservatives Won the Heart of America.* New York: Picador.

Fraser, Nancy. 2014. "Can Society Be Commodities All the Way Down? Post-Polanyian Reflections on Capitalist Crisis." *Economy and Society* 43 (4): 541–58. doi:10.1080/0 3085147.2014.898822.

Fraser, Nancy. 2013. "How Feminism Became Capitalism's Handmaiden–and How to Reclaim It." *The Guardian,* 14 October. https://www.theguardian.com/commentisfree/2013/oct/14/feminism-capitalist-handmaiden-neoliberal (accessed 3 April 2016).

Fraser, Nancy. 2009. "Feminism, Capitalism and the Cunning of History." *New Left Review* 56: 97–117.

Fraser, Nancy. 1996. "Social Justice in the Age of Identity Politics: Redistribution, Recognition and Participation." Presentation at The Tanner Lectures on Human Values, Stanford University, Stanford, CA, 30 April–2 May.

Friedman, Milton. 1982. *Capitalism and Freedom.* 2nd ed. Chicago: University of Chicago Press.

Fudge, Judy. 2012. "Precarious Migrant Status and Precarious Employment: The Paradox of International Rights for Migrant Workers." *Comparative Law and Policy Journal* 34: 101–37.

Fudge, Judy, and Fiona MacPhail. 2009. "The Temporary Foreign Worker Program in Canada." *Comparative Labor Law & Policy Journal* 31: 101–39.

Fuller, Sylvia, and Leah F. Vosko. 2008. "Temporary Employment and Social Inequality in Canada: Exploring Intersections of Gender, Race and Immigration Status." *Social Indicators Research* 88 (1): 31–50. doi:10.1007/s11205-007-9201-8.

Gallie, Walter Bryce. 1956. "Essentially Contested Concepts." *Proceedings of the Aristotelian Society* 56 (1): 167–98. doi:10.1093/aristotelian/56.1.167.

Gauthier, David P. 1986. *Morals by Agreement.* New York: Clarendon Press-Oxford University Press.

Ghosh, Amitav. 1992. "Petrofiction: The Oil Encounter and the Novel." *New Republic* 206 (9): 29–34.

Gilens, Martin, and Benjamin I. Page. 2014. "Testing Theories of American Politics: Elites, Interest Groups, and Average Citizens." *Perspectives on Politics* 12 (3): 564–81.

Gill, Stephen. 1995. "Globalization, Market Civilization, and Disciplinary Neoliberalism." *Millennium* 23 (3): 399–423. doi:10.1177/03058298950240030801.

Gill, Stephen, and A. Claire Cutler, eds. 2014. *New Constitutionalism and World Order.* Cambridge: Cambridge University Press. doi:10.1017/CBO9781107284142.

Goldberg, David Theo. 2001. *The Racial State.* New York: Wiley Blackwell.

Goldring, Luin, Carolina Berinstein, and Judith Bernhard. 2009. "Institutionalizing Precarious Migrant Status in Canada." *Citizenship Studies* 13 (3): 239–65. doi:10.1080/13621020902850643.

Goldring, Luin, and Patricia Landolt, eds. 2013. *Producing and Negotiating Non-Citizenship: Precarious Legal Status in Canada.* Toronto: University of Toronto Press.

Goodwin, Jeff, James M. Jasper, and Francesca Polletta. 2001. "Introduction: Why
    Emotions Matter." In *Passionate Politics: Emotions and Social Movements*, edited by
    Jeff Goodwin, James M. Jasper, and Francesca Polletta, 1–24. Chicago: University of
    Chicago Press. doi:10.7208/chicago/9780226304007.003.0001.

Gothoskar, Ruchika. 2015. "Gender Goes Beyond Genitals: What the Amendments
    to Bill C-279 Mean for Trans People." *The Silhouette: McMaster University's Student
    Newspaper*, 12 March. http://www.thesil.ca/gender-goes-beyond-genitals (accessed
    19 January 2016).

Gould, Deborah. 2002. "Life during Wartime: Emotions and the Development of ACT
    UP." *Mobilization: An International Quarterly* 7 (2): 177–200.

Gourevitch, Peter. 1986. *The Politics of Hard Times*. Ithaca, NY: Cornell University Press.

Goutor, David. 2007. *Guarding the Gates: The Canadian Labour Movement and Immigration,
    1872–1934.* Vancouver: UBC Press.

Government of Alberta. 2016. "Oil Prices: Price Per Barrel of WCS Oil in US Dollars."
    http://economicdashboard.alberta.ca/OilPrice (accessed 10 October 2017).

Government of British Columbia. 2013. "Aboriginal Post-Secondary Education and
    Training Policy Framework and Action Plan. 2020 Vision for the Future." Minister
    of Advanced Education, Innovation and Technology. http://www2.gov.bc.ca/
    assets/gov/education/post-secondary-education/aboriginal-education-training/
    aboriginal_action_plan.pdf (accessed 10 October 2017)

Government of Canada. 2016. "Bill C-16: An Act to Amend the Canadian Human
    Rights Act and the Criminal Code." Parliament of Canada.
    https://openparliament.ca/bills/42-1/C-16/ (accessed 7 October 2017).

Government of Canada. 2014. "Overhauling the Temporary Foreign Worker Program:
    Putting Canadians First." http://www.amssa.org/wp-content/uploads/2015/05/
    Overhauling-the-TFWP-Putting-Canadians-First.pdf (accessed 7 October 2017).

Gramsci, Antonio. 1971. *Selections from the Prison Notebooks.* Translated by Geoffrey
    Smith and Quintin Hoare. London: Lawrence & Wishart.

Grant, Tavia. 2017. "Immigrants Will Comprise Growing Share of Canada's Population
    by 2036: StatsCan." *The Globe and Mail*, 25 January. https://beta.theglobeandmail.
    com/news/national/immigrant-nation-newcomers-will-comprise-a-growing-
    share-of-canadas-population/article33755105/?ref=http://www.theglobeandmail.
    com& (accessed 1 February 2017).

Green, David A., and Jonathan R. Kesselman. 2011. *Dimensions of Inequality in Canada*.
    Vancouver: UBC Press.

Greenblatt, Alan. 2007. "Putnam's Paradox: Diversity Accomplishes Many Things–
    but It May Not Make Us Better Citizens." *Governing* (November). http://www.
    governing.com/topics/health-human-services/Putnams-Paradox.html (accessed 3
    December 2016).

Griffith, Andrew. 2016. "We Need a Baseline of Information about Diversity in Judicial
    Appointments, in Order to Evaluate the Government's Promises." *Policy Options*,
    4 May. http://policyoptions.irpp.org/2016/05/04/diversity-among-federal-
    provincial-judges/ (accessed 3 January 2017).

Gross, Dominique. 2014. "Temporary Foreign Workers in Canada: Are They Really
    Filling Labour Shortages?" C.D. Howe Institute Commentary No. 407.
    https://www.cdhowe.org/public-policy-research/temporary-foreign-workers-

canada-are-they-really-filling-labour-shortages (accessed 12 January 2016). doi:10.2139/ssrn.2428817.

Grossi, Renata. 2012. "The Meaning of Love in the Debate for Legal Recognition of Same-Sex Marriage in Australia." *International Journal of Law in Context* 8 (4): 487–505. doi:10.1017/S1744552312000341.

Guidotto, Nadia. 2011. "Looking Back: The Bathhouse Raids in Toronto, 1981." In *Captive Genders: Trans Embodiment and the Prison Industrial Complex*, edited Eric A. Stanley and Nat Smith, 63–76. Edinburgh: AK Press, 2011.

Guo, Shibao, and Zenobia Jamal. 2007. "Nurturing Cultural Diversity in Higher Education: A Critical Review of Selected Models." *Canadian Journal of Higher Education* 43 (5): 27–49.

Haber, Stephen, and Victor Menaldo. 2011. "Do Natural Resources Fuel Authoritarianism? A Reappraisal of the Resource Curse." *American Political Science Review* 105 (1): 1–26. doi:10.1017/S0003055410000584.

Hall, Peter A. 2015. "The Changing Role of the State in Liberal Market Economies." In *Oxford Handbook on the Transformation of the State*, edited by Stephan Leibfried, Evelyne Huber, Matthew Lange, Jonah D. Levy, and Frank Nullmeier, 426–44. Oxford: Oxford University Press.

Hall, Stuart. 1986. "Gramsci's Relevance for the Study of Race and Ethnicity." *Journal of Communication Inquiry* 10 (2): 5–27. doi:10.1177/019685998601000202.

Hall, Stuart, and Doreen Massey. 2012. "Interpreting the Crisis." In *Soundings on the Neoliberal Crisis*, edited by Jonathan Rutherford and Sally Davidson, 55–69. London: Soundings.

Haluza-DeLay, Randy, and Angela V. Carter. 2014. "Joining Up and Scaling Up: Analysing Resistance to Canada's 'Dirty Oil.'" *Cultural Studies of Science Education* 9: 343–62.

Haque, Eve. 2012. *Multiculturalism within a Bilingual Framework*. Toronto: University of Toronto Press.

Harper, Tim. 2012. "Diane Finley Wants More Canadians Working at McDonald's." *The Toronto Star,* 24 May. https://www.thestar.com/news/canada/2012/05/24/tim_harper_diane_finley_wants_more_canadians_working_at_mcdonalds.html (accessed 12 January 2016).

Harris, John. 2011. "Global Protests: Is 2011 a Year that Will Change the World?" *The Guardian,* 15 November. https://www.theguardian.com/world/2011/nov/15/global-protests-2011-change-the-world (accessed 11 January 2016).

Hedges, Chris. 2013. "Let's Get This Class War Started." *Truthdig,* 20 October. https://www.truthdig.com/articles/lets-get-this-class-war-started/ (accessed 20 October 2013).

Helsen, Werner, Jan van Winckel, and A. Mark Williams. 2005. "The Relative Age Effect in Youth Soccer across Europe." *Journal of Sports Sciences* 23 (6): 629–36. doi:10.1080/02640410400021310.

Henry, Frances. 2004. "Understanding the Experiences of Visible Minority and Aboriginal Faculty Members at Queen's University: Report on the 2003 Study." Kingston, ON: Queen's University. http://www.queensu.ca/provost/sites/webpublish.queensu.ca.provwww/files/files/SystemicRacism.pdf (accessed 26 January 2016).

Henry, Frances, and Carol Tator. 2009. "Introduction: Racism in the Canadian University." In *Racism in the Canadian University: Demanding Social Justice, Inclusion and Equity*, edited by Frances Henry and Carol Tator, 3–21. Toronto: University of Toronto Press.

Henry, Frances, Enakshi Dua, Audrey Kobayashi, Carl James, Peter Li, Howard Ramos, and Malinda S. Smith. 2017a. *The Equity Myth: Racialization and Indigeneity in Canadian University*. Vancouver: UBC Press.

Henry, Frances, Enakshi Dua, Audrey Kobayashi, Carl James, Peter Li, Howard Ramos, and Malinda S. Smith. 2017b. "Race, Racialization and Indigeneity in Canadian Universities." *Race, Ethnicity and Education* 20 (3): 300–14. doi:10.1080/13613324.2016.1260226.

Hewlett, Sylvia Ann, Melinda Marshall, and Laura Sherbin. 2013. "How Diversity Can Drive Innovation." *Harvard Business Review*, December. https://hbr.org/2013/12/how-diversity-can-drive-innovation (accessed 4 December 2016).

Heylen, Freddy, and Gerdie Everaert. 2000. "Success and Failure of Fiscal Consolidation in the OECD: A Multivariate Analysis." *Public Choice* 105 (1–2): 103–24. doi:10.1023/A:1005130929435 (accessed 11 October 2017).

Higgs, Malcolm, Ulrich Plewnia, and Jorg Ploch. 2005. "Influence of Team Composition and Task Complexity on Team Performance." *Team Performance Management* 11 (7/8): 227–50. doi:10.1108/13527590510635134.

Hixson, Walter L. 2013. *American Settler Colonialism: A History*. New York, NY: Palgrave-MacMillan. doi:10.1057/9781137374264.

Hobbes, Thomas. 1996. *Leviathan*. Cambridge: Cambridge University Press.

Hoberg, George. 2014. "Canada: The Overachieving Petro-State." *Green Policy Prof*, 20 January. http://greenpolicyprof.org/wordpress/?p=952 (accessed 14 January 2016).

Holmes, Mary. 2004. "Feeling Beyond Rules: Politicizing the Sociology of Emotion and Anger in Feminist Politics." *European Journal of Social Theory* 7 (2): 209–27. doi:10.1177/1368431004041752.

Homer-Dixon, Thomas. 2013. "The Tar Sands Disaster." *New York Times*, 31 March. http://www.nytimes.com/2013/04/01/opinion/the-tar-sands-disaster.html?_r=0 (accessed 14 January 2016).

Hong, Lu, and Scott E. Page. 2004. "Groups of Diverse Problem Solvers Can Outperform Groups of High-ability Problem Solvers." *Current Issue* 101 (46): 16385–89.

hooks, bell. 1996. *Killing Rage: Ending Racism*. New York: First Owl Books.

Hubbard, Phil. 2004. "Revenge and Injustice in the Neoliberal City: Uncovering Masculinist Agendas." *Antipode* 36 (4): 665–86. doi:10.1111/j.1467-8330.2004.00442.x.

Hui, Stephen. 2013. "Five Reasons Why We Should Stop Calling White People 'Caucasian.'" *The Georgia Straight*, 8 November. https://www.straight.com/blogra/526526/five-reasons-why-we-should-stop-calling-white-people-caucasian (accessed 20 October 2017).

Hunt, Vivian, Dennis Layton, and Sara Prince. 2015. "Why Diversity Matters." McKinsey & Company, January. http://www.mckinsey.com/business-functions/organization/our-insights/why-diversity-matters (accessed 15 January 2017).

Huntington, Samuel P. 1991. *The Third Wave: Democratization in the Late Twentieth Century*. Norman: University of Oklahoma Press.

Innis, Harold. [1930] 1977. *The Fur Trade in Canada: An Introduction to Canadian Economic History*. Toronto: University of Toronto Press.

International Energy Agency (IEA). 2014. *World Energy Outlook 2014*. London: IEA.

Iverson, Susan VanDeventer. 2007. "Camouflaging Power and Privilege: A Critical Race Analysis of University Diversity Policies." *Educational Administration Quarterly* 43 (5): 586–611. doi:10.1177/0013161X07307794.

Jackson, Andrew. 2013. "The Distribution of Wealth: Implications for the Neoliberal Justification for Economic Inequality." *The Broadbent Blog*, 23 January. https://www.pressprogress.com/en/blog/andrew-jackson-distribution-wealth-implications-neo-liberal-justification-economic-inequality (accessed 14 January 2016).

Jackson, Ben. 2005. "The Conceptual History of Social Justice." *Political Studies Review* 3 (3): 356–73. doi:10.1111/j.1478-9299.2005.00028.x.

James, Carl. 2009. "'It Will Happen Without Putting in Place Special Measures': Racially Diversifying Universities." In *Racism in the Canadian University: Demanding Social Justice, Inclusion and Equity*, edited by Frances Henry and Carol Tator, 128–59. Toronto: University of Toronto Press.

James, Carl. 2012. "Strategies of Engagement: How Racialized Faculty Negotiate the University System." *Canadian Ethnic Studies* 44 (2): 133–52. doi:10.1353/ces.2012.0007.

James Bay and Northern Quebec Agreement (JBNQA). 1974. http://www.gcc.ca/pdf/LEG000000006.pdf#page16 (accessed 14 January 2016).

Jedwab, Jack. 2016. "Many Canadians Don't Realize They're Part of a Majority-Minority." *Huffington Post Living Blog*, 8 August. http://www.huffingtonpost.ca/jack-jedwab/many-canadians-unaware-th_b_11389308.html (accessed 15 January 2017).

Jennex, Craig. 2015. "No More Shit! Complicated Collectivity, Past and Present." GUTS 3 (January). http://gutsmagazine.ca/slider/no-shit (accessed 19 January 2016).

Jenson, Jane, and Martin Papillon. 2000. *Backgrounder: Citizenship and the Recognition of Cultural Diversity: The Canadian Experience*. Ottawa: Canadian Policy Research Network.

Jiménez, Marina. 2007. "Do ethnic enclaves impede integration?" Globe and Mail (February 8). https://beta.theglobeandmail.com/news/national/do-ethnic-enclaves-impede-integration/article1070403/

Johnson, Calmers. 1982. *MITI and the Japanese Miracle: The Growth of Industrial Policy, 1925–1975*. Stanford, CA: Stanford University Press.

Johnson, Darlene. 2005. "Connecting People to Place: Great Lakes Aboriginal History in Cultural Context." Prepared for The Ipperwash Commission of Inquiry. https://www.attorneygeneral.jus.gov.on.ca/inquiries/ipperwash/transcripts/pdf/P1_Tab_1.pdf (accessed 4 December 2016).

Johnston, Basil. 1982. *Ojibway Heritage*. Toronto: McClelland and Stewart.

Kahler, Miles, and David Lake. 2013. "Introduction: Anatomy of Crisis: The Great Recession and Political Change." In *Politics in the New Hard Times: The Great Recession in Comparative Perspective*, edited by Miles Kahler and David Lake, 1–9. Ithaca, NY: Cornell University Press.

Kamier, Rawiya. 2015. "How Social Justice Became Cool." *The Fader*, 25 November. http://www.fader.com/2015/11/25/how-social-justice-became-cool (accessed 4 July 2016).

Kaplan, Soren. 2012. *Leapfrogging: Harness the Power of Surprise for Business Breakthroughs.* San Francisco: Berrett-Koehler Publishers.

Karl, Terry Lynn. 1997. *The Paradox of Plenty: Oil Booms and Petro-States.* Oakland: University of California Press.

Kawachi, Ichiro, and S.V. Subramanian. 2014. "Income Inequality." In *Social Epidemiology*, edited by Lisa Berkman, Ichiro Kawachi, and M. Maria Glymour, 126–52. Oxford: Oxford University Press.

Kelly, Erin, ed. 2001. *Justice as Fairness: A Restatement—John Rawls.* Cambridge, MA: Harvard University Press.

Kelly, Erin, David Schindler, P.V. Hodson, J.W. Short, R. Radmanovich, and C.C. Nielsen. 2010. "Oil Sands Development Contributes Elements Toxic at Low Concentrations to the Athabasca River and Its Tributaries." *Proceedings of the National Academy of Sciences of the United States of America* 107 (37): 16178–83. doi:10.1073/pnas.1008754107.

Kelly, Sean. 2012. "Avoid 'Group Think': Diverse Teams Are More Creative." *Creativity Seminar Blog,* July. http://creativityseminar.blogspot.ca/2012/07/choose-someone-whos-different-diverse.html (accessed 15 January 2017).

Khan, Razib. 2011. "Stop Using the Word 'Caucasian' to Mean White." *Discover,* 22 January. http://blogs.discovermagazine.com/gnxp/2011/01/stop-using-the-word-caucasian-to-mean-white/#.WETM_NOGP-Y (accessed 16 October 2017).

Kinsman, Gary, and Patrizia Gentile. 2010. *The Canadian War on Queers: National Security as Sexual Regulation.* Vancouver: UBC Press.

Kintz, Linda. 1997. *Between Jesus and the Market: The Emotions that Matter in Right-Wing America.* Durham, NC: Duke University Press. doi:10.1215/9780822382102.

Klein, Naomi. 2015. *This Changes Everything: Capitalism vs. The Climate.* Toronto: Knopf Canada.

Klein, Naomi. 2013. "Dancing the World into Being: A Conversation with Idle No More's Leanne Simpson." *Yes! Magazine,* 3 March. http://www.yesmagazine.org/peace-justice/dancing-the-world-into-being-a-conversation-with-idle-no-more-leanne-simpson (accessed 20 January 2016).

Kobayashi, Audrey, Laura Cameron, and Andrew Baldwin, eds. 2011. *Rethinking the Great White North: Race, Nature and the Historical Geographies of Whiteness in Canada.* Vancouver: UBC Press.

Kouri-Towe, Natalie. 2011. "Sanitizing Pride." *Briar Patch*, 6 May. https://briarpatchmagazine.com/articles/view/sanitizing-pride (accessed 7 October 2017).

Lackenbauer, Whitney P. 2008. "Carrying the Burden of Peace: Mohawks, the Canadian Forces and the Oka Crisis." *Journal of Military and Strategic Studies* 10 (2): 1–71.

LaDuke, Winona. 2002. *The Winona LaDuke Reader: A Collection of Essential Readings.* Penticton, BC: Theytus Books.

LaDuke, Winona. 2013. "Why First Nations Movement Is Our Best Chance for Clean Land and Water." *Yes! Magazine,* 9 January. http://www.yesmagazine.org/people-power/first-nations-movement-is-best-chance-for-clean-land-water (accessed 11 January 2016).

Lambertus, Sandra. 2004. *Wartime Images, Peacetime Wounds: The Media and the Gustafsen Lake Standoff.* Toronto: University of Toronto Press.

LaRoque, Emma. 2010. *When the Other Is Me: Native Resistance Discourse, 1850–1990.* Winnipeg: University of Manitoba Press.

Lascelles, Eric. 2016. "The Postcrisis Shift is Underway: What Took So Long?" *Globe and Mail*, 26 April, A12.

Lavelle, Ashley. 2013. *The Death of Social Democracy: Political Consequences in the 21st Century.* London: Ashgate.

Laxer, Michael. 2015. "Reinforcing Male Privilege: The Trudeau Cabinet, Andrew Coyne, and the Mythology of 'Merit.'" *Feminist Current*, 4 November. http://www.feministcurrent.com/2015/11/04/reinforcing-male-privilege-the-trudeau-cabinet-andrew-coyne-and-the-mythology-of-merit/ (accessed 1 March 2017).

Leach, Andrew. 2013. "Canada, the Failed Petrostate?" *Maclean's*, 4 November. http://www.macleans.ca/economy/economicanalysis/canada-the-failed-petrostate/ (accessed 14 January 2016).

Leap Manifesto. 2015. "The Leap Manifesto: A Call for a Canada Based on Caring for the Earth and One Another." https://leapmanifesto.org/en/the-leap-manifesto/ (accessed 10 January 2016).

Leavitt, Sarah. 2016a. "Police Forces Fail When Not Reflective of Diverse Population, Activists Say." *CBC News*, 24 March. http://www.cbc.ca/news/canada/montreal/quebec-police-forces-diversity-1.3505293 (accessed 4 January 2017).

Leavitt, Sarah. 2016b. "Quebec's Police Forces Still Overwhelmingly White." *CBC News*, 23 March. http://www.cbc.ca/news/canada/montreal/quebec-police-hiring-visible-minorities-1.3502667 (accessed 4 January 2017).

LeBaron, Genevieve. 2015. "Unfree Labor Beyond Binaries: Insecurity, Social Hierarchy, and Labor Market Restructuring." *International Feminist Journal of Politics* 17 (1): 1–19. doi:10.1080/14616742.2013.813160.

LeMenager, Stephanie. 2014. *Living Oil: Petroleum Culture in the American Century.* Oxford: Oxford University Press. doi:10.1093/acprof:oso/9780199899425.001.0001.

Lemieux, Tracy, and Jean-Francois Nadeau. 2015. *Temporary Foreign Workers in Canada: A Look at Regions and Occupational Skill.* Ottawa: Office of the Parliamentary Budget Officer. http://www.pbo-dpb.gc.ca/web/default/files/files/files/TFW_EN.pdf (accessed 12 January 2016).

Lenard, Patti Tamara, and Christine Straehl, eds. 2012. *Legislated Inequality: Temporary Labour Migration in Canada.* Montreal: McGill-Queen's University Press.

Lenon, Suzanne. 2011. "Why Is Our Love an Issue? Same-Sex Marriage and the Racial Politics of the Ordinary." *Social Identities* 17 (3): 351–72. doi:10.1080/13504630.2011.570975.

Leo, Geoff. 2014. "Waitresses in Saskatchewan Lose Jobs to Foreign Workers." *CBC News*. 18 April. http://www.cbc.ca/news/canada/saskatchewan/waitresses-in-saskatchewan-lose-jobs-to-foreign-workers-1.2615157 (accessed 12 January 2016).

Leung, Angela Ka-yee, William W. Maddux, Adam D. Galinsky, and Chi-yue Chiu. 2008. "Multicultural Experience Enhances Creativity: The When and How." *American Psychologist* 63 (3): 169–81. doi:10.1037/0003-066X.63.3.169.

Levine, Sheen S., Evan P. Apfelbaum, Mark Bernard, Valerie L. Bartelt, Edward J. Zajac, and David Stark. 2014. "Ethnic Diversity Deflates Price Bubbles." *Current Issue* 111 (82): 18524–29.

Levine, Sheen, and David Stark. 2015. "Diversity Makes You Brighter." *New York Times*, 9 December. https://www.ncbi.nlm.nih.gov/pmc/articles/PMC4284549/ (accessed 7 October 2017).

Lewis, Hannah, Peter Dwyer, Stuart Hodkinson, and Louise Waite. 2014. "Hyper-Precarious Lives: Migrants, Work, and Forced Labour in the Global North." *Progress in Human Geography*. http://eprints.whiterose.ac.uk/85419/1/Prog_Hum_Geogr_2014_Lewis_0309132514548303.pdf (accessed 12 January 2016).

Li, Peter. 2012. "Differences in Employment: Income of University Professors." *Canadian Ethnic Studies* 44 (2): 39–48. doi:10.1353/ces.2012.0012.

Linklater, Andrew. 2014. "Anger and World Politics: How Collective Emotions Shift Over Time." *International Theory* 6 (03): 574–78. doi:10.1017/S1752971914000293.

Logie, Carmen H., and Marie-Jolie Rwigema. 2014. "'The Normative Idea of Queer is a White Person': Understanding Perceptions of White Privilege among Lesbian, Bisexual, and Queer Women of Colour in Toronto, Canada." *Journal of Lesbian Studies* 18 (2): 174–91. doi:10.1080/10894160.2014.849165.

Long, John S. 2010. *Treaty No. 9: Making the Agreement to Share the Land in Far Northern Ontario in 1905*. Montreal: McGill-Queen's University Press.

Lorde, Audre. 1984. *Sister Outsider*. New York: Random House.

Lyman, Peter. 2004. "The Domestication of Anger: The Use and Abuse of Anger in Politics." *European Journal of Social Theory* 7 (2): 133–47. doi:10.1177/1368431004041748.

Lynk, Michael. 2009. "Labour and the New Inequality." *University of New Brunswick Law Journal* 59: 14–40.

Lyons, Oren. 1986. "Indian Self-Government in the Haudenosaunee Constitution." *Nordic Journal of International Law* 55 (1): 117–21. doi:10.1163/157181086X00337.

MacDonald, Fiona. 2011. "Indigenous Peoples and Neoliberal 'Privatization' in Canada: Opportunities, Cautions and Constraints." *Canadian Journal of Political Science* 44 (2): 257–73. doi:10.1017/S000842391100014X.

Mann, Arshy. 2016a. "Black Lives Matter to Be Honoured Group at Toronto Pride." *Daily Xtra Online*, 16 February. https://www.dailyxtra.com/black-lives-matter-to-be-honoured-group-at-toronto-pride-70195 (accessed 20 December 2016).

Mann, Arshy. 2016b. "Pride Toronto Backtracks from Black Lives Matter Promises." *Daily Xtra Online*, 4 July. https://www.dailyxtra.com/pride-toronto-backtracks-from-black-lives-matter-promises-71431 (accessed 20 December 2016).

Marcoux, Jacques, Katie Nicholsen, Vera-Lynn Kubinec, and Holy Moore. 2016. "CBC Investigates: Police Diversity Fails to Keep Pace with Canadian Populations." CBC *News*, 14 July. http://www.cbc.ca/news/canada/police-diversity-canada-1.3677952 (accessed 5 January 2017).

Marinakis, Christina. 2015. "What Are the Benefits of Having Diversity in a Jury Panel?" *Litigation Insights*, 30 September. http://litigationinsights.com/jurors/benefits-diversity-jury/ (accessed 7 October 2017).

Marsden, Sara. 2011. "Assessing the Regulation of Temporary Foreign Workers in Canada." *Osgoode Hall Law Journal* 49: 39–70.

Matulewicz, Kaitlyn. 2015. "Law and the Construction of Institutionalized Sexual Harassment in Restaurants." *Canadian Journal of Law and Society* 30 (3): 401–19. doi:10.1017/cls.2015.12.

Maugeri, Leonardo. 2013. "The Shale Oil Boom: A U.S. Phenomenon." Discussion Paper—Belfer Center for Science and International Affairs, Harvard Kennedy School, June. https://www.belfercenter.org/publication/shale-oil-boom-us-phenomenon (accessed 14 January 2016).

McEwen, Joan I. 1995. *Report in Respect of the Political Science Department of the University of British Columbia.* Vancouver: University of British Columbia.

McFarland, Janet. 2015. "Women, Minorities Making Gains on Canadian Corporate Boards: Report." *The Globe and Mail*, 19 November. https://beta.theglobeandmail.com/report-on-business/women-minorities-making-gains-on-corporate-boards-report/article27325474/?ref=http://www.theglobeandmail.com& (accessed 4 January 2017).

McFarland, Janet. 2014. "Women Gain on Corporate Boards but Visible Minority Representation Dips." *The Globe and Mail*, 19 November. https://beta.theglobeandmail.com/report-on-business/corporate-boards-now-have-more-women-fewer-minorities/article21641463/?ref=http://www.theglobeandmail.com& (accessed 4 January 2017).

McFarland, Janet. 2013. "Percentage of Visible Minority Directors on Canadian Corporate Boards Dropping." *The Globe and Mail*, 25 November. https://beta.theglobeandmail.com/report-on-business/careers/management/percentage-of-visible-minority-directors-on-canadian-corporate-boards-getting-smaller/article15588021/?ref=http://www.theglobeandmail.com& (accessed 5 January 2017).

McMaster University, Office of Human Rights and Equity Services. 2001. *Recognizing Sexual Diversity at McMaster University: Experiences of Gay, Lesbian, Bisexual and Queer Students, Staff and Faculty Members.* http://equity.mcmaster.ca/documents/recognizing-sexual-diversity-at-mcmaster.pdf/view (accessed 8 August 2016).

Meissner, Fran, and Steven Vertovec. 2015. "Comparing Super-Diversity" *Ethnic and Racial Studies* 38 (4): 541–55. doi:10.1080/01419870.2015.980295.

Mercer, Ilana. 2007. "Greater Diversity Equals More Misery." *Orange County Register*, 22 July. http://www.ocregister.com/opinion/putnam-59065-diversity-social.html (accessed 15 July 2016).

Miller, Peter, and Nikolas Rose. 2008. *Governing the Present: Administering Economic, Social and Personal Life.* Cambridge: Polity Press.

Mills, Charles W. 1997. *The Racial Contract.* Ithaca, NY: Cornell University Press.

Mills, Suzanne, and Brenden Sweeney. 2013. "Employment Relations in the Neo-Staples Resource Economy: Impact Benefit Agreements and Aboriginal Governance in Canada's Nickel Mining Industry." *Studies in Political Economy* 91 (1): 7–34. doi:10.1080/19187033.2013.11674980.

Mirza, Munera. 2010. "Rethinking Race." *Prospect* 22 (175): 30–32.

Mitchell, Michael. 1989. "An Unbroken Assertion of Sovereignty." In *Drumbeat: Anger and Renewal in Indian Country*, edited by Boyce Richardson, 105–36. Toronto: Summerhill Press.

Mitchell, Timothy. 2011. *Carbon Democracy: Political Power in the Age of Oil.* London: Verso Books.

Mochama, Vicky. 2016. "Are Canada's Newspapers Too White? Most Refused to Say." *Canadaland*, 2 March. http://www.canadalandshow.com/are-canadas-newspapers-too-white-most-refused-say/ (accessed 15 January 2017).

Momani, Bessma, and Jillian Stirk. 2017. "Opinion: The Diversity Dividend: Canada's Global Advantage." *Vancouver Sun*, 24 February. http://vancouversun.com/opinion/opinion-the-diversity-dividend-canadas-global-advantage (accessed 10 March 2017).

Monbiot, George. 2016. "Neoliberalism—the Ideology at the Root of All Our Problems." *The Guardian,* 15 April. https://www.theguardian.com/books/2016/apr/15/neoliberalism-ideology-problem-george-monbiot? (accessed 20 May 2016).

Monture, Rick. 2014. *We Share Our Matters: Two Centuries of Writing and Resistance at Six Nations of the Grand River.* Winnipeg: University of Manitoba Press.

Morris, Lydia. 2001. "Stratified Rights and the Management of Migration: National Distinctiveness in Europe." *European Societies* 3 (4): 387–411. doi:10.1080/14616690120112190.

Nakache, Delphine. 2013. "The Canadian Temporary Foreign Worker Program: Regulations, Practices, and Protection Gaps." In *Producing and Negotiating Non-Citizens: Precarious Legal Status in Canada,* edited by Luin Goldring and Patricia Landolt, 71–98. Toronto: University of Toronto Press.

Nakache, Delphine, and Sarah D'Aoust. 2012. "Provincial/Territorial Nominee Programs: An Avenue to Permanent Residency for Low-Skilled Temporary Foreign Workers?" In *Legislated Inequality: Temporary Labour Migration in Canada,* edited by Patti Tamara Lenard and Christine Straehle, 158–77. Montreal: McGill-Queen's University Press.

Nikiforuk, Andrew. 2010. *Tar Sands: Dirty Oil and the Future of a Continent.* Vancouver: Greystone Books.

Nisga'a Lisims Government. 1998. *Understanding the Treaty.* http://www.nisgaanation.ca/understanding-treaty (accessed 20 January 2016).

Noble, Greg. 2011. "'Bumping into Alterity': Transacting Cultural Complexities." *Continuum (Perth)* 25 (6): 827–40. doi:10.1080/10304312.2011.617878.

Nolan, Joseph E., and Grace Howell. 2010. "Hockey Success and Birth Date: The Relative Age Effect Revisited." *International Review for the Sociology of Sport* 45 (4): 507–12. doi:10.1177/1012690210371560.

Norris, Pippa. 2011. *Democratic Deficit: Critical Citizens Revisited.* New York: Cambridge University Press. doi:10.1017/CBO9780511973383.

Nozick, Robert. 1974. *Anarchy, State, and Utopia.* New York: Basic Books.

Nuttall, Jeremy. 2013. "Chinese Miner Permits Investigated by BC Government." *The Canadian Press,* 21 October. http://www.huffingtonpost.ca/2012/10/23/chinese-miner-recruitment-investigated_n_2004352.html (accessed 12 January 2016).

Offe, Claus. 2011. "Crisis and Innovation of Liberal Democracy: Can Deliberation Be Institutionalised?" *Czech Sociological Review* 3: 447–72.

O'Keefe, Derek. 2013. "Seize the Moment, Stand with Elsipogog." *The Straight,* 18 October. http://www.straight.com/news/509291/derrick-okeefe-seize-moment-stand-elsipogtog (accessed 20 January 2016).

Organisation for Economic Co-Operation and Development (OECD). 2014. "Does Income Inequality Hurt Economic Growth?" *Focus on Inequality and Growth.*

http://www.oecd.org/social/Focus-Inequality-and-Growth-2014.pdf (accessed 14 January 2016).

Organisation for Economic Co-Operation and Development (OECD). 2011. *Divided We Stand: Why Inequality Keeps Rising*. http://www.oecd.org/els/soc/49170768.pdf (accessed 14 January 2016).

Organisation for Economic Co-Operation and Development (OECD). 2008. *Growing Unequal? Income Distribution and Poverty in OECD Countries*. http://www.oecd.org/els/soc/41527936.pdf (accessed 14 January 2016).

Ost, David. 2004. "Politics as the Mobilization of Anger: Emotions in Movements and in Power." *European Journal of Social Theory* 7 (2): 229–44. doi:10.1177/1368431004041753.

Ostry, Jonathan, Prakash Loungani, and Davide Furceri. 2016. "Neoliberalism: Oversold?" *Finance & Development* 53 (2): 38–41.

Oxfam. 2017. "An Economy for the 99%." Oxfam Briefing Paper. 16 January. https://www.oxfam.org/en/research/economy-99 (accessed 1 February 2017).

Oxfam. 2016. "An Economy for the 1%." 210 Oxfam Briefing Paper. 18 January. https://www.oxfam.org/sites/www.oxfam.org/files/file_attachments/bp210-economy-one-percent-tax-havens-180116-en_0.pdf (accessed 3 April 2016).

Pachner, Joanna. 2016. "How to Make Corporate Boards More Diverse." *Canadian Business*, 7 January. http://www.canadianbusiness.com/innovation/building-better-boards-diversity/ (accessed 4 January 2017).

Page, Jillian. 2015. "#wejustneedtopee: Transgender Rights Movement Growing in Canada, U.S." *Montreal Gazette,* 14 March. http://montrealgazette.com/life/wejustneedtopee-transgender-revolution-growing-in-canada-u-s (accessed 19 January 2016).

Palmater, Pamela. 2016. "Ontario Policing: Gang Rape, Murder, and Child Porn." *TeleSUR*, 1 February.

Pateman, Carole, and Charles Mills. 2007. *The Contract and Domination*. New York: Polity.

Paul, Joshua. 2014. "Post-Racial Futures: Imagining Post-Racialist Anti-Racisms." *Journal of Ethnic and Racial Studies* 37 (4): 702–18. doi:10.1080/01419870.2014.857031.

Peake, Linda, and Brian Ray. 2001. "Racializing the Canadian Landscape. Whiteness, Uneven Geography and Social Justice." *Canadian Geographer* 45 (1): 168–76.

Peck, Jamie. 1996. *Work-Place: The Social Regulation of Labor Markets*. London: Guilford Press.

Perdue, Anne. 2009. "Out and Proud: How Students, Faculty, Staff and Alumni Brought Queer Activism to the University of Toronto and Changed the Campus Forever." *University of Toronto Magazine* (Autumn). http://magazine.utoronto.ca/cover-story/out-and-proud-history-of-gay-lesbian-activism-toronto-anne-perdue/ (accessed 19 January 2016).

Pew Research Center. 2011. "Occupy Wall Street and Inequality." Pew Research Centre: U.S., Politics & Policy, 15 December. http://www.people-press.org/2011/12/15/section-2-occupy-wall-street-and-inequality (accessed 11 January 2016).

Phillips, Katherine W. 2014. "How Diversity Makes Us Smarter." *Scientific American*, 1 October. https://www.scientificamerican.com/article/how-diversity-makes-us-smarter/ (accessed 3 January 2017).

Piketty, Thomas. 2016. "Panama Papers: Act Now. Don't Wait for Another Crisis." *The Guardian*, 9 April. https://www.theguardian.com/commentisfree/2016/apr/09/panama-papers-tax-havens-thomas-piketty (accessed 20 July 2016).

Piketty, Thomas. 2014. *Capital in the Twenty-First Century*. Cambridge, MA: Belknap Press. doi:10.4159/9780674369542.

Plattner, Marc F. 2013. "Reflections on Governance." *Journal of Democracy* 24 (4): 17–28. doi:10.1353/jod.2013.0058.

Polanyi, Karl. 2001. *The Great Transformation: The Political and Economic Origins of Our Time*. 2nd ed. Boston: Beacon Press.

Porter, Ann. 2013. "Privatizing Social Policy in an Age of Austerity: The Canadian Case." Presentation at the New Policies of Privatization International Conference on Public Policy, Grenoble, France, 26–28 June. http://archives.ippapublicpolicy.org/IMG/pdf/panel_39_s1_porter.pdf (accessed 12 January 2016).

Powell, John. 2013. "Tracing the History of Racial Inclusion and Debunking the Colour-Blind/Post-Racial Myth." *Human Rights* 40. http://racism.org/index.php?option=com_content&view=article&id=1751:tracing-the-history-of-racial-inclusion-and-debunking-the-color-blind-post-racial-myth&catid=34&Itemid=152 (accessed 10 July 2016).

Probyn, Fiona. 2005. "Review of Whitening Race." *Australian Humanities Review*. http://australianhumanitiesreview.org/2005/06/01/review-of-whitening-race (accessed 10 July 2016).

Putnam, Robert. 2007. "E Pluribus Unum: Diversity and Community in the Twenty-First Century – The 2006 Johan Skytte Prize Lecture." *Scandinavian Political Science* 30 (2): 137–74. doi: 10.1111/j.1467-9477.2007.00176.x.

Queen's University. 1991. "Towards Diversity and Equity at Queen's: A Strategy for Change." Final Report of the Principal's Advisory Committee on Race Relations (The Barry Report), 28 February. http://www.queensu.ca/provost/sites/webpublish.queensu.ca.provwww/files/files/TowardsDiversityandEquityatQueens.pdf (accessed 11 October 2017).

Quijano, Anibal. 2007. "Coloniality and Modernity/Rationality." *Cultural Studies* 21 (2–3): 168–78. doi:10.1080/09502380601164353.

Ramsaroop, Chris, and Adrian A. Smith. 2014. "The Inherent Racism of the Temporary Foreign Worker Program." *The Toronto Star*, 21 May. https://www.thestar.com/opinion/commentary/2014/05/21/the_inherent_racism_of_the_temporary_foreign_worker_program.html (accessed 16 January 2016).

Rawlinson, Kevin. 2017. "White Men 'Endangered Species' in UK Boardrooms, Says Tesco Chairman." *The Guardian*, 11 March. https://www.theguardian.com/business/2017/mar/10/white-men-endangered-species-in-uk-boardrooms-says-tesco-chairman (accessed 12 March 2017).

Rawls, John. 1999. *A Theory of Justice*. Cambridge, MA: Harvard University Press.

Rayside, David. 2009. "Two Pathways to Revolution: The Differences that Context Makes in Canada and the United States." In *Who's Your Daddy? And Other Writings on Queer Parenting*, edited by R. Epstein, 202–09. Toronto: Sumach Press.

Razack, Sherene H. 1998. *Looking White People in the Eye: Gender, Race and Culture in Courtrooms and Classrooms*. Toronto: University of Toronto Press.

Rebick, Judy. 2009. *Transforming Power: From the Personal to the Political*. Toronto: Penguin Canada.

Reitz, Jeffrey. 2011. *Pro-Immigration Canada: Social and Economic Roots of Popular Views. Study No. 20.* Montreal: Institute for Research on Public Policy.

Relly, Jeannine E., and Carol B. Schwalbe. 2016. "How Business Lobby Networks Shaped the U.S. Freedom of Information Act: An Examination of 60 Years of Congressional Testimony." *Government Information Quarterly* 33 (3): 404–16.

Restaurants Canada. 2014. "Temporary Foreign Worker Moratorium: Take Action." *Restaurants Canada* (16 May). https://www.restaurantscanada.org/temporary-foreign-worker-moratorium-take-action/ (accessed 12 January 2016).

Ross, Michael Lewin. 2009. "Oil and Democracy Revisted." Preliminary Draft. UCLA Department of Political Science. https://www.sscnet.ucla.edu/polisci/faculty/ross/papers/working/Oil%20and%20Democracy%20Revisited.pdf (accessed 14 January 2016).

Ross, Michael Lewin. 2001. "Does Oil Hinder Democracy?" *World Politics* 53 (3): 325–61. doi:10.1353/wp.2001.0011.

Rozworski, Michal. 2015. "Creative Resistance: Interview with Andreas Karitzis." *Political Eh-Conomy Blog,* 5 November. http://rozworski.org/political-eh-conomy/2015/11/05/creative-resistance-interview-with-andreas-karitzis/ (accessed 11 January 2016).

Ruhs, Martin. 2013. *The Price of Rights: Regulating International Labor Migration.* Princeton: Princeton University Press. doi:10.1515/9781400848607.

Saez, Emmanuel. 2013. "Striking It Richer: The Evolution of Top Incomes in the United States." http://eml.berkeley.edu/~saez/saez-UStopincomes-2012.pdf (accessed 14 January 2016).

Said, Edward. 1993. *Culture and Imperialism.* New York: Vintage Books.

Savoia, Antonia, Josh Easaw, and Andrew McKay. 2010. "Inequality, Democracy and Institutions: A Critical Review of Recent Research." *World Development* 38 (2): 142–54. doi:10.1016/j.worlddev.2009.10.009.

Scott, Peter D. 2014. *The American Deep State: Wall Street, Big Oil, and the Attack on U.S. Democracy.* Boulder, CO: Rowman and Littlefield Publishing.

Sen, Amartya. 1999. *Development as Freedom.* Oxford: Oxford University Press.

Sharma, Nadita. 2012. "The 'Difference' that Borders Make: 'Temporary Foreign Workers' and the Social Organization of Unfreedom in Canada." In *Legislated Inequality: Temporary Labour Migration in Canada,* edited by Patti Tamara Lenard and Christine Straehle, 26–47. Montreal: McGill-Queen's University Press.

Sharma, Nadita. 2006. *Home Economics: Nationalism and the Making of "Migrant Workers" in Canada.* Toronto: University of Toronto Press.

Shepard, Benjamin. 2002. "The Aids Coalition to Unleash Power: A Reassessment." *ResearchGate.* https://www.researchgate.net/publication/265199168_The_AIDS_Coalition_to_Unleash_Power_A_Reassessment (accessed 19 January 2016).

Shrivankova, Klara. 2010. *"Between Decent Work and Forced Labour: Examining the Continuum of Exploitation."* JRF Programme Paper. York, UK: Joseph Rowntree Foundation.

Shrivastava, Meenal. 2015a. "Theory and Praxis of Liberal Democracy in Oil-Exporting Countries: Relevance of the Staples Theory in a Fluid Global Oil Market." In *Alberta Oil and the Decline of Democracy in Canada,* edited by Meenal Shrivastava and Lorna Stefanick, 31–68. Edmonton: Athabasca University Press. doi:10.15215/aupress/9781771990295.01.

Shrivastava, Meenal. 2015b. "Of Democracy and Deficits: Surviving Neoliberalism in Oil-Exporting Economies." In *Alberta Oil and the Decline of Democracy in Canada*, edited by Meenal Shrivastava and Lorna Stefanick, 391–410. Edmonton: Athabasca University Press. doi:10.15215/aupress/9781771990295.01.

Shrivastava, Meenal, and Lorna Stefanick. 2012. "Do Oil and Democracy Only Clash in the Global South? Petro Politics in Alberta." *New Global Studies* 6 (1): 1–27. doi:10.1515/1940-0004.1147.

Siegfried, Andre. 1907. *The Race Question in Canada*. London: Eveleigh Nash.

Siksay, Bill. 2011. "An Act to Amend the Canadian Human Rights Act and the Criminal Code (Gender Identity and Gender Expression)." Private Members Bill, House of Commons of the Parliament of Canada, 7 February. https://openparliament.ca/bills/40-2/C-389/ (accessed 19 January 2016).

Simon, Mary. 2011. "Embracing the Maple Leaf." CBC *Radio Ideas with Paul Kennedy*, 27 January. http://www.cbc.ca/radio/ideas/embracing-the-maple-leaf-1.2979048 (accessed 15 January 2017).

Simpson, Audra. 2014. *Mohawk Interruptus: Political Life Across Settler Borders*. Durham, NC: Duke University Press. doi:10.1215/9780822376781.

Simpson, Leanne. 2008. "Looking after Gdoo-naaganinaa: Precolonial Nishnaabeg Diplomatic and Treaty Relationships." *Wicazo Sa Review* 23 (2): 29–42. doi:10.1353/wic.0.0001.

Smith, Dorothy. 2002. "Regulation or Dialogue." In *Academic Freedom and the Inclusive University*, edited by Sharon E. Kahn and Dennis Pavlich, 150–58. Vancouver: UBC Press.

Smith, Malinda S. 2016. "The Diversity Gap in Canadian University Leadership." Edmonton: Academic Women's Association). https://uofaawa.wordpress.com/awa-diversity-gap-campaign/the-diversity-gap-in-university-leadership/

Smith, Malinda. 2014. "Commissioning 'Founding Races' and Settler Colonial Narratives." *Canadian Ethnic Studies* 46 (2): 141–49. doi:10.1353/ces.2014.0024.

Smith, Malinda S. 2012. "Queering In/Equality: LGBTQ, 'It Gets Better' and Beyond." In *Beyond the Queer Alphabet: Conversations in Gender, Sexuality and Intersectionality*, edited by Malinda S. Smith and Fatima Jaffer, 15–18. Ottawa: Canadian Federation for the Humanities and Social Sciences.

Smith, Malinda. 2010. "Gender, Whiteness and the 'Other Others' in the Academy." In *States of Race: Critical Race Feminism for the 21st Century*, edited by Sherene Razack, Malinda Smith, and Sunera Thobani, 37–58. Toronto: Between the Lines.

Smith, Malinda S. 2008. "Racism and Motivated Ignorance." *Ardent: Anti-Racism and Decolonization Review* 1 (1): vi–vii.

Smith, Malinda S. 2003. "Race Matters and Race Manners." In *Reinventing Canada: Politics of the 21st Century*, edited by Janine Brodie and Linda Trimble, 108–30. Toronto: Prentice Hall.

Smith, Mariam. 2010. "Federalism and LGBT Rights in the U.S. and Canada: A Comparative Policy Analysis." In *Federalism, Feminism, and Multilevel Governance*, edited by Melissa Haussman, Marian Sawer, and Jill Vickers, 97–110. Farnham, UK: Ashgate.

Smith, Mariam. 1999. *Lesbian and Gay Rights in Canada: Social Movements and Equality Seeking, 1971–1995.* Toronto: University of Toronto Press.

Solomon, Yoram. 2016. "9 Diversity Factors That Will Increase Team Creativity." *Inc.* (25 May). https://www.inc.com/yoram-solomon/9-diversity-factors-that-will-increase-team-creativity.html (accessed 12 January 2017).

Sommers, Samuel R. 2006. "On Racial Diversity and Group Decision Making: Identifying Multiple Effects of Racial Composition on Jury Deliberations." *Journal of Personality and Social Psychology* 90 (4): 597–612. https://www.apa.org/pubs/journals/releases/psp-904597.pdf (accessed 15 July 2016).

St. Clair, Darlene, and Kyoko Kishimoto. 2010. "Decolonizing Teaching: A Cross Curricular and Collaborative Model for Teaching about Race in the University." *Multicultural Education* 18 (1): 18–24.

St. Germain, Jill. 2009. *Broken Treaties: United States and Canadian Relations with the Lakotas and the Plains Cree, 1868–1885.* Idaho: University of Nebraska Press.

Standing, Guy. 2014. *A Precariat Charter: From Denizens to Citizens.* London: Bloomsbury.

Standing, Guy. 2011. *The Precariat: The New Dangerous Class.* London: Bloomsbury.

Statistics Canada. 2017. "Study: A Look at Immigration, Ethno-cultural Diversity and Languages in Canada up to 2036, 2011 to 2036." *The Daily,* 25 January. http://www.statcan.gc.ca/daily-quotidien/170125/dq170125b-eng.pdf (accessed 12 February 2017).

Statistics Canada. 2010. "Projections of the Diversity of the Canadian Population, 2006–2031." Ottawa: Ministry of Industry. http://www.statcan.gc.ca/pub/91-551-x/91-551-x2010001-eng.pdf (accessed 15 January 2017).

Stefanick, Lorna. 2015. "Blurring the Boundaries of Private, Partisan, and Public Interests: Accountability in an Oil Economy." In *Alberta Oil and the Decline of Democracy in Canada,* edited by Meenal Shrivastava and Lorna Stefanick, 363–89. Edmonton: Athabasca University Press, 2015.

Stiglitz, Joseph E. 2013. *The Price of Inequality: How Today's Divided Society Endangers Our Future.* New York: W.W. Norton.

Stiglitz, Joseph. 2012. *The Price of Inequality.* New York: W.W. Norton & Co.

Strauss, Kendra. 2013. "Unfree Labour and the Regulation of Temporary Agency Work in the UK." In *Temporary Work, Agencies, and Unfree Labour: Insecurity in the New World of Work,* edited by Judy Fudge and Kendra Strauss, 164–83. New York: Routledge.

Streeck, Wolfgang. 2016. *How Will Capitalism End?* London: Verson Books.

Streeck, Wolfgang. 1995. "From Market Making to State Building? Reflections on the Political Economy of European Social Policy." In *European Social Policy: Between Fragmentation and Integration,* edited by Stephan Leibfriend and Paul Pierson, 389–431. Washington DC: Brookings Institute.

Streeck, Wolfgang, and Jerome Roos. 2015. "Politics in the Interregnum: A Q & A with Wolfgang Streeck." *Roar Magazine* (23 December). https://roarmag.org/essays/wolfgang-streeck-capitalism-democracy-interview/ (accessed 5 April 2016).

Surak, Kristen. 2013. "Guestworkers: A Taxonomy." *New Left Review* 84: 84–102.

Sutherland, Harry. 1982. *Track Two*. Documentary Film. Toronto: Independent Release.

Szeman, Imre. 2012. "Introduction to Focus: Petrofictions." *American Book Review* 33 (3): 3.

Taylor, Tiffany. 2004. "Anger Privilege: Deconstructing the Controlling Image of the 'Angry Black Woman.'" Presentation at the Annual Meeting of the American Sociological Association, San Francisco, CA, 14–17 August.

Teivainen, Teivo. 2002. *Enter Economism, Exit Politics*. London: Zed Books.

Thobani, Sunera. 2007. *Exalted Subjects: Studies in the Making of Race and Nation in Canada*. Toronto: University of Toronto Press.

Thompson, Simon. 2006. "Anger and the Struggle for Justice." In *Emotion, Politics, and Society*, edited by Simon Clarke, Paul Hoggett, and Simon Thomspon, 123–44. New York: Palgrave MacMillan. doi:10.1057/9780230627895_8.

Tolley, Erin. 2015. "Visible Minority and Indigenous Members of Parliament." In *Canadian Election Analysis 2015: Communication, Strategy, and Democracy*, edited by Alex Marland and Thierry Giasson, 50–51. Vancouver: UBC Press.

Tomassello, Michael. 2001. *The Cultural Origins of Human Cognition*. Cambridge, MA: Harvard University Press.

Tomlinson, Kathy. 2014a. "McDonald's Accused of Favouring Foreign Workers." *CBC Go Public*, 14 April. http://www.cbc.ca/news/canada/british-columbia/mcdonald-s-accused-of-favouring-foreign-workers-1.2598684 (accessed 12 January 2016).

Tomlinson, Kathy. 2014b. "McDonald's Foreign Workers Call It 'Slavery.'" *CBC Go Public*, 15 April. http://www.cbc.ca/news/canada/edmonton/mcdonald-s-foreign-workers-call-it-slavery-1.2612659 (accessed 12 January 2016).

Tomlinson, Kathy. 2013. "RBC Replaces Canadian Staff with Foreign Workers." *CBC*, 15 April. http://www.cbc.ca/news/canada/british-columbia/rbc-replaces-canadian-staff-with-foreign-workers-1.1315008 (accessed 12 January 2016).

Trehin, Simren. 2010. "My Experience Is Just One: The Voices of Four Racialized Women at Queen's University." PhD diss., Queen's University.

Treuer, Anthony. 2011. *The Assassination of Hole in the Day*. Minneapolis, MN: Borealis.

Trudeau, Justin. 2015. "Diversity Is Canada's Strength: La diversité est la force du Canada." London, United Kingdom, Canada House, 26 November. http://pm.gc.ca/eng/news/2015/11/26/diversity-canadas-strength (accessed 3 January 2017).

Tsilhqot'in National Government. 1998. "A Declaration of Sovereignty." http://www.tsilhqotin.ca/PDFs/98DeclarationSovereignty.pdf (accessed 20 January 2016).

Tsui, Kevin K. 2011. "More Oil, Less Democracy? Evidence from Worldwide Crude Oil Discoveries." *The Economic Journal* 121 (551): 89–115. doi: 10.1111/j.1468-0297.2009.02327.x.

Tutton, Michael. 2016. "Canada Must Boost Racial Diversity in 'Judiciary of Whiteness,' Advocates Urge." *The Toronto Star*, 18 July. https://www.thestar.com/news/queenspark/2016/07/18/canada-must-boost-racial-diversity-in-judiciary-of-whiteness-advocates-urge.html (accessed 5 January 2017).

Union of British Columbia Indian Chiefs (UBCIC). 1998. *Modern Land Claim Agreements: Through the Nisga'a Looking Glass*. https://d3n8a8pro7vhmx.cloudfront.net/ubcic/pages/1440/attachments/original/1484861477/

19_ubcic_modernagreements_lookingglass.pdf?1484861477 (accessed 20 January 2016).

United Food and Commercial Workers Canada (UFCW). 2014. "Justice and Dignity for Temporary Foreign Workers." *UFCW Canada*. http://www.ufcw.ca/Theme/UFCW/images/en/socialjustice/downloadables/trifold_leaflet_EN_online.pdf (accessed 12 January 2016).

United Nations Conference on Trade and Development (UNCTAD). 2012. *Trade and Development Report, 2012: Policies for Inclusive and Balanced Growth.* New York: United Nations.

van Kempen, Ronald. 2013. *Hyper-Diversity: A New Perspective on Urban Diversity.* Policy Brief No. 1, Divercities. Brussels: European Commission. https://www.urbandivercities.eu/wp-content/uploads/2013/05/DIVERCITIES_Policy_Brief_1.pdf (accessed 15 January 2017).

Various Authors. 2015. "Harper's Policy State Anti-Terrorism Bill C-51 'Dangerous': 100+ Academics." *The Canadian Progressive Blog*, 28 February. http://www.canadianprogressiveworld.com/2015/02/28/harpers-police-state-anti-terrorism-bill-c-51-dangerous-100-academics/ (accessed 14 January 2016).

Venne, Sharon. 1998. "Understanding Treaty #6." In *Aboriginal and Treaty Rights in Canada: Essays on Law, Equity, and Respect for Difference*, edited by Michael Asch, 173–207. Vancouver: University of British Columbia Press.

Veracini, Lorenzo. 2010. *Settler Colonialism: A Theoretical Overview.* New York: Palgrave-MacMillan. doi:10.1057/9780230299191.

Vertovec, Steven. 2007. "Super-Diversity and Its Implications." *Ethnic and Racial Studies* 30 (6): 1024–54. doi:10.1080/01419870701599465.

Vertovec, Steven. 2005. "Opinion: Super-diversity Revealed." *BBC News*, 20 September. http://news.bbc.co.uk/2/hi/uk_news/4266102.stm (accessed 15 January 2017).

Voyageur, Cora, and Brian Calliou. 2000/2001. "Various Shades of Red: Diversity within Canada's Indigenous Community." *London Journal of Canadian Studies* 16: 109–24.

Walberg, Rebecca. 2014. "Why Aren't Canadian Corporate Boards Getting Any Less Male, or White?" *Financial Post*, 29 September. http://business.financialpost.com/executive/leadership/why-arent-canadian-corporate-boards-getting-any-less-male-or-white (accessed 3 January 2017).

Walsh, James. 2014. "From Nations of Immigrants to States of Transience: Temporary Migration in Canada and Australia." *International Sociology* 29 (6): 584–606. doi:10.1177/0268580914538682.

Wang, Amy X. 2015. "Diversity Actually Makes Us Smarter," *Quartz* (11 December). https://qz.com/570732/diversity-actually-makes-us-smarter/ (accessed 3 January 2017).

Wantchekon, Leonard. 2002. "Why Do Resource Dependent Countries Have Authoritarian Governments?" *Journal of African Finance and Economic Development* 5 (2): 57–77.

Ware, Alan. 1992. "Liberal Democracy: One Form or Many?" *Political Studies* 40 (1_suppl Supp. 1): 130–45. doi:10.1111/j.1467-9248.1992.tb01817.x.

Warner, Tom. 2002. *Never Going Back: A History of Queer Activism in Canada.* Toronto: University of Toronto Press.

Warrell, Margie. 2013. *Stop Playing Safe: Rethink Risk, Unlock the Power of Courage, Achieve Outstanding Success.* Melbourne: Wrightbooks.

Warrell, Margie. 2009. *Find Your Courage: 12 Acts for Becoming Fearless at Work and in Life.* Columbus, OH: McGraw-Hill.

Watkins, Melville H. 2013. "The Staple Theory @ 50: Bitumen as Staple." *The Progressive Economics Forum,* December.. http://www.progressive-economics. ca/2013/12/26/the-staple-theory-50-mel-watkins/ (accessed 14 January 2016).

Watkins, Melville H. 2007. "Staples Redux." *Studies in Political Economy* 79: 213–26.

Watkins, Melville H. 1977. "The Staple Theory Revisited." *Journal of Canadian Studies/ Revue d'Etudes Canadiennes* 12 (5): 83–95. doi:10.3138/jcs.12.5.83.

Wilkinson, Richard, and Kate Pickett. 2009. *The Spirit Level: Why Greater Equality Makes Societies Stronger.* New York: Bloomsbury Press.

Williams, Raymond. 1977. *Marxism and Literature.* Oxford: Oxford University Press.

Williams, Robert. 1992. *The American Indian in Western Legal Thought: The Discourses of Conquest.* New York: Oxford University Press.

Wilson, Codi. 2016. "Pride Organizer Says He Has Not Agreed to Exclude Police Floats from Parade." *CP24: Toronto's Breaking News.* http://www.cp24.com/mobile/ news/pride-organizer-says-he-has-not-agreed-to-exclude-police-floats-from-parade-1.2971974 (accessed 20 December 2016).

Wise, Tim. 2010. *Colour-Blind: The Rise of Post-Racial Politics and the Retreat from Racial Equity.* San Francisco: City Light Books/Open Media Series.

Wolfe, Patrick. 2006. "Settler Colonialism and the Elimination of the Native." *Journal of Genocide Research* 8 (4): 387–409. doi:10.1080/14623520601056240.

Woodsworth, James S. 1909. *Strangers within Our Gates, or Coming Canadians.* Toronto: F.C. Stenvenson.

Workers Action Centre. 2015. *Still Working on the Edge.* Toronto: Workers Action Centre. http://www.workersactioncentre.org/updates/new-report-released-still-working-on-the-edge/ (accessed 12 January 2016).

World Bank (WB). 2015. "Oil Rents (% of GDP)." http://data.worldbank.org/ indicator/NY.GDP.PETR.RT.ZS (accessed 14 January 2016).

WEF (World Economic Forum). 2016. *The Global Risks Report.* 11th ed. Geneva: World Economic Forum. http://www3.weforum.org/docs/GRR/WEF_GRR16.pdf (accessed 11 October 2017).

Wright, Teresa. 2014. "Q&A: Employment Minister Jason Kenney on EI and TFW." *The Guardian* (Charlottetown), 19 September. http://www.theguardian.pe.ca/ news/local/2014/9/19/strong-q-a-strong-employment-ministe-3875241.html (accessed 12 January 2016).

Yalnizyan, Armine. 2013. "Study of Income Inequality in Canada—What Can Be Done." Presentation to the House of Commons Standing Committee on Finance, 30 April. Ottawa: Canadian Centre for Policy Alternatives. https://www.policyalternatives.ca/publications/reports/study-income-inequality-canada%E2%80%94what-can-be-done (accessed 7 October 2017).

York University. 1984. *Majority Report and Minority Report.* Special Review Committee on Charges of Racial and Sexual Harassment at York University.

Young, Iris Marion. 1990. *Justice and the Politics of Difference.* Princeton N.J.: Princeton University Press.

Zembylas, Michalinos. 2007. "Mobilizing Anger for Social Justice: The Politicization of Emotions in Education." *Teaching Education* 18 (1): 15–28. doi:10.1080/10476210601151516.

INDEX